An Introduction to the United States-Mexico-Canada Agreement

T0313987

Dedicated to Catherine Anne Fagan

My wife, best friend, steadfast supporter and partner in our life adventures, both great and small

An Introduction to the United States-Mexico-Canada Agreement

Understanding the New NAFTA

David A. Gantz

Will Clayton Fellow for Trade and International Economics, Rice University's Baker Institute for Public Policy, Center for the United States and Mexico and Samuel M. Fegtly Professor Emeritus, James E. Rogers College of Law, University of Arizona, USA

Cheltenham, UK • Northampton, MA, USA

Published by
Edward Elgar Publishing Limited
The Lypiatts
15 Lansdown Road
Cheltenham
Glos GL50 2JA
UK

Edward Elgar Publishing, Inc.
William Pratt House
9 Dewey Court
Northampton
Massachusetts 01060
USA

Paperback edition 2021

A catalogue record for this book
is available from the British Library

Library of Congress Control Number: 2020940527

This book is available electronically in the **Elgar**online
Law subject collection
http://dx.doi.org/10.4337/9781839105326

ISBN 978 1 83910 531 9 (cased)
ISBN 978 1 83910 532 6 (eBook)
ISBN 978 1 80088 454 0 (paperback)

Printed and bound by CPI Group (UK) Ltd, Croydon, CR0 4YY

Contents

About the author

David A. Gantz, AB Harvard College, JD, JSM Stanford Law School, is the Will Clayton Fellow for Trade and International Economics at the Center for the United States and Mexico of the Baker Institute at Rice University, and the Samuel M. Fegtly Professor of Law Emeritus at the University of Arizona. David teaches, writes and lectures in the areas of international trade and investment law, regional trade agreements, international business transactions, public international law and international environmental law. He served earlier in the Office of the Legal Adviser, US Department of State and practiced law in Washington DC. David is the author, co-author or editor of six books and has written and published more than 75 law journal articles and book chapters. He has served as an arbitrator in multiple proceedings under Chapters 11, 19 and 20 of the North American Free Trade Agreement (NAFTA) and as a consultant for the US Agency for International Development, the World Bank Group and the UN Development Programme, among others.

January 2020

Preface

The United States-Mexico-Canada Agreement (USMCA) is the most significant free trade agreement (FTA) negotiated by the United States since NAFTA, particularly if one discounts the Trans-Pacific Partnership (TPP), negotiated by President Obama but rejected by President Trump two days after he became president in January 2017. The original NAFTA has been responsible for developing integrated supply chains among the three parties, generating annually more than $1.3 billion worth of trade in goods and services, more than the total trade between the United States and the European Union (including the United Kingdom) and well over total trade with China. There is every reason to believe that USMCA will maintain or even increase that volume of trade once implemented.

USMCA in the view of many observers represents a retreat from NAFTA in such areas as much-weakened protection of investors, overly protectionist automotive rules of origin and unwise "sunset" provisions, among others. Realistically, however, there is no such thing as a free trade agreement, and it may be telling that the term "free" does not appear in the USMCA title. NAFTA and every regional trade agreement negotiated by the United States following NAFTA contemplated at least a significant degree of managed trade. USMCA's auto rules of origin and related provisions have the dubious honor of achieving a new height of protectionism. Still, this is a difference of degree rather than kind as no one can reasonably suggest that the parallel rules in NAFTA were not in themselves designed to favor the NAFTA parties over foreign competitors, albeit with a more North American and less United States focus. Also, in terms of managed trade, USMCA pales in comparison to the level of governmental controls found in the United States-China "Phase One" trade agreement signed January 15, 2020.

Moreover, and probably much more important in the real world of trade agreements, USMCA also provides badly needed modernization of a NAFTA negotiated 28 years ago. It does so by addressing such topics as small and medium-sized enterprises, state-owned enterprises, e-commerce and digital trade, and intellectual property, many of which were originally negotiated by the parties to the TPP.

Perhaps most significantly, USMCA contains enforceable labor and environmental provisions that go well beyond even the TPP, with the unprecedented "facility-specific rapid response labor mechanism" insisted upon by the Democratic Congress and incorporated in the USMCA Protocol of Amendment signed December 10, 2019 and in the consolidated USMCA text a few days later. USMCA is thus to a considerable degree a combination of NAFTA, the TPP and new concepts negotiated by the Trump Administration and the Democratic congressional leadership (strongly supported by the AFL-CIO and the Teamsters' Union) with input from Mexico and Canada. The bipartisan support reflected in the vote in the House, 385–41, and in the Senate, 89–10, demonstrates that with strong and enforceable labor provisions, and effective negotiators such as House Speaker Nancy Pelosi, Democratic Party support of trade agreements *can* be achieved.

In assessing USMCA, as with other regional trade agreements, it is wise to take a long-term view. In many respects, assessing the strengths and weaknesses of NAFTA is much more accurate and productive today than it was 25 years ago. The same will likely be true with USMCA after it has been in force for 10 or 15 years (and it may benefit from the "sunset" provisions that mandate a trilateral reconsideration beginning after six years and continuing). There are even some optimists, including one of the senior Mexican government officials at the time NAFTA was negotiated, who believe that despite the many challenges there is hope of eventually converting USMCA into a customs union with a common external tariff. (He notes that 60 percent of the tariffs of the USMCA parties are already the same or nearly the same.) Thus, the initial assessments, including those offered in this volume, should be read with this caveat in mind.

The first chapter of this book provides an overview of USMCA, the areas where in my view USMCA improves NAFTA, maintains NAFTA benefits, or represents steps backward. The remaining ten chapters of this book address the major chapters of USMCA, including in each a short analysis of the substance with an emphasis on the changes from NAFTA, and provide a brief analysis of other factors that may affect the success of USMCA. While it is impossible in a study of this length to cover every detail of USMCA, I have attempted to include discussions of all the major and most of the minor provisions of significance. Those readers whose primary interests, for example, are in rules of origin for autos, textiles and apparel or agricultural tariff-rate quotas will have to seek out writings focused on those sectors.

Also, other than briefly in Chapter 1, the overview chapter, and in Chapter 11, I have not discussed the complex negotiations that took place between the Trump Administration, House Speaker Nancy Pelosi and her colleagues and Mexican government officials, negotiations that resulted in the approval of USMCA by the House of Representatives overwhelmingly on December 19, 2019 (one day after the same House impeached President Trump) and by the Senate on January 16, 2020. Senate approval was never in much doubt given that under the Trade Promotion Authority only a majority was required in the Senate and no filibuster would have been possible even if desired by some Senators, but the overwhelming bipartisan support for USMCA in the House was unprecedented in the past quarter-century, as was the support of the AFL-CIO and the Teamsters' Union.

In the course of assembling the book I have drawn on a variety of primary and secondary sources, in particular the texts of NAFTA, CPTPP[1] and USMCA, along with the US implementing legislation and various documents and reports provided by the US Trade Representative's Office discussing the USMCA provisions in particular. I note that the USMCA text signed by the three parties on November 30, 2019 was modified by a Protocol of Amendment signed December 10, 2019. Except where necessary for clarity, all references are to the consolidated USMCA text as of December 13, 2019.[2]

The reports of the many advisory committees convened by the Office of the United States Trade Representative (USTR) on most of the subjects addressed in USMCA are useful in some cases. Also, given the similarity of many CPTPP chapters with USMCA chapters, I have also relied on the chapter-by-chapter summaries of the CPTPP chapters prepared by the Obama Administration, summaries that remain

---

[1]   In most instances I have referred to the "Comprehensive and Progressive Trans-Pacific Partnership" (CPTPP) even though in most instances the changes made by the remaining 11 members after US withdrawal in January 2017 are relatively limited and minor. See Government of Canada, "Comprehensive and Progressive Agreement for Trans-Pacific Partnership" (CPTPP), www.international.gc.ca/ trade-commerce/trade-agreements-accords-commerciaux/agr-acc/ cptpp-ptpgp/index.aspx?lang=eng.

[2]   Agreement Between the United States of America, the United Mexican States, and Canada, consolidated text of December 13, 2019, https://ustr.gov/trade-agreements/free-trade-agreements/united -states-mexico-canada-agreement/agreement-between. See also Protocol of Amendment to the Agreement Between the United States of America, the United Mexican States, and Canada, December 10, 2019, https://ustr.gov/sites/default/files/files/agreements/FTA/ USMCA/Protocol-of-Amendments-to-the-United-States-Mexico -Canada-Agreement.pdf, which is useful for comparison purposes.

available on USTR's fine website. These and other sources are listed in the "Selected Bibliography" at the end of the book.

Most of the chapters of this book were originally published individually as a series of reports on the website of the Baker Institute, Center for the United States and Mexico of Rice University in Houston,[3] although all such have been extensively revised and updated since they were first issued. The idea for the series originally came in conversations with Dr Tony Payan, the director of the Center, and was strongly supported by Ambassador Edward P. Djerejian, the director of the Institute; the project was ably supported by Lisa Guaqueta, the Center's program manager. All of us were convinced that a need existed for a series of short, timely articles on the major USMCA provisions. I was also encouraged to publish the full collection (with updates as necessary) as a book, with the caveat that it should be (a) published as soon as practicable; and (b) in a format or formats that would be sufficiently inexpensive to engender a broader readership. Hopefully, we shall have accomplished both goals.

I am also thankful to Will Garwood of the Clayton foundation for the fellowship that made this book possible. Regina Denis, Joelle Paulson, Lianne Hart and Kristin Hoffmeister did an excellent job of editing my drafts, and who, like all good editors, were not afraid of saying, in effect, "David, this sentence doesn't make sense; please rewrite it." Their work also gave me some confidence that the text would be understandable to persons who are not experienced trade lawyers, including the hopefully many readers who are not attorneys. Of course, I am solely responsible for what undoubtedly are occasional errors of fact or legal interpretation. Also, the views expressed in various parts of the book are mine alone, and are not necessarily shared by Dr Payan, Ambassador

---

[3]   www.bakerinstitute.org/experts/david-a-gantz/.

Djerejian or other employees or staff of the Center or Institute, or of Rice University.

David A. Gantz
January 31, 2020

Table of cross-referencing

USMCA	NAFTA	CPTPP/TPP	This Book
1. Initial Provisions/ General Definitions	1. Objectives 2. General Definitions	1. Initial Provisions & General Definitions	
2. Nat'l Treatment & Market Access (Goods)	3. Nat'l Treatment & Market Access	2. Nat'l Treatment & Market Access	2
3. Agriculture	7. Agriculture & SPS Measures	2. Section C, Agriculture	6
4. Rules of Origin	4. Rules of Origin	3. Rules of Origin & Origin Procedures	2
5. Origin Procedures	4. Rules of Origin	3. Rules of Origin & Origin Procedures	2
6. Textiles & Apparel	3. Annex 300-B, Textiles & Apparel	4. Textiles & Apparel	6
7. Customs & Trade Facilitation	5. Customs Procedures	5. Customs Administration & Trade Facilitation	2
8. Mexican Hydrocarbons	6. Energy & Basic Hydrocarbons	(No Equivalent)	5
9. Sanitary & Phyto-Sanitary Measures	7. Agriculture & SPS Measures	7. SPS Measures	8
10. Trade Remedies, AD/CVD Review	8. Safeguards 19. AD/CVD Review	6. Trade Remedies	3
11. Technical Barriers to Trade	9. Standards Related Measures	8. Technical Barriers to Trade	8
12. Sectoral Annexes	(No Equivalent)	(No Equivalent)	8
13. Government Procurement	10. Government Procurement	15. Government Procurement	9

USMCA	NAFTA	CPTPP/TPP	This Book
14. Investment	11. Investment	9. Investment	3, 5
15. Cross-Border Trade in Services	12. Cross-Border Trade in Services	10. Cross-Border Trade in Services	7
16. Temporary Entry	16. Temporary Entry	12. Temporary Entry	9
17. Financial Services	14. Financial Services	11. Financial Services	7
18. Telecommunications	13. Telecommunications	13. Telecommunications	7
19. Digital Trade	(No Equivalent)	14. Electronic Commerce	7
20. Intellectual Property	17. Intellectual Property	18. Intellectual Property	7
21. Competition Policy	15. Competition Policy, Monopolies, State Enterprises	16. Competition	8
22. SOEs	NAALC	17. SOEs	
23. Labor	NAALC	19. Labour	4
24. Environment	NAAEC	20. Environment	4
25. Small & Medium-Sized Enterprises	(No Equivalent)	24. Small & Medium-Sized Enterprises	8
26. Competitiveness	(No Equivalent)	22. Competitiveness & Business Facilitation	8
27. Anticorruption	(No Equivalent)	26. Transparency & Anticorruption	8
28. Good Regulatory Practices	18. Publication, Notification & Administration of Laws	25. Regulatory Coherence	9
29. Publication & Administration		26. Transparency & Anticorruption	8

USMCA	NAFTA	CPTPP/TPP	This Book
30. Administrative & Institutional Provisions	20. Institutional Arrangements/Dispute Settlement	27. Administrative & Institutional Provisions	9
31. Dispute Settlement		28. Dispute Settlement	3
32. Exceptions & General Provisions	21. Exceptions	29. Exceptions & General Provisions	9
33. Macroeconomic Policies and Exchange Rates	(No Equivalent)	(No Equivalent)	10
34. Final Provisions	22. Final Provisions	30. Final Provisions	10

Abbreviations

AB	Appellate Body (WTO)
AD	antidumping [duties]
AFL-CIO	American Federation of Labor/Congress of Industrial Organizations
AMLO	Andrés Manuel López Obrador (Mexico's President)
APEC	Asia-Pacific Economic Cooperation Forum
BPD	barrels per day
CAFTA-DR	Central American-United States-Dominican Republic Free Trade Agreement
CEC	Commission for Environmental Cooperation
CETA	Comprehensive Economic and Trade Agreement [EU-Canada]
CFE	Comisión Federal de Electricidad
CPTPP	Comprehensive and Progressive TPP
CVD	countervailing duty
EU	European Union

FTA	free trade agreement
G-7	Canada, France, Germany, Italy, Japan, the United States and the United Kingdom
GATS	General Agreement on Trade in Services (WTO)
GATT	General Agreement on Tariffs and Trade
GI	geographical indications
ILAB	Bureau of International Labor Affairs (US)
IP	intellectual property
IPRC	Committee on Intellectual Property Rights
ISDS	investor–state dispute settlement
MEA	multilateral environmental agreement
MFN	most-favored nation treatment
MNE	multinational enterprises
NAAEC	North American Agreement on Environmental Cooperation
NAALC	North American Agreement on Labor Cooperation
NAFTA	North American Free Trade Agreement
OECD	Organisation for Economic Co-operation and Development

PAN	National Action Party (Mexico)
Pemex	Petroleos Mexicanos
PRD	Party of the Democratic Revolution (Mexico)
PRI	Institutional Revolutionary Party (Mexico)
SMEs	small and medium-sized enterprises
SOEs	state-owned enterprises
SPS	Sanitary and Phytosanitary Measures Agreement
TBT	Technical Barriers to Trade Agreement (WTO)
TBT	technical barriers to trade provisions
TN	Trade National (visa)
TPF	transparency and pro-cedural fairness [for pharmaceuticals]
TPP	Trans-Pacific Partnership
TRIMS	WTO Agreement on Trade-Related Investment Measures
TRIPS	WTO Agreement on Trade-Related Aspects of Intellectual Property
USMCA	United States-Mexico-Canada Agreement (also T-MCA; CUSMA)

| USTR | Office of the United States Trade Representative |
| WTO | World Trade Organization |

1. Overview of "NAFTA 2.0"

I   INTRODUCTION

The United States-Mexico-Canada Agreement (USMCA) has been approved by the three governments. After all required legal and constitutional procedures, it is to enter into force July 1, 2020.[1] This modified and modernized version of NAFTA[2] will continue to govern most economic relationships in North America, including the more than $1.3 trillion in annual trade of goods and services, for at least 16 years and probably much longer. USMCA preserves the bulk of the NAFTA structures that permit North American manufacturers to compete effectively in North American and foreign markets with their counterparts in Europe and Asia. The most likely alternative—termination of NAFTA by the Trump

---

[1]   See Protocol Replacing the North American Free Trade Agreement with the Agreement Between the United States of America, the United Mexican States and Canada, November 30, 2018, https://ustr.gov/sites/default/files/files/agreements/FTA/USMCA/Text/USMCA_Protocol.pdf. Paragraph 2 provides that the Protocol and its Annex (the USMCA) "shall enter into force on the first day of the third month following the last notification." The Canadian parliamentary process was expected to be completed in April. "Mexican Trade Official in Washington to Plan USMCA Implementation by July 1st" (2020), World Trade Online, January 17, https://insidetrade.com/daily-news/mexican-trade-official-washington-plan-usmca-implementation-july-1st?s=na.

[2]   North American Free Trade Agreement [US-Mex.-Can.], December 15, 1992, www.nafta-sec-alena.org/Home/Texts-of-the-Agreement/North-American-Free-Trade-Agreement.

Administration—would have been far worse for the three economies and might have created a constitutional crisis in the United States between the president and Congress. The chilling effect on investment and new hiring generated by three years of uncertainty over NAFTA's future should also be largely resolved once USMCA goes into force.

Those in Canada and Mexico who rightly viewed the negotiations first and foremost as a damage-limiting exercise can take comfort that in the case of Canada, the NAFTA cultural industries exception was preserved, the trade dispute settlement mechanism survived, and Canada was required to reduce its restrictions on milk product imports and accept higher pharmaceutical prices to only a limited degree. For Mexico, despite attacks on its auto industry, under the new rules the industry will probably survive mostly intact and may actually expand (see below) although aggregate results are virtually impossible to predict. Labor obligations permitting independent unions and effective collective bargaining, if properly implemented, should assist Mexico's new President Andrés Manuel López Obrador (AMLO) in increasing Mexican wages and reducing inequality, and most other industrial and agricultural sectors will be relatively unaffected. Both Mexico and Canada benefitted from successful Congressional insistence that ten-year biologic drug protection be excised from USMCA and improved state-to-state dispute settlement be added in the USMCA Protocol. Most significantly, both Mexico and Canada preserve their access to the United States market, on which more than 75 percent of their respective exports are dependent.

Given that NAFTA was negotiated in 1991–92 and signed in 1993, it is obvious that many changes have occurred affecting regional and global trade in the ensuing 27 years. USMCA consists of 34 chapters compared to 22 in NAFTA, plus numerous annexes and side letters.[3] The new subject matter includes small and medium-sized enterprises, state-owned enterprises, corruption, e-commerce, digital trade and general regulatory practices, some of which may set the standard for future trade agreements concluded by the parties. Significant economic or political changes in NAFTA include rules governing the automotive trade, dispute settlement, intellectual property and agriculture.

As with NAFTA, compliance with USMCA rules will create significant administrative burdens, particularly for the automotive industry and particularly for small and medium-sized enterprises. Whether USMCA will result in measurable increases in manufacturing employment in the United States, or a reduction in the trade deficit, remains to be seen.

Congressional approval of USMCA came only after an extensive series of negotiations among the Administration (headed by US Trade Representative Robert Lighthizer), the Democratic congressional leadership (led by Speaker Nancy Pelosi and House Ways and Means Committee Chairman Richard Neal) and toward the end by Mexican officials (led by Undersecretary of Foreign Relations Jesus Seade). That negotiation resulted in a Protocol of Amendment encompassing major changes in such areas as dispute settlement, intellectual property protection, environmental rights and most importantly, labor rights and their enforcement.

---

[3]   Agreement Between the United States of America, the United Mexican States and Canada November 30, 2019, https://ustr.gov/trade-agreements/free-trade-agreements/united-states-mexico-canada-agreement/agreement-between, as modified by Protocol of Amendment to the Agreement Between the United States of America, the United Mexican States, and Canada, December 10, 2019, https://ustr.gov/trade-agreements/free-trade-agreements/united-states-mexico-canada-agreement/protocol-amendments. Unless the context requires otherwise, all references are to the consolidated December 13, 2019, text.

This chapter provides an introduction and overview to USMCA, focusing on the most significant changes embodied in the final version. The discussion is divided into three major sections, addressing positive and negative changes, and a few key areas where Canada and Mexico prevailed against US pressures, forcing the United States to compromise. It also reflects major changes negotiated by the Trump Administration, the Democratic House leadership and Mexico, resulting in the Protocol of Amendment. The three divisions are the author's and do not necessarily reflect those of other observers. Overall, the changes in the USMCA Protocol, widely trumpeted as improvements by the Democratic House leadership,[4] were treated with skepticism by some business groups, although almost all the latter supported the USMCA nonetheless.[5]

Subsequent chapters of the book explore major features of the agreement in much greater detail, reflecting a highly complex agreement that is undoubtedly the most economically significant US regional trade agreement since the original NAFTA.

II   POSITIVE CHANGES IN USMCA COMPARED TO NAFTA

While there has been much, often justified, criticism of USMCA as a movement from open regional trade to more managed trade, particularly in the automotive sector and (in

---

[4]   See House Committee on Ways and Means, "Improvements to the USMCA," https://waysandmeans.house.gov › documents › USMCA win factsheet.

[5]   "Business Groups Push for USMCA's Approval Despite Biologics Changes" (2019), World Trade Online, December 11, https://insidetrade.com/trade/business-groups-push-usmcas -approval-despite-biologics-changes.

my view) in the area of dispute settlement,[6] this does not change the fact that the 26-year-old NAFTA was badly in need of modernization, to deal with many new areas such as data and e-commerce, and to improve coverage of areas such as labor, the environment and small and medium-sized enterprises.

A   Modernization of NAFTA

USMCA updates or adds to NAFTA (and to some later US FTAs) coverage of customs and customs procedures, state-owned enterprises, competition policy, small and medium-sized enterprises, corruption, good regulatory practices, technical barriers to trade, sanitary and phytosanitary standards, digital trade, good regulatory practices, and various industry-specific standards.[7] The most important modernizations for American businesses, particularly financial institutions and enterprises in the high-tech area are probably those that prohibit localization requirements for data storage and govern e-commerce.[8] For North American business and labor the most significant benefit of USMCA, as noted earlier, is that it continues NAFTA in a manner that will largely preserve North American supply chains, intra-regional trade and a strong ability to maintain high-level manufacturing, innovation and services with its major competitors, China and the European Union.

Many of the USMCA innovations reflect the Trans-Pacific Partnership text that the Obama Administration concluded

---

[6]   See, for example, Jeffrey J. Schott (2018), "For Mexico, Canada, and the United States, a Step Backward on Trade and Investment," Peterson Institute for International Economics, October 2,   https://piie.com/blogs/trade-investment-policy-watch/mexico -canada-and-united-states-step-backwards-trade-and.

[7]   USMCA, Chs 7, 9, 11, 12, 21, 22, 25, 27, 28.

[8]   USMCA, Ch. 19.

(along with Canada and Mexico), and which was rejected in January 2018 by the Trump Administration.[9] A major objective of TPP, which entered into force in modified form as the "Comprehensive and Progressive TPP" on December 30, 2018 for six of the remaining 11 parties, and Vietnam shortly thereafter,[10] was to set new standards for future trade agreements worldwide. Incorporation of many TPP provisions in USMCA suggests that some officials of the Trump Administration are mindful of the desirable precedential effects of incorporating provisions developed in regional trade agreements.

B   Enhanced Labor and Environmental Protection

Improved protection for labor and the environment has been incorporated in every free trade agreement concluded by the United States since NAFTA, beginning in 2003 with the agreements with Australia, Chile and Singapore.[11] The principal objective of NAFTA critics during this period was to assure that future FTAs would incorporate labor and environmental protection in the body of the agreement (rather than in add-on supplemental agreements as with the NAFTA "side"

---

[9] Presidential Memorandum Regarding Withdrawal of the United States from the Trans-Pacific Partnership Negotiations and Agreement, January 23, 2017, www.whitehouse.gov/presidential-actions/presidential-memorandum-regarding-withdrawal-united-states-trans-pacific-partnership-negotiations-agreement/.

[10] Comprehensive and Progressive Trans-Pacific Partnership [Australia, Brunei, Canada, Chile, Japan, Malaysia, Mexico, New Zealand, Peru, Singapore and Vietnam], March 8, 2018, www.mfat.govt.nz/assets/CPTPP/Comprehensive-and-Progressive-Agreement-for-Trans-Pacific-Partnership-CPTPP-English.pdf; see "What Is the CPTPP," Government of Canada, www.international.gc.ca/trade-commerce/trade-agreements-accords-commerciaux/agr-acc/cptpp-ptpgp/index.aspx?lang=eng (noting the entry into force of CPTPP).

[11] See "Labor Rights and Environmental Protection Under NAFTA and Other U.S. Free Trade Agreements" (2011), *University of Miami Inter-American Law Review*, **42**, 297.

agreements, so as to assure that violation of those provisions would be subject to the same dispute settlement mechanism and trade sanctions as violations of the trade obligations. However, due to Bush Administration intransigence, this was not achieved until a group of late Bush Administration agreements with Colombia, Panama, Peru and South Korea were amended at the demand of the Democratic Congress in 2007.[12]

USMCA labor provisions focus on the support for independent unions in Mexico, on the assumption that more effective unions will mean higher wages and greater purchasing power for Mexican workers.[13] One addition, presumably added at the initiative of Canada, requires the implementation of policies against, inter alia, "employment discrimination on the basis of sex, including with regard to pregnancy, sexual harassment, sexual orientation, gender identity, and caregiving responsibilities ..."[14]

The USMCA Protocol went much further, by incorporating a "Rapid Response Labor Mechanism" in the state-to-state dispute settlement chapter. This annex provides for monitoring of alleged labor abuses and creates a special type of arbitration panel designed to address specific labor violations in Mexican enterprises producing goods or services.[15] In the event that an enterprise is found to have denied labor rights, remedies include suspension of preferential tariff treatment and other penalties.[16] The Protocol added, controversially, five new labor attachés to be based in Mexico for monitoring

---

[12]   Ibid.

[13]   See Harley Shaiken (2017), "Improved Workers' Rights for Mexicans Will Benefit Americans," *New York Times*, January 30, www.nytimes.com/roomfordebate/2017/01/30/new-terms-for-nafta-7/improved-workers-rights-for-mexicans-will-benefit-americans.

[14]   USMCA, Art. 23.9.

[15]   USMCA, Annex 31-A.

[16]   USMCA, Annex 31-A, Art. 31-A.10.

purposes and established a rebuttable presumption that labor violations are trade related.[17]

The environmental provisions draw heavily on the TPP environmental chapter, which addresses conservation in such areas as fisheries subsidies, shark finning, invasive species and cooperation on marine litter and air quality.[18] The USMCA Protocol restores some provisions from earlier FTA environmental chapters, including a NAFTA-based declaration that where there is a conflict between USMCA and multilateral environmental agreements (MEAs) to which the USMCA parties are party, the latter prevail.[19] Also, the parties accept a specific obligation to implement a listed series of MEAs found in many earlier US FTAs, including the Montreal Protocol on the Ozone Layer, and to consider adding further MEAs to the list.[20] (Needless to say the Paris Agreement on Climate Change is not included in the list.) As with the labor chapter modifications, there exists a rebuttable presumption that an alleged environment violation is trade related.[21]

C   Currency Manipulation

For the first time in a trade agreement, USMCA incorporates measures to guard against currency manipulation.[22] While the importance of incorporating such safeguards in USMCA is limited, given that neither Canada nor Mexico has been accused of currency manipulation in the past, the US negotiators—very wisely in my view—saw the USMCA

---

[17] USMCA, Art. 23.3, fn. 5. Parallel changes are made in other provisions, making it unnecessary for claimants to prove that a labor violation is trade related.

[18] USMCA, Ch. 24.

[19] USMCA, Art. 1.3.

[20] USMCA, Art. 24.8.4.

[21] USMCA Art. 24.4, fn. 5.

[22] USMCA, Ch. 33.

negotiations as an opportunity to develop language that could be incorporated in future Administration trade agreements, such as those contemplated with the European Union, Japan and the United Kingdom.[23] The relatively limited reach of the provisions likely reflects the reluctance of the US Treasury Department to address currency issues in trade agreements.

D   Agriculture

Press reports on the negotiations between Canada and the United States suggest that the most difficult issues to resolve were Canada's insistence on maintaining the NAFTA dispute settlement mechanism for reviewing national unfair trade practice actions (see below) and US demands for improved access to the Canadian dairy market and for some changes to Canada's wheat management system. The United States achieved a modest opening for milk solids exports, comprising about 3.6 percent of the Canadian market.[24] In addition, cheese exporters to Mexico preserved a lucrative export market for their branded products, including protection against EU efforts in a pending trade agreement with Mexico to limit usage of certain product names to EU suppliers.[25] More importantly, the United States, Mexico and Canada preserve a vibrant, mutually beneficial series of trade relationships. American farmers and food processors will continue to enjoy access to their largest (Canada) and third-largest (Mexico) export markets.[26] Mexico was also successful in preserving

---

[23]   USTR (2018), "Trump Administration Announces Intent to Negotiate Trade Agreements with Japan, the European Union and the United Kingdom," October, https://ustr.gov/about-us/policy-offices/press-office/press-releases/2018/october/trump-administration-announces.

[24]   Annex 3-B, Sec. C (Dairy Pricing and Imports).

[25]   See Ch. 20, Sec. D (country names).

[26]   See "U.S. Agricultural Exports by Country" (2015) *FCA Economic Report*, www.fca.gov/template-fca/download/Economic

access to the US market for winter fruits and vegetables, defeating a Trump Administration demand for new trade remedies that could have hampered such access.[27]

III   THE DOWNSIDES OF USMCA

As indicated above, it is likely that the areas which have been most severely criticized in USMCA, that is, automotive rules of origin and dispute settlement, have overshadowed some of the positive aspects discussed in Section II above. Still, these two areas are not the only ones that for many observers, including me, represent steps backward in the long process of evolution of US FTAs since NAFTA.

A   Automotive Rules of Origin and Related Restrictions

By far and away the most controversial area of the USMCA negotiations related to the auto and auto parts sector. The United States initially made a series of draconian demands, including raising the North American content requirements from 62.5 percent to 85 percent, of which 50 percent would have to be US content![28] These were not surprisingly rejected out of hand by Mexico and Canada. Ultimately, in the nego-

---

Reports/3 U.S.AgriculturalExports-KeyDestinationsAndCountryCo ncentrationRisk.pdf (showing Canada first with $21.8 billion and Mexico third with $18.3 billion).

27   Caitlin Dewey (2017), "How a Group of Florida Tomato Growers Could Help Derail NAFTA," *Washington Post*, October 16, www.washingtonpost.com/business/economy/how-a-group-of-florida-tomato-growers-could-help-derail-nafta/2017/10/16/e1ec5438-b27c-11e7-a908-a3470754bbb9_story.html?utm_term=.88330100e6bc.

28   See David A. Gantz (2018), "The Risks and Rewards of Renegotiating the North American Trade Relationship," *Maryland Journal of International Law*, **33**, 127, 135.

tiations between the United States and Mexico that took place in July and August 2018, compromises were reached, although the US focus remained on increasing US content, indirectly if not directly. Most of the changes will be phased in over a three-year period beginning with the entry into force of USMCA.

First, the North American "regional value content" (RVC) required for NAFTA treatment was raised from 62.5 percent to 75 percent, to be phased in over several years.[29] Second, 70 percent of the steel and aluminum used in auto production must come from North American sources. The scope of this requirement specifies that for steel products to count toward the 70 percent, after seven years the steel must be "melted and poured" in North America, that is, "all steel manufacturing processes must occur in one or more of the Parties."[30]

Third, 40 percent of the product value of autos and 45 percent of trucks must be made in facilities where workers are paid at least $16/hour, meaning that except for R&D and some engineering, only facilities located in the United States or Canada would qualify.

For Canada the $16/hour requirement is no more a bar than in the United States, given the similar wage costs in Canada. For Mexico it is a much more serious challenge since typical auto industry wages in Mexico are approximately $3.60–$3.90 per hour (attributable by some studies in part to lack of union support for workers).[31] This means that most of that 40–45 percent of auto content must be produced in the United States or Canada. Still, some high-waged Mexican employees, for example, engineers, R&D and management personnel, are

---

[29] Appendix to Annex 4-B, Product-Specific Rules of Origin for Automotive Goods.

[30] USMCA, Annex 4-B, Art. 6.1, fn. 74.

[31] "Study Points to Large Wage Gaps for Mexican Auto Workers" (2018), *Mexico News Daily*, July 2, https://mexiconewsdaily.com/news/study-points-large-wage-gaps-mexican-auto-workers/.

paid up to $22 per hour, and this may be counted toward the total, perhaps encouraging auto manufacturers to undertake more R&D in Mexico.[32] Mexican officials estimate that about 70 percent of Mexican auto production would already meet the 75 percent RVC requirements.[33] Those vehicles that do not qualify for USMCA rules of origin would be eligible for the current MFN duty of 2.5 percent, if the applied MFN rate remains at 2.5 percent, as do the MFN rates on auto parts. For small cars produced in Mexico this may be the preferred solution, with the alternative being to import such vehicles from China or other low labor-cost countries.

Vehicles that would have met the NAFTA rules of origin but not USMCA rules would continue to benefit from the current MFN duties, but only up to 1.6 million vehicles per year.[34] Such imports would be feasible for autos at the 2.5 percent MFN tariff but not for small trucks, where the US tariff is 25 percent. Side letters effectively establish a tariff-rate quota for both Mexican and Canadian vehicles if the United States imposes "national security" tariffs on autos and auto parts. Under USMCA, 2.6 million passenger vehicles per year and a quantity of auto parts ($32.4 billion for Canada and $108 billion for Mexico), as well as light trucks from both countries, would be excluded from the "national

---

[32]   See Rosella Brevetti (2018), "Tough NAFTA Auto Rules Will Help Spur Investment in Mexico (1)," *International Trade Daily* (BBNA), October 12, http://news.bna.com/itln/display/batch_print _display.adp?searchid=31860977 (quoting Mexican trade negotiator Jesus Seade).

[33]   See Sharay Angulo (2018), "Most Mexican Auto Exports Can Meet New NAFTA Rules, Says Minister", *Reuters*, August 27, www.reuters.com/article/us-trade-nafta-mexico-autos/most-mexi can-auto-exports-can-meet-new-nafta-rules-says-minister-idUSKCN1LC2HC (quoting Mexican Economy Minister Ildefonso Guajardo).

[34]   USMCA, Annex 2-C, para. 5.

security" measures if applied elsewhere.[35] All such volumes are well above current Canadian and Mexican exports to the United States.

Tracing the parts and components produced in facilities paying $16/hour or more will likely be a significant administrative burden for auto and auto parts producers as well as for the three governments, as would be the costs of new facilities that are redundant. However, changes in the rules that set specific regional value content for certain major components may modestly reduce administrative costs attributed under NAFTA to the complex tracing requirements.[36]

The net impact of the stiffer rules of origin on North American vehicle production and employment is difficult to predict. It is possible that they will result in increased investment in steel and aluminum as well as in auto parts production in the United States and Mexico, but the magnitude is impossible to predict. It is also likely that a higher percentage of vehicle and parts production for the US market will occur in the United States, but if prices increase as many expect, the total number of vehicles sold in North America may decrease. US-made vehicles which are currently exported to third countries such as China may be exported in smaller numbers in the future because of increased costs leading to reduced competitiveness. Thus, the Trump Administration objective of increasing US auto industry employment and decreasing the trade deficit with Mexico may not ultimately be realized, even if the effects of greater automation (to offset some of the higher wage costs) are ignored.

---

[35] USMCA, US Canada 232 side letter, US Mexico 232 side letter.

[36] See NAFTA, Annex A-300; appendix to Annex 4-B.

B   **Reduced Investor Protections**

Specified rights for foreign investors and investor–state dispute settlement (ISDS) have been included in NAFTA (Chapter 11) and all subsequent US FTAs except the agreement with Australia,[37] and similar ISDS provisions are found in several thousand bilateral investment treaties, including more than 40 concluded by the United States.[38] However, such protection is not favored by the Trump Administration, whose officials believe that ISDS violates US sovereignty and may encourage American enterprises to move the facilities to lower-wage countries such as Mexico.[39]

Chapter 14 of USMCA, except for "legacy" claims under NAFTA Chapter 11 (which would survive for a period of three years),[40] significantly reduces the protection for most investors in Mexico, primarily by depriving them of the right to pursue actions against the Mexican government in ISDS for denial of "fair and equitable treatment" or indirect expropriation.[41] In addition, the new provisions do not apply to establishment claims (prior to the actual investment) and impose a 30-month period for exhaustion of local remedies before international arbitration can be sought.[42]

The full ISDS protections, including the frequently cited denial of fair and equitable treatment and indirect expropriation, remain only for investors in Mexico that have concluded

---

[37]   Australia refused to accept ISDS in that agreement but did so in the TPP and the CPTPP 15 years later.

[38]   US Dept of State (undated), "United States Bilateral Investment Treaties," www.state.gov/e/eb/ifd/bit/117402.htm.

[39]   See "Brady-Lighthizer Exchange [on ISDS]" (2018), International Economic Law and Policy Blog, March 21, https://worldtradelaw.typepad.com/ielpblog/2018/03/brady-lighthizer-isds-exchange.html.

[40]   USMCA, Annex 14-C.

[41]   USCMA, Annex 14-D.

[42]   Ibid.

contracts with the government or government entities in oil and gas, telecommunications, certain infrastructure projects, power generation and telecommunications.[43] Given the importance for Mexico of attracting foreign investment to the hydrocarbons sector, the preservation of ISDS for that sector probably will afford potential investors a greater level of confidence when they invest billions of dollars in long-term projects. For investors in the relatively unprotected sectors, questions arise as to whether there will be a substantial impact on investment levels, given the relatively few ISDS actions (about 20 in 25 years) against Mexico.

The situation with Canada is different; ISDS claims will not be permitted at all between the United States and Canada after the legacy period.[44] Disputes between Canadian investors and the Mexican government and vice versa would be covered by CPTPP.[45] With Canada, which has the dubious honor of being the most frequent NAFTA respondent, one may speculate that many government lawyers and other officials are weary of defending ISDS cases in a country where the national courts have a well-deserved reputation for competence and independence.

C   Hydrocarbon Sector Investment in Mexico

Many, if not all, trade agreements are subject to after-the-fact criticism about what was not accomplished. NAFTA was criticized for permitting Mexico to retain its long-time monopoly over hydrocarbons and electric power generation under the Mexican Constitution.[46] Some observers had hoped that

---

[43]   USMCA, Annex 14-E, para. 6(b).

[44]   See USMCA, Annexes 14-D and 14-E (not applicable to Canada).

[45]   CPTPP, Ch. 9; but see CPTPP text, Annex, para. 2 (suspending certain investment-related provisions of TPP).

[46]   NAFTA, Ch. 6.

USMCA would instead offer the same opportunities for private foreign investors in those sectors as are provided by the Peña-Nieto Administration's 2013 legal and constitutional reforms.[47] Key elements of the reforms overwhelmingly approved by Mexico's Congress included procedures to permit and govern investment in service and other profit-sharing contracts in hydrocarbon development as well as in the refining, transport, storage, natural gas processing, and petrochemicals sectors.[48]

However, USMCA does not in so many words guarantee that the Peña-Nieto reforms cannot be changed. Rather, in language that was presumably insisted upon by López Obrador's representatives in the negotiations, Mexico explicitly retains the right to change its hydrocarbon laws and related constitutional provisions at any time.[49] Still, this language does not provide the protection for AMLO that appears to be the case. Elsewhere in the USMCA, Mexico must afford treatment to the United States and to US investors in the energy sector, among others, that is no less favorable than treatment Mexico has offered in parallel trade and investment agreements, such as the Trans-Pacific Partnership.[50] In Mexico's TPP annexes, Mexico must afford the other parties no less favorable treatment than what is set out in the Peña-Nieto energy legislation.[51]

---

[47]   See Diana Villiers Negroponte (2018), "Mexico's Energy Reforms Become Law", Brookings, August 14, www.brookings.edu/articles/mexicos-energy-reforms-become-law/.

[48]   Clare Ribando Selke, Michael Ratner, M. Angeles Villarreal and Phillip Brown (2015), "Mexico's Oil and Gas Sector: Background, Reform Efforts, and Implications for the United States," Congressional Research Service, September 28, https://fas.org/sgp/crs/row/R43313.pdf.

[49]   USMCA, Ch. 8.

[50]   USMCA, Art. 32.11.

[51]   CPTPP, Annex I-Mexico-17 through Annex I-Mexico-27.

D   Sixteen-Year Sunset Clause

The best thing that can be said about the sunset clause[52] is that the process in USMCA calling for the beginning of a review six years after USMCA enters into force, with termination ten years thereafter if there is no agreement on extending it, is far better than the original US government proposal, which was a five-year sunset provision. Such a short period of time would have resulted in great uncertainty for investors in all three countries—probably the reason the Administration proposed it in the first place—and was roundly criticized by all stakeholders. Sixteen years is long enough to cover the useful lives of most investment outside the extractive industries and should have relatively little impact on investment decisions in North America. Still, if negotiations beginning in six years become acrimonious, investor confidence could be shaken.

E   Ten-Year Term for Protection for Biologic Drugs (Deleted)

While the United States was unable to negotiate a ten-year period for biologic drug patent protection in the TPP (effectively eight years[53]), Canada and Mexico both initially agreed on ten years in USMCA.[54] (Other intellectual property sections of the initial USMCA are generally similar to those in TPP, providing for enhanced protection against generic producers of agricultural chemicals and pharmaceutical products.[55]) While US law provides for an 11-year term, such lengthy pro-

---

[52] USMCA, Art. 34.7.

[53] TPP, Art. 18.51 (deleted from the Comprehensive and Progressive TPP concluded by the remaining 11 TPP Parties in 2018).

[54] USMCA, Ch. 20, Section F, Art. 20.F.14.

[55] USMCA, Ch. 20, Subsections B (agricultural chemicals), C (pharmaceutical products).

tection is generally opposed elsewhere, including by Canada and Mexico, because it increases the costs of such drugs, most of which accrue to national government healthcare systems.

Perhaps surprisingly, given the power of the pharmaceutical industry in the United States, the fall 2019 negotiations between the Democratic congressional leadership and the Trump Administration led to the elimination of any special protection for biologic drugs in the USMCA.[56] Other changes demanded by the Congress and accepted by the Administration reduced modestly the protections afforded in the USMCA (and in TPP) to branded drug producers when they seek to discourage generic production of similar drugs.[57] The result is somewhat more similar to the balance achieved in the US FTAs with Peru, Colombia and Panama.[58]

F   Prohibition of Mexico or Canada from Concluding an FTA with a Non-Market Economy (e.g., China)

Another unique provision insisted upon by the Trump Administration is designed to give the United States the option of withdrawing from USMCA upon six months' notice if either Canada or Mexico were to negotiate a trade agreement with a non-market economy.[59] However, any country with which a party has a free trade agreement at the time of the signature of USMCA is excluded. Thus Vietnam, which is

---

[56]   USMCA Protocol, para. 3E, eliminated what in the original USMCA test was Art. 20.49.

[57]   USMCA, esp. Art. 20.50.

[58]   See House Committee on Ways and Means (2019), "Improvements to the USMCA," December 10, https://waysandmeans .house.gov › documents › USMCA win factsheet (referring to the May 10, 2007 compromise between the Democratic Congress and the Bush Administration).

[59]   USMCA, Art. 32.10.

a party to the existing CPTPP along with Canada and Mexico, is excluded from the prohibition.

G   Steel and Aluminum Tariffs

Section 232 steel and aluminum tariffs that have resulted in US "national security" tariffs on steel and aluminum imported from most countries remained in place under USMCA, and so too retaliatory tariffs imposed by many US trading partners, including Mexico and Canada. Canada was, before the tariffs, the largest source of both steel and aluminum imports into the United States, and Mexico was fourth largest in terms of steel imports.[60] Fortunately for the future of USMCA, the Trump Administration lifted these tariffs with respect to Canada and Mexico in May 2019.[61]

IV   PRESERVING CERTAIN KEY ASPECTS OF NAFTA

The fact that USMCA carried over certain NAFTA elements was undoubtedly critical to obtaining Canada's last-minute inclusion in the agreement. In addition to the general preservation of duty-free, tariff-free trade established under NAFTA, and very limited changes in the NAFTA rules of origin, which NAFTA stakeholders have learned to live with over the past 26 years, several specific areas are notable.

---

[60]   "Top US Import Sources of Steel, Aluminum" (2018), VOA News, March 1, www.voanews.com/a/top-us-import-sources-steel -aluminum/4277212.html.

[61]   See USTR (2019), "United States Announces Deal with Canada and Mexico to Lift Retaliatory Tariffs," May 17, https://ustr .gov/about-us/policy-offices/press-office/press-releases/2019/may/ united-states-announces-deal-canada-and.

A   Review of Dumping and Subsidies Trade Determinations

The NAFTA mechanism ("Chapter 19") for review of national administrative agency determinations of dumping or illegal subsidization by binational panels in place of domestic federal courts was preserved without significant changes[62] despite initially strong opposition from the Trump Administration. While the September 30 draft initially applied the mechanism only between the United States and Canada, with Mexico having agreed to its elimination, USMCA was soon revised to expand the mechanism to Mexico as well. For Canada, Chapter 19 was a red line, given that it was material—the "crown jewel" with "iconic significance"—in Canadian approval of the 1988 US-Canada Free Trade Agreement, as well as NAFTA five years later.[63]

B   Canadian Cultural Industries Exception

The other red-line issue was Canada's "cultural industries" exception, also incorporated in the United States-Canada FTA and in NAFTA, and now in USMCA.[64] The exception, which applies in the final text to all three parties, reflects long-standing Canadian concerns "of having its indigenous cultural expression drowned in a flood of U.S. films, televi-

---

[62] NAFTA, Ch. 19; USMCA, Ch. 10, Section D.

[63] United States-Canada Free Trade Agreement, January 2, 1988; see Jesse McLean (2018), "Will Chapter 19 Be a Deal-Breaker for Canada in NAFTA Talks," *The Star (Toronto)*, September 2, www .thestar.com/news/canada/2018/09/02/will-chapter-19-be-a-deal -breaker-for-canada-in-nafta-talks.html (quoting USCFTA chief Canadian negotiator, Gordon Ritchie).

[64] USMCA, Art. 32.6; NAFTA, Annex 2106 (incorporating relevant provisions of the US-Canada FTA).

sion programs, sound recordings, books, and magazines."[65] Given that most of Canada's citizens live within 100 miles of the Canadian border and some 94 percent of films and 75 percent of TV shows shown in Canada originate in the United States (as of 2010), these concerns do not seem unreasonable if exercised responsibly, even if, technically, restrictions on such media would otherwise violate free trade principles. (Please see Chapter 9 of this book for additional discussion ("exceptions").) Under the USMCA, the cultural exception was extended to Mexico, with some limitations applicable to either Canada or Mexico.[66]

C   State-to-State Dispute Settlement

Another area of strong interest to Canada and Mexico, given the enormous disparities between the size of their economies and the United States and their dependence on the United States as their major export market, was preservation of a strong state-to-state dispute settlement mechanism. This aspect of NAFTA was targeted for curtailment by the United States, which had proposed making compliance with dispute settlement panel rulings voluntary.[67] Canada and Mexico ultimately prevailed to a limited degree, with the NAFTA provisions carried over to USMCA with minimal substantive changes.[68] While the NAFTA mechanism has proved susceptible to long delays by any party if that party refuses to cooperate in appointing panelists, even an imperfect system was likely even more necessary in USMCA given that the United

---

[65]   Alan Z. Hertz, "The NAFTA Cultural Industries Exception" (2010), Audi Alteram Partem, October 7, www.allenzhertz.com/2010/10/cultural-industries-exception.html.

[66]   USMCA, Art. 32.6.

[67]   See Gantz, "Risks and Rewards," 135.

[68]   See NAFTA, Ch. 20; USMCA, Ch. 31.

States seems intent on emasculating the binding dispute settlement mechanism in the WTO.[69]

Fortunately for Canada and Mexico, the Democratic Congress insisted on major improvements in the chapter, changes which will likely make it more difficult for the United States to prevent dispute settlement by blocking appointment of panelists, and included specific rules of evidence for panel proceedings.[70] The essence of the complex changes, discussed in detail in Chapter 3, provides that if one party (for example, the United States) refuses to appoint its 10-member panel roster, the complaining party may appoint panelists from those persons appointed to the rosters by other parties.[71] This is presumably intended to create an incentive for all parties to promptly appoint their respective panel rosters.

D   Government Procurement

NAFTA's government procurement provisions were also attacked by the United States during the negotiations. Initially, the United States demanded that government procurement be reciprocal on a dollar-for-dollar basis, that is, Canadian and Mexican enterprises would benefit from sales to US government entities only to the extent that the Canadian and Mexican governments made purchases from US enterprises.[72]

---

[69]   Understanding on Rules and Procedures Governing the Settlement of Disputes, Annex 2 of the WTO Agreement, April 15, 1994; see Kirtika Suneja (2018), "US Blocking Appointment to Key WTO Body, Trump May Soon Be the Only Winner in Any Trade Dispute," *The Economic Times*, March 6, https:// economictimes.indiatimes.com/news/economy/foreign-trade/trade -wars-us-blocking-appointment-of-members-of-wtos-appellate -body/articleshow/63177200.cms.

[70]   USMCA, Art. 31.6.

[71]   USMCA, Arts 31.8, 31.9.

[72]   Eric Martin, Josh Wingrove and Andrew Mayeda (2017), "U.S. Demands on NAFTA Said to Risk Scuttling Trade Talks," International Trade Report (BBNA), **34**, 1316.

This approach was impractical given that the US economy and population are many times the size of the other economies, and ultimately was abandoned. The USMCA provisions make minor changes but in general the NAFTA provisions are carried over.[73] However, the USMCA provisions apply *only* to procurements between the United States and Mexico; procurement between the United States and Canada is governed by WTO rules.[74] (Canada and the United States are parties to the WTO Agreement on Government Procurement; Mexico is not.[75])

V   CONCLUDING OBSERVATIONS

The Trump Administration's broader trade policies will also affect North American trade, particularly if tariffs or quotas are imposed on imports of autos and auto parts from Europe and Asia, and particularly if the trade war with China continues or escalates. Mexico could benefit from a higher North American content requirement for auto production if some current Chinese production is shifted to Mexico. Still, if the major threat to the US economy in the future is China, a robust North American economy, which in most respects preserves regional supply chains, becomes critical.

---

[73] See Jean Heilman Grier (2018), "USMCA-Modernized NAFTA: Government Procurement," Perspectives on Trade, October 5, https://trade.djaghe.com/?p=5174; USMCA, Ch. 13.

[74] USMCA, Art. 13.2.3.

[75] See WTO, "Agreement on Government Procurement: Parties, Observers and Accessions," www.wto.org/english/tratop_e/gproc_e/memobs_e.htm.

2. Tariffs, customs and rules of origin

I INTRODUCTION

Chapter 1 provided an overview and initial analysis of USMCA.[1] This chapter analyzes what most see as the essence of a preferential trade agreement—tariffs, customs, and rules of origin that govern bilateral trade in goods. Discussion of these issues is simplified because the United States-Mexico-Canada Agreement (USMCA)[2] makes relatively few significant changes to the North American Free Trade Agreement (NAFTA) rules, whereby virtually all manufactured goods and most agricultural goods are traded duty-free and quota-free.[3] However, in several sectors, particularly the automotive industry, USMCA incorporates major changes compared to the NAFTA provisions, and in my view stands as an example of managed trade that has seldom been

---

[1]   See David A. Gantz (2018), *The United States-Mexico-Canada Agreement: Overview and Analysis*, Baker Institute Report no. 12.11.18, Rice University's Baker Institute for Public Policy, Houston, Texas, www.bakerinstitute.org/media/files/files/1f9f406a/bi-report-121118-mex-usmca.pdf.

[2]   Agreement Between the United States of America, the United Mexican States, and Canada, November 30, 2018 (not yet in force), https://ustr.gov/trade-agreements/free-trade-agreements/united-states-mexico-canada-agreement/agreement-between.

[3]   See North American Free Trade Agreement, US-Mex.-Can., December 15, 1992, www.nafta-sec-alena.org/Home/Texts-of-the-Agreement/North-American-Free-Trade-Agreement, Ch. 3.

seen in US trade agreements except in the areas of textiles and clothing.

Other major areas of significant changes in USMCA compared to NAFTA include the new de minimis rules for imposing tariffs on small package delivery services. Changes in customs administration and trade facilitation, improved compared to NAFTA, are also reviewed. Other sector-specific changes are noted but not discussed in detail. Changes in the treatment of textiles and clothing and in agricultural products, including the politically sensitive opening of Canada's dairy market and rules relating to geographical indications, will both be addressed in Chapter 6.

For those who have not studied the details of trade under preferential trade agreements such as NAFTA and USMCA, one key fact is worth emphasizing: such agreements do *not* provide for duty-free trade of all products traded among the states that are parties to the agreement. Rather, duty-free trade applies only to products that "originate" in North America, usually those that meet specific rules of origin. Such rules are variously based on regional value content, utilization of specific major components produced in the region, or a shift in tariff headings (i.e., the classification of goods).[4] (The general rules of origin in USMCA are very similar to those in NAFTA.[5]) Rules of origin are designed to ensure that goods that enjoy duty-free trade status in the region ("originating goods") have substantial regional content rather than being trans-shipped from Asia or assembled from parts and components that are completely or largely imported from outside North America.[6] Thus, for example, a finished product made in China and imported into the United States would not

---

[4]   See NAFTA, Chs 3 and 4; USMCA, Chs 2 and 4.

[5]   See USMCA, Art. 4.2; NAFTA, Art. 401.

[6]   See David A. Gantz (1995), "Implementing the NAFTA Rules of Origin: Are the Parties Helping or Hurting Free Trade?" *Arizona Journal of International and Comparative Law*, **12**, 367.

qualify for duty-free entry into Mexico or Canada unless the article was duty-free under Mexico and/or Canada's WTO tariffs.

As in other regional trade agreements, demonstrating that a good produced entirely in one or more of the USMCA parties is an originating good, such as copper ore mined and smelted in Arizona or Mexico, is typically a straightforward process.[7] Similarly, a good produced entirely from originating materials in the territory of one or more USMCA parties,[8] such as flour milled in one of the USMCA countries from wheat grown in the United States or Canada, rarely raises questions about origin. However, manufactured goods often depend on global supply chains and use materials and components from many different sources both within and outside North America. Such goods must satisfy product-specific rules of origin—or in some instances meet a minimum regional value content (RVC) requirement—to qualify as an originating good and enjoy duty-free trade status in North America.[9]

The procedures for establishing that a product is an originating good under the rules of origin are often complex and thus costly to meet, particularly for small and medium-sized enterprises that do not have in-house lawyers or customs experts to assure compliance. It is not unusual for importers of goods that are subject to low or zero most-favored-nation (MFN) tariffs (not including footwear, clothing and small trucks)[10] to opt against seeking NAFTA treatment because

---

[7] USMCA, Art. 4.3.

[8] USMCA, Art. 4.2(c).

[9] USMCA, Art. 4.2(b) and (d), Annex 4-B.

[10] Duties assessed on US imports amounted to only 1.4 percent of all imported goods; more than two-thirds of all imported goods were not subject to any tariffs at all. See Drew Desilver (2018), "U.S. Tariffs Vary a Lot, but the Highest Duties Tend to Be on Imported Clothing," Pew Research Center, Factank (blog), March 28, www .pewresearch.org/fact-tank/2018/03/28/u-s-tariffs-vary-a-lot-but-the -highest-duties-tend-to-be-on-imported-clothing/.

of the high compliance costs and the risk that a subsequent customs audit will discover errors, resulting in charges to the importer for additional duties, interest and penalties.

The Office of the US Trade Representative (USTR), in announcing USMCA, characterized these aspects of the agreement as follows:

> The United States, Mexico, and Canada have concluded substantive discussions on new rules of origin and origin procedures, including product-specific rules for passenger vehicles, light trucks, and auto parts. This update to the rules of origin will provide greater incentives to source goods and materials in the United States and North America.[11]

Further,

> This deal exceeds NAFTA 1.0 and the TPP [Trans-Pacific Partnership] by establishing procedures that streamline certification and verification of rules of origin and that promote strong enforcement. This includes new cooperation and enforcement provisions that help to prevent duty evasion before it happens.
>
> The new rules will help ensure that only producers using sufficient and significant North American parts and materials receive preferential tariff benefits.[12]

Overall, USTR explains that USMCA for the most part retains the NAFTA market access provisions albeit with some important modifications:

- maintaining duty-free treatment for originating goods;

---

[11]   Office of the United States Trade Representative (2018), "United-States-Mexico-Canada Trade Fact Sheet: Rebalancing Trade to Support Manufacturing," October, https://ustr.gov/about-us/policy-offices/press-office/fact-sheets/2018/october/united-states%E2%80%93mexico%E2%80%93canada-trade-fa-0. (Small trucks are dutiable at 25 percent—see Harmonized Tariff Schedule of the United States 8704.)

[12]   Ibid.

- maintaining the prohibition on export duties, taxes, and other charges and the waiver of specific customs processing fees;
- adding new provisions for transparency in import and export licensing procedures;
- prohibiting parties from: (a) requiring the use of local distributors in importation; (b) restricting the import of commercial goods that contain cryptography; (c) placing import restrictions on used or remanufactured goods; and (d) requiring consular transactions and their associated fees and charges;
- updating provisions for the duty-free temporary admission of goods to include shipping containers or other substantial holders used in the shipment of goods;[13]
- eliminating the standard customs form for certification of origin, allowing electronic completion and permitting the importer as well as the foreign producer or exporter to complete and certify the USMCA origin of the good, with liability for errors remaining with the importer;[14]
- the de minimis level of non-originating goods permitted increases from 7 percent to 10 percent.[15]

It is evident that North American trade will benefit from some strengthened standards in areas such as trade facilitation and transparency. Changes in rules of origin and customs procedures are relatively minor except as indicated herein, although importers will want to review carefully the specific rules of origin for their imported products to assure that they are aware of any changes compared to the NAFTA rules of origin. This is particularly true with the extensively modified and highly complex automotive goods rules.[16]

---

[13]   Ibid.

[14]   USMCA, Art. 5.2.

[15]   USMCA, Art. 4.12.

[16]   USMCA, Annex 4-B, Appendix, esp. Art. 2.

One positive change in the rules of origin is the increase in the de minimis exception for non-originating goods from 7 percent to 10 percent.[17] This means that in most instances where a specific rule of origin specifies that *all* materials used in the production of a good originate in North America in order to meet a rule of origin that is based on a complete tariff shift (where the parts and components are all classified under one or more four-digit subchapters of the harmonized tariff system), origin is conferred when the finished product is classified in a different four-digit subchapter; but under the new rules, up to 10 percent of the materials are not required to meet the tariff shift.

II   AUTOMOTIVE GOODS

Automobiles and auto parts account for more than 20 percent of total NAFTA trade and for about 950,000 jobs in the United States.[18] Some automotive components cross the Canadian and/or Mexican borders as many as eight times before they are assembled into a finished automobile in one of the three NAFTA countries.[19] It is thus not surprising that this was the focus of the NAFTA renegotiations. The elements of USMCA that directly address the auto industry include modifications to the NAFTA rules of origin and related content requirements,

---

[17]   USMCA, Art. 4.12.

[18]   Bureau of Labor Statistics (2018), "Automotive Industry: Employment, Earnings and Hours," October, www.bls.gov/iag/tgs/iagauto.htm. Another 3.3 million are employed in vehicle and parts dealerships.

[19]   See Kristin Dziczek, Bernard Swiecki, Yen Chen, Valerie Brugeman, Michael Schultz and David Andrea (2017), "NAFTA Briefing: Trade Benefits to the Automotive Industry and Potential Consequences of Withdrawal from the Agreement," Center for Automotive Research, January, www.cargroup.org/publication/nafta -briefing-trade-benefits-to-the-automotive-industry-and-potential -consequences-of-withdrawal-from-the-agreement/.

plus some protections for Mexico and Canada should the Trump Administration impose 20–25 percent tariffs on US auto and auto part imports (presumably on "national security" grounds under Section 232 of the Trade Expansion Act of 1962).[20] Automotive trade was extensively "managed" under NAFTA and is dictated to even more so under USMCA. Whether the increasingly strict rules under USMCA will help or hurt the North American auto and auto parts industries in the medium or long term will not be known for at least half a decade.

In assessing the new USMCA rules, we first discuss what the United States did *not* achieve in the negotiations. The US sought to depart from the *regional* content rules used in NAFTA and other US free trade agreements reached over the past 20 years. Rather than NAFTA's requirement that 62.5 percent of the net cost of the auto be made of North American content, the US initially demanded raising the threshold to 82.5 percent North American content, of which 50 percent must be from the *United States* (including steel and aluminum).[21] Due to strong opposition from Mexico during bilateral negotiations in August and September 2018, the United States was forced to compromise. Still, by adding a $16/hour wage requirement to the agreement, as discussed below, the United States indirectly assured that a higher percentage of total automotive content would be produced in the US (or Canada), given the higher wages in the US compared to Mexico.

The final changes for the automotive industry include raising the percentage of regional value content required for automobiles and light trucks from 62.5 percent to 75 percent. These requirements are to be phased in over three years from

---

[20]   19 U.S.C. Sec. 1862—Safeguarding National Security.

[21]   "US Seeks to Include Steel, Aluminum in NAFTA Autos: Sources" (2017), CNBC, October 13, https://uk.reuters.com/article/uk-trade-nafta-steel-exclusive/exclusive-u-s-seeks-to-include-steel-aluminum-in-nafta-autos-rules-sources-idUKKBN1CI1XC.

the date the USMCA goes into effect; certain "core" components such as engines, advanced batteries for electric cars and
transmissions must originate in North America.[22] In addition,
70 percent of the steel used in the manufacture of cars and
small trucks must originate in USMCA countries.[23] The full
significance of the 70 percent rule was clarified only in the
December 10, 2019 Protocol of Amendment. In a further step,
apparently designed by the Trump Administration rather than
the Democratic Congress, the steel rules (but not those relating to aluminum), were further tightened. Steel automotive
products, such as chassis and bodies, will not count toward the
70 percent after a seven-year grace period unless the steel is
"melted and poured" in North America.[24]

This presumably means that manufacturers can no longer
import slab or sheet steel from suppliers, such as those in
Turkey, Brazil and China, and simply conduct the fabrication
in the United States. The specific language is as follows:

> Beginning seven years after entry into force of this Agreement,
> for steel to be considered as originating under this Article, all steel
> manufacturing processes must occur in one or more of the Parties,
> except for metallurgical processes involving the refinement of
> steel additives. Such processes include the initial melting and
> mixing and continue through the coating stage. This requirement
> does not apply to raw materials used in the steel manufacturing
> process, including steel scrap; iron ore; pig iron; reduced, pro-
> cessed, or pelletized iron ore; or raw alloys.[25]

In addition, the USMCA Protocol added a requirement that,
ten years after the USMCA enters into force, the parties will
consider similar requirements to be applicable to aluminum.[26]

---

22 USMCA, App. to Annex 4-B, Art. 3.1.
23 USMCA, App. to Annex 4-B, Art. 6.
24 USMCA, App. 4-B, Art. 6.1, fn. 74.
25 USMCA, Annex 4-B, Art. 6.1, fn. 74.
26 Ibid.

Mexico apparently resisted these changes until a seven-year grace period was added, and refused to see such rules applied to aluminum, since Mexico does not produce raw aluminum.[27] The full impact of the 70 percent rule (and for regional value calculations) will not be known until the USMCA parties have established uniform regulations, a process that is expected to last well into 2020. For example, does the rule mean 70 percent by company? By brand? By plant, or something else?[28]

Also significantly for Mexico, 40 percent of the materials for cars and 45 percent of the components for light trucks must be produced by enterprises that pay workers at least $16/hour.[29] Some employees of automotive enterprises that conduct research and development and/or assemble advanced components such as batteries, engines and transmissions in Mexico would count toward up to 15 percent of these thresholds if the workers are paid at this level. These calculations are subject to complex tracing rules,[30] which likely will add to auto manufacturing costs in North America, although some of the NAFTA tracing rules for parts and components have been relaxed.[31]

Since typical auto industry hourly wages in Mexico are approximately $3.60–$3.90 (a level some studies attribute

---

[27] See "Foreign Minister: Mexico Considering U.S. Steel Demand, with Conditions" (2019), World Trade Online, December 8, https://insidetrade.com/daily-news/foreign-minister-mexico-considering-us-steel-demand-conditions.

[28] See "Seade: Uniform Regulations for USMCA Auto Rules Under Development" (2019), World Trade Online, January 13, https://insidetrade.com/daily-news/seade-uniform-regulations-usmca-auto-rules-under-development (discussing the ongoing negotiations of uniform regulations for autos and auto parts).

[29] USMCA, App. to Annex 4-B, Art. 7.

[30] See, for example, USMCA, App. to Annex 4-B, Arts 3.4–3.6, 3.8–3.9.

[31] USMCA, App. to Annex 4-B, Arts 3.4, 3.5.

in part to the lack of union support for workers),[32] this wage requirement means most of the materials and components counting toward the 40–45 percent content rule must be produced in the United States or Canada. It is possible that wages in Mexico will eventually increase to the $16/hour level; Mexican President Andrés Manuel López Obrador (AMLO) presumably will seek to implement policies encouraging higher wages for Mexican workers, including policies that support workers' rights to organize independent unions, as required under USMCA.[33]

Moreover, at least at present, the $16/hour rate is not indexed to inflation, although with inflation in the United States averaging about 2 percent per year (i.e., $0.32 on $16), the lack of indexing probably would not significantly help Mexico.

Mexican officials have asserted that about 70 percent of the country's current auto production would meet the 75 percent RVC requirements.[34] Automobiles that would have met the NAFTA rules of origin, but not the new USMCA rules, would continue to benefit from the current most-favored-nation (MFN) duties (with some limits at the discretion of the United States); this excludes small trucks, where the US tariff is 25 percent of the customs value. This high tariff on imported trucks is potentially a significant limitation on Mexico's production of vehicles intended for export to the United States.

---

[32]   "Study Points to Large Wage Gaps for Mexican Auto Workers" (2018), *Mexico News Daily*, July 2, https://mexiconewsdaily.com/news/study-points-large-wage-gaps-mexican-auto-workers/.

[33]   See USMCA, Annex 23-A (Worker Representation in Collective Bargaining in Mexico) and Chapter 4 of this volume.

[34]   See Sharay Angulo (2018), "Most Mexican Auto Exports Can Meet New NAFTA Rules, Says Minister," Reuters, August 27, www.reuters.com/article/us-trade-nafta-mexico-autos/most-mexican-auto-exports-can-meet-new-nafta-rules-says-minister-idUSKCN1LC2HC (quoting Mexican Economy Minister Ildefonso Guajardo).

Without that 25 percent tariff, auto producers in Mexico would not face potentially higher costs of meeting the new regional value content/minimum wage rules and their accompanying administrative burdens; they could simply pay the US MFN tariff of 2.5 percent.

Separately, side letters effectively establish a tariff-rate quota for vehicles produced in both Mexico and Canada, whereby 2.6 million passenger vehicles per year and a set amount of auto parts (valued at $32.4 billion for Canada and $108 billion for Mexico), as well as light trucks from both countries, would be excluded from the additional Section 232 tariffs if applied by the Trump Administration.[35] All such figures are well above current Canadian and Mexican exports to the United States.

An obscure but possibly very important provision buried in the automotive annexes appears to afford any party (e.g., the United States) the opportunity, with some limitations,[36] including a five-year cap unless extended by agreement of the parties, to fashion alternative rules of origin:

> A Party may apply an alternative staging regime described in this Article on a producer-by-producer basis. Upon request of one of the Parties, the Parties shall discuss and agree on any appropriate extensions or other modifications to the alternative staging regime described in paragraphs 1 through 4 if the Parties consider that such an extension or modification would result in

---

[35]   USMCA, US Canada 232 side letter, US Mexico 232 side letter. (The many side letters included in the USMCA package to address specific issues are binding on the parties in the same manner as if they were part of the text of the agreement and will be approved as part of the same process in which the US and Mexican congresses and the Canadian Parliament approve USMCA.)

[36]   USMCA, App. to Annex 4-B, Art. 8. These alternative rules in addition to the five-year time period are limited generally to 10 percent of a producer's total production, but the time period may be extended as noted in the quotation if the result would be new investment in North American automobile or parts production.

new investment for vehicle or parts production in the territories of the Parties.[37]

It may be that the principal purpose of this exception is to temporarily assist a producer that demonstrates that it is unable to meet certain requirements for duty-free trade.[38] However, this exception could be significant. For example, suppose the United States government (under Mr Trump or a successor president) tells an auto producer in North America, "If you build or expand your factory in the United States instead of Mexico, we will relax certain of the rules of origin in a manner to reduce your costs." Similarly, it is conceivable that the Trump Administration could provide more favorable rules of origin in exchange for the producer declining to support California's stricter vehicle emissions rules.[39] Another possible approach to keep auto production in the United States was raised in November 2019, and would increase the phase-in period for compliance with the rules of origin from three years to five years if companies were to agree that 100 percent of their production would meet the regional value contents of USMCA.[40] Any use of alternative staging methods by the United States would require the approval of Canada and

---

[37] USMCA, App. to Annex 4-B, Art. 8.5.

[38] United States-Mexico-Canada Agreement Implementation Act, introduced December 13, 2019, Sec. 202A(d)(2), H.R. 5430, 116th Congress, 1st Session.

[39] See Umair Irfan (2019), "Trump's Fight with California over Vehicle Emissions Rules Has Divided Automakers," Vox, November 5, www.vox.com/policy-and-politics/2019/11/5/20942457/california-trump-fuel-economy-auto-industry.

[40] "Sources: USTR Wants Auto Companies to Agree All Production Will Comply with USMCA" (2019), World Trade Online, November 7, https://insidetrade.com/daily-news/sources-ustr-wants-auto-companies-agree-all-production-will-comply-usmca?s=iust.

Mexico. Additional details on the regime are provided in the implementing legislation.[41]

Few objective observers would agree that the more protectionist rules for vehicles and auto parts will benefit auto manufacturers or consumers, and it remains to be seen whether the changes will benefit workers in the industry. Accurately estimating the additional North American production costs because of the more restrictive rules of origin and related minimum salary requirements is almost impossible, in part because they likely will vary company by company and vehicle model by vehicle model. The $16/hour wage requirement may impose a significant tracking and record-keeping burden on enterprises that produce finished passenger vehicles or light trucks and on associated parts suppliers, at least temporarily.[42] This will add to vehicle manufacturing costs in North America, compared to automotive production costs in Asia or the European Union. Still, one can reasonably expect that within a few years, the major auto producers will have devised means of minimizing the costs, given the phase-in period and potential detailed regulatory guidance the US government may provide.[43]

As noted earlier, the rules of origin for autos under NAFTA have been a significant burden, in part because of the requirement to track the production origin of not only major components but also parts of major components,[44] a tracing requirement that has been relaxed under USMCA. However, auto manufacturers in North America appear to have learned how to minimize the administrative costs of compliance. As

---

[41]   United States-Mexico-Canada Agreement Implementation Act, introduced December 13, 2019, Sec. 202A(a), (d). H.R. 5430, 116th Congress, 1st Session.

[42]   USMCA, App. to Annex 4-B, Art. 7.

[43]   See USMCA, App. to Annex 4-B, Art. 3.

[44]   See NAFTA, Annex 300-A.

industry representatives noted in the supplementary advisory report,

> While the changes to the automotive rules of origin methodology and the increases in the Regional Value Content (RVC) levels present challenges, and increased costs in the near term, ITAC-2 automotive industry representatives appreciate that helpful flexibilities were maintained in the automotive rules of origin [tracing] that temper some of those challenges and minimizes many of the longer-term administrative burdens and costs.[45]

The overall economic impact of these provisions on the North American auto industry depends on several other factors, such as the increased cost of steel and aluminum due to US tariffs and quotas on steel and aluminum imported from most countries other than Australia that the Trump Administration imposed in June 2018 on Section 232 "national security" grounds (with Canada and Mexico exempted in May 2019).[46] Given the costs to North American auto producers of complying with the requirements of the rules of origin, particularly those relating to sourcing of steel, one can reasonably expect US and other North American vehicle sales to fall, although predicting the magnitude of the decrease—and the resulting job losses, if any—is difficult. As one observer has noted,

> This is the part of the USMCA that takes a lot of the free trade out of the North American Free Trade Agreement. The specific

---

[45]   "Addendum to the Earlier (September 28, 2018) Report of the Industry Trade Advisory Committee on Automotive Equipment and Capital Goods," October 24, 2018, https://ustr.gov/sites/default/files/files/agreements/FTA/AdvisoryCommitteeReports/ITAC_2_REPORT-Automotive_Equipment_and_Capital_Goods_Addendum.pdf, 4.

[46]   Australia is the only country exempted to date, as of December 2018. See Michael Cowden (2018), "Australia Joins 232 Tariff Exemption Parade," Fastmarkets AMM, March 12, www.amm.com/Article/3793254/Australia-joins-232-tariff-exemption-parade.html.

impact will depend on how the provisions are implemented, which is likely to involve a big fight among various interest groups. It could also lead to the auto supply chain being significantly scaled back, with companies retaining the option of simply paying the 2.5% most-favored-nation tariff for cars instead of complying with the more stringent USMCA rules. At any rate, we can expect auto production costs to increase.[47]

The increased production costs for autos and light trucks in North America come at a time of other significant uncertainties in the industry. Major producers such as GM, Ford, Mercedes-Benz, Nissan, Honda and Volkswagen are reducing their workforces in various markets by thousands of jobs and closing factories to save money. Global vehicle sales are expected to decline by about 3.1 million units through 2019.[48] Further, every major manufacturer will be spending billions of dollars over the next five to ten years on electric and self-driving car technology and production; these cost-saving measures are designed in part to protect such investments in the event of another recession, in the United States or elsewhere.[49]

In the future, some of the auto parts production now in Mexico may move to the United States or Canada because of the $16/hour wage rule. (The extent to which additional US workers are hired depends in part on the extent to which manufacturers invest in robots and other labor-saving equipment.) Moreover, the increase in North American content requirements by 12.5 percent will apply to lower-priced parts now

---

[47]   Inu Manak and Simon Lester (2019), "Evaluating the New USMCA," Cato Institute, December 11, www.cato.org/blog/evaluating-new-usmca-0.

[48]   Michael Wayland (2019), "GM, Ford and Others Cut Thousands of Jobs and Closed Factories to Save Billions in 2019," CNBC, December 23, www.cnbc.com/2019/12/23/automakers-cut-jobs-close-factories-to-save-billions-in-2019.html.

[49]   Ibid.

imported from Asia and are thus most likely to be produced in Mexico rather than Canada or the United States because of Mexico's much lower labor costs. At the same time, while the RVC is increasing from 62.5 percent to 75 percent, 25 percent of the total content may still be obtained from non-North American sources.

For Mexican auto production, sourcing some components from China, elsewhere in Asia, and the European Union will still be feasible, even if the Trump Administration ultimately imposes 20–25 percent tariffs on auto parts from those countries under Section 232. For some USMCA market producers, these additional tariffs many encourage a shift in auto parts production for direct importation into the United States from China to alternatives such as Malaysia, Vietnam, South Korea or Mexico. This could further increase the cost advantage of producing auto parts in Mexico, but only if uncertainties regarding the investment climate under AMLO are favorably resolved.[50] One may also speculate that the steel content requirements, with the increased fabrication ("melted and poured") requirements for USMCA treatment, will stimulate investment in Mexico's basic steel production because production costs will likely be lower in Mexico than in Canada or the United States, even as steel production in the developed parties becomes increasingly automated.

---

[50] See, for example, Colby Smith (2018), "Investors Face Big Call as Mexico's López Obrador Prepares Budget," *Financial Times*, December 11, www.ft.com/content/52a1e866-fc4e-11e8-ac00-57a2a 826423e.

III CUSTOMS ADMINISTRATION AND TRADE FACILITATION

As was summarized by the Heritage Foundation in its analysis of USMCA, Chapter 7

focuses on streamlining the trade process so that it is more efficient and transparent. There is an emphasis on the use of online
publication and information technology, which is evidence of
the success of modernization. The promotion of information
sharing with regard to resources, such as documentation and
data, for importation, exportation and transit, as well as laws,
regulations, procedures, duties, taxes and other fees will help to
minimize costs in trading, allowing for greater efficiency and
transparency.[51]

The provisions address, inter alia, the need for simplified
procedures for the release of goods by the national customs
services; express shipments (discussed separately below); risk
management, post-clearance audits; and protection of trade
information.[52] The chapter also creates a trade facilitation
committee composed of government officials for sharing of
information. As some have suggested, the committee would
be more useful if business representatives, particularly those
from SMEs, were made part of the process.[53] As with similar
committees created under this and other trade agreements, its
efficacy will depend in significant part on whether the parties
make an effort to convene it regularly.

Another change that could have beneficial results for
smaller shipments is a requirement that the USMCA parties

---

[51] Tory Whiting and Gabriella Beaumont-Smith (2019),
"Backgrounder: An Analysis of the United States-Mexico-Canada
Agreement," Heritage Foundation, January 28, www.heritage.org/
trade/report/analysis-the-united-states-mexico-canada-agreement,
17.

[52] USMCA, Arts 7.7, 7.8, 7.12, 7.13, 7.22.

[53] Whiting and Beaumont-Smith, "Backgrounder," 18.

adopt simplified customs formalities for shipments valued at less than US$2,500 for US entries and less than CAD$3,300 for Canadian entries.[54] This will be helpful for shipments that exceed the de mimimis limits discussed below, but are still relatively small in value.

IV   TARIFF AND CUSTOMS TREATMENT OF EXPRESS SHIPMENTS

When NAFTA was originally negotiated, online shopping barely existed because most of the technology was not available, and low-value parcels were not a significant aspect of international trade within North America. At the time, the de minimis threshold for the United States was only $200. But by 2017, the number of packages delivered by the US Postal Service, most of them generated by Internet-based sellers such as Amazon.com, had increased from fewer than a billion in 1992 to 5.7 billion.[55]

Given the importance of Internet-based shopping today, companies that ship goods from the US to Canada and Mexico, including but not limited to the US Postal Service and Amazon, have long objected to the very low thresholds for expedited customs services and duty exemptions imposed by Mexico and Canada. Exemption from customs duties and value-added (Mexico) or national sales taxes (Canada) for small, relatively low-value packages shipped from the United States would facilitate international sales by online retailers in the United States. US law provides that shipments

---

[54]   USMCA, Art. 7.8.2.

[55]   See Gary Clyde Hufbauer and Euijin Jung (2018), "Higher de Minimis Thresholds: A Win in the USMCA," Peterson Institute for International Economics, Trade and Investment Policy Watch (blog), October 15, https://piie.com/blogs/trade-investment-policy-watch/higher-de-minimis-thresholds-win-usmca.

worth up to $800 may be imported into the US without facing customs duties and with expedited processing requirements.[56] In significant contrast, these thresholds are currently CAD$20 (US$15) for packages exported to Canada and $50 for Mexico.[57] These levels often mean that the administrative costs for completing the shipments exceed the value of the goods shipped.

The USMCA requires Mexico to increase these thresholds to $117 for customs duties and $50 for value-added taxes, while Canada's limits must increase to CAD$150 (US$112.50) for customs duties and CAD$40 (US$30) for national sales taxes.[58] Industry spokespersons have expressed disappointment that the US trade negotiators were "unable to secure more ambitious commitments from Canada and Mexico." However, they also expressed concern regarding a provision in USMCA that would permit the United States to decrease the de minimis level for express shipments from Mexico and Canada below $800, effectively in retaliation for their intransigence. This, according to the industry, would be the wrong response[59] (presumably because US importers of goods from all countries, not just Canada and Mexico, benefit from the relatively high US threshold). It seems likely, given the relative unresponsiveness of Canada and Mexico to US requests, that there will be further negotiations among the USMCA parties on de minimis levels in the future. Still, it appears that authority for the United States government

---

[56]   Addendum to Industry Trade Advisory Report on Services, October   19,   2018,   https://ustr.gov/sites/default/files/files/agreements/FTA/AdvisoryCommitteeReports/ITAC_10_REPORT-Services_Addendum.pdf, 2.

[57]   Addendum to Industry Trade Advisory Report on Services, 2.

[58]   USMCA, Art. 7.8(1)(f).

[59]   USMCA, Art. 7.8, n. 3.

to decrease de minimis levels was omitted from the United States-Mexico-Canada Implementation Act.[60]

V   OTHER PRODUCT AREAS AND PROCEDURES

Changes to the rules of origin are not limited to automotive goods. Other affected areas include chemicals, steel-intensive products, and glass and optical fiber goods, but are not discussed in detail in this report. All can be found in the product-specific rules of origin Annex.[61] Similarly, this report does not address changes, many reflecting desired modifications 28 years after NAFTA negotiations were concluded, to rules of origin in areas such as information and communication technology, pharmaceuticals, medical devices, cosmetics and chemicals.[62] Those interested in these sectors are directed to USMCA's sectoral annexes and to the industry trade advisory committee reports.[63]

The Office of the US Trade Representative has also identified some significant procedural changes relating to rules of origin, including "allowing importers as well as exporters and producers to makes [*sic*] certifications of origin and enhancing

---

[60]   H.R. 5430, 116th Congress, 1st Session, December 13, 2019, www.cbo.gov/publication/55960; see Andrea Shalal (2019), "U.S. to Drop Item on Tax-Free Threshold from North American Trade Pact: Sources," Reuters, December 10, www.reuters.com/article/us-usa -trade-usmca-taxbreaks/u-s-to-drop-item-on-tax-free-threshold-from -north-american-trade-pact-sources-idUSKBN1YE2TI (reporting on the Trump Administration decision after pressure from small business owners).

[61]   USMCA, Annex to Ch. 4.

[62]   See USMCA, Ch. 12 (sectoral annexes).

[63]   See USMCA, Ch. 12, https://ustr.gov/sites/default/files/ files/agreements/FTA/USMCA/Text/12_Sectoral_Annexes.pdf; Advisory Committee Reports, https://ustr.gov/trade-agreements/free -trade-agreements/united-states-mexico-canada-agreement/advisory -committee.

cooperation and enforcement tools for compliance with rules for all goods."[64] This appears to be a significant improvement over the current NAFTA rules. In my experience as a former customs lawyer with rules of origin under NAFTA, the importers, who are responsible under US law for paying any applicable customs duties, interest on those duties, and penalties for negligence,[65] were often concerned that their exporter/ producers in Canada or Mexico might have made errors in completing the certificates of origin, the liability for which would fall on the importers. Importer concerns about inaccurate certificates of origin, which might, after an audit several years later, result in higher duty liability for past imports, interest on additional duties and penalties for negligence or even gross negligence, were a factor that discouraged some importers, particularly SMEs, from seeking NAFTA treatment for their imports.[66]

---

[64]   Office of the US Trade Representative (2019), "Changes in Existing Law Required to Bring the United States into Compliance with Obligations Under the Agreement Between the United States of America, the United Mexican States and Canada (USMCA)," January 29, www.finance.senate.gov/imo/media/doc/USMCA%20 Changes%20To%20Existing%20US%20Law%20Document.pdf, 2. See USMCA, Art. 5.2.1 (providing that a "certification of origin [may be] completed by the exporter, producer or importer").

[65]   NAFTA, Art. 501.3(a).

[66]   See 19 U.S.C. Sec. 1592(f)(1): "[I]t is unlawful for any person to certify falsely, by fraud, gross negligence, or negligence, in a NAFTA Certificate of Origin (as defined in section 1508(b)(1) of this title) that a good to be exported to a NAFTA country (as defined in section 3301(4) of this title) qualifies under the rules of origin set out in section 3332 of this title."

3.   Settlement of disputes

I   INTRODUCTION

The North American Free Trade Agreement (NAFTA)[1] incorporated three distinct dispute settlement mechanisms. These address (1) investor–state disputes (ISDs) between foreign investors and host states; (2) binational panel review of national administrative agency rulings under domestic anti-dumping (AD) and subsidy/countervailing duty (CVD) laws; and (3) state-to-state disputes challenging another party's application or interpretation of the agreement.[2] The United States-Mexico-Canada Agreement (USMCA)[3] incorporates the same three mechanisms, two of which are extensively modified.

Retention of these three mechanisms was *not* a US objective in the NAFTA renegotiation. Rather, the original proposals made to Canada and Mexico contemplated:

*   a provision that would allow a party (e.g., the United States) to opt out of ISDS protection for foreign investment, without necessarily providing reciprocal protection for investors from Mexico and Canada;

---

[1]   See North American Free Trade Agreement, US-Mex.-Can., December 15, 1992, http://bit.ly/2FZ8d3z.
[2]   See NAFTA Chapters 11, 19, and 20, respectively.
[3]   Agreement Between the United States of America, the United Mexican States, and Canada, November 30, 2018 (not yet in force), http://bit.ly/2YSXFL9.

- elimination of Chapter 19 (AD/CVD binational panel) reviews of unfair trade practice remedies imposed by national agencies;
- converting state-to-state dispute settlement (Chapter 20) into a less legal and more diplomatic means for resolving disputes over the interpretation and application of NAFTA provisions, by allowing the United States to disregard panel decisions the US views as "clearly erroneous."[4]

Wisely, in my view, the US negotiators demonstrated a significant degree of flexibility in modifying or abandoning these objectives, without which the renegotiation probably would not have been successfully concluded and the US House of Representatives would not have approved USMCA.

II   INVESTOR PROTECTIONS AND INVESTOR–STATE DISPUTE SETTLEMENT

Worldwide, more than 3,300 international investment agreements—most of which are stand-alone bilateral investment treaties (BITs) or investment chapters in regional trade agreements such as NAFTA Chapter 11—have been negotiated, and more than two-thirds are in force.[5] As noted in Chapter 1, most of these incorporate investor–state dispute settlement (ISDS) with binding third-party international arbitration. This includes the Trans-Pacific Partnership (now the Comprehensive and Progressive Agreement for Trans-Pacific

---

4   Josh Wingrove and Eric Martin (2017), "U.S. Proposes Gutting NAFTA Legal Dispute Tribunals," Bloomberg Markets, October 14 (subscription), https://bloom.bg/2Uo23Cr.
5   UNCTAD (2018), "Investment Policy Monitor," December, Issue 20, http://bit.ly/2IaP0xC.

Partnership) negotiated by the Obama Administration but rejected by President Donald Trump.[6]

In its trade negotiations, the Trump Administration has departed from policies of previous US administrations, dating back to Ronald Reagan, which favored robust investor protections subject to ISDS. Rather, the president and Robert Lighthizer, his trade representative and chief USMCA negotiator, appear to be convinced that ISDS infringes on US sovereignty and may encourage American enterprises to move their production facilities to lower-wage countries such as Mexico.[7] These views are not confined to the Trump Administration. For example, law professor Jason Yackee has argued that the inclusion of ISDS in treaties such as TPP (or by extension, USMCA) is "unlikely to provide significant benefits" to investors or host countries and that because of ISDS "costs" the "rational way to proceed" is to exclude ISDS altogether.[8] Under such circumstances, supporters of ISDS should probably be relieved that ISDS was not eliminated entirely from USMCA.

The investment protection provisions of USMCA can be divided into four categories:

---

[6]   Trans-Pacific Partnership, February 4, 2016 (Australia, Bahrain, Canada, Chile, Japan, Malaysia, Mexico, New Zealand, Peru, Singapore, United States and Vietnam) (superseded), Ch. 8, http://bit.ly/2uLoYcb. TPP has been replaced for all parties other than the United States by the Comprehensive and Progressive Trans-Pacific Partnership, March 8, 2018, http://bit.ly/2UgPSIb. (The TPP and CPTPP must be read together. The CPTPP made minor modifications in the investment chapter not relevant to this discussion.)

[7]   See "Brady-Lighthizer Exchange [on ISDS]" (2018), International Economic Law and Policy Blog, March 21, http://bit.ly/2UmJkYM.

[8]   See Jason Yackee (2015), "New Trade Agreements Don't Need ISDS," Cato Unbound, May 19, http://bit.ly/2HW3UZ6.

A   Basic Investor Protections

The basic protections for "covered" investors and their investments, such as national treatment, most-favored-nation treatment, fair and equitable treatment, free choice of management, protection against performance requirements, free transfer of capital and profits, and protection against direct and indirect expropriation, generally apply under USMCA as under NAFTA and the TPP.[9] However, in USMCA, these host country obligations are enforceable against host governments only in national courts rather than in international arbitration, except as set out below.

B   Elimination of ISDS for Canada and the United States

For Canadian enterprises investing in Mexico and the United States, and Mexico- and US-based companies investing in Canada, no USMCA investor–state dispute enforcement protections will apply after a three-year transition period from NAFTA for "legacy" investment claims and pending claims that remain subject to NAFTA Chapter 11.[10] The absence of ISDS affects most significantly US investors in Canada and Canadian investors in the United States. Both will be required to rely on national courts for their disputes, courts that with a few exceptions are generally considered to be competent, unbiased, and free of corruption.[11] Still, there is no equiva-

---

[9]   USMCA, Arts 14.4–14.11; Annexes 14-A, 14-B; NAFTA, Arts 1102–1110; TPP, Arts 9.1–9.11.

[10]   USMCA, Annex 14-C.

[11]   *Loewen Group, Inc. and Raymond L. Loewen v. United States of America*, ICSID Case no. ARB(AFT)/98/3, http://bit.ly/2UiIewU, wherein what some believe was a gross miscarriage of justice in the Mississippi state courts was effectively upheld by the Chapter 11 tribunal, with the tribunal noting, inter alia, "A reader following our account of the injustices which were suffered by Loewen and Mr.

lent in Canada to the Fifth Amendment's prohibition on the seizure of private property for public use without providing just compensation, although such seizures are prohibited in some instances by statute. One study further concludes that of 35 Chapter 11 claims filed against Canada, awards would have been equivalent in only four cases had they been adjudicated by Canadian federal courts.[12] (No similar study exists for the United States since the US has not yet lost a NAFTA Chapter 11 case.) It is evident both the Canadian and US governments welcomed the elimination of ISDS from USMCA because the change "strengthened the Canadian government's right to regulate in the public interest," according to one official.[13] Those Canadian officials in Global Affairs Canada and the Ministry of Justice who have been responsible for defending actions in which Canada has paid out more than $200 million in awards and spent an estimated $65 million on outside legal fees[14] and other officials involved in defending Canada's interests may well have been pleased to avoid further NAFTA actions.[15]

From the point of view of Canadian investors in Mexico and Mexican investors in Canada, the CPTPP will provide a high degree of protection, similar to that currently provided by NAFTA's Chapter 11, for investor claims that arise

---

Raymond Loewen in the Courts of Mississippi could well be troubled to find that they emerge from the present long and costly proceedings with no remedy at all" (para. 241).

[12] See Armand de Mestral and Robin Morgan (2016), "Does Canadian Law Provide Remedies Equivalent to NAFTA Chapter 11 Arbitration?" CIGI Investor–State Arbitration Series Paper no. 4, May, http://bit.ly/2YMgz6a, 11. Others would have received only administrative remedies and no monetary damages.

[13] See James Munson (2019), "Canada Told to Pay $7 million in NAFTA Quarry Case," Bloomberg Law, February 26, http://bit.ly/2IhYMOB.

[14] See "Stop Investor-State Dispute Settlement" (2016), ISDS Platform, March, https://isds.bilaterals.org/?-isds-nafta-.

[15] Discussions with a former senior member of Canada's legal defense team, November 19, 2019.

after January 1, 2019, when the CPTPP entered into force for Canada, Mexico and five other parties.[16] However, the agreement excludes coverage for investment agreements and investment authorizations that were originally incorporated in the TPP.[17]

C   Investment in Mexican Government Projects

A limited group of potential ISDS claims against Mexico or Mexican government entities "relating to covered government contracts" will enjoy protections like those under NAFTA Chapter 11 and TPP Chapter 9. However, the list of covered sectors is narrow:

(i)   activities with respect to oil and natural gas that a national authority of an Annex Party controls, such as exploration, extraction, refining, transportation, distribution, or sale;

(ii)   the supply of power generation services to the public on behalf of an Annex Party;

(iii)   the supply of telecommunications services to the public on behalf of an Annex Party;

(iv)   the supply of transportation services to the public on behalf of an Annex Party; or

(v)   the ownership or management of roads, railways, bridges, or canals that are not for the exclusive or predominant use and benefit of the government of an Annex Party ...[18]

The first three categories are mostly self-evident. With (i), for example, both the United States and Mexico likely had concerns that without ISDS, it would be difficult to convince foreign investors to participate in exploration and devel-

---

[16] CPTPP, Ch. 9. As of December 30, 2018, the parties that had ratified the CPTPP were Australia, Canada, Japan, Mexico, New Zealand, Singapore and Vietnam. Ratification is pending in Brunei, Chile, Malaysia and Peru.

[17] TPP, Ch. 9; CPTPP, Annex, para. 2.

[18] USMCA, Annex 14.E, para. 6(b).

opment of Mexico's oil and gas reserves, particularly after initial decisions by Mexican President Andrés Manuel López Obrador that have increased investors' uneasiness. These include terminating construction of a new Mexico City airport (financed with about $6 billion in foreign-held bonds) using dubious "referendum" procedures, even though it was about one-third complete, and postponing auctions for new oil leases until 2021.[19]

Category (v) has generated the greatest interest and concern among stakeholders. In the initial draft of USMCA, the infrastructure scope was considerably more open ended. Under the version signed November 30, 2018, infrastructure such as dams, seaports and airports was not covered. While the USMCA provisions have no impact on the Mexico City airport bondholders—they would presumably be subject to dispute settlement under NAFTA Chapter 11—investment in future infrastructure projects could be jeopardized. For example, long-running efforts by stakeholders in Sonora, Mexico, and southern Arizona to expand the Port of Guaymas, Sonora, through private funding are probably less likely to succeed under USMCA.[20]

D   Other US Investments in Mexico

For investments between Mexico and the United States outside the scope of category (iii) above, ISDS is available but significantly circumscribed compared to NAFTA Chapter 11 or CPTPP Chapter 9. Significantly, ISDS claims are limited to alleged violations of national treatment, most-favored-nation

---

[19]   Colby Smith (2018), "Investors Face Big Call as Mexico's López Obrador Prepares Budget," *Financial Times*, December 11, https://on.ft.com/2UwkZ1K.

[20]   See Gabriela Rico (2013), "Port of Guaymas Set to Double Its Capacity, Seeks Arizona Ties," *Arizona Daily Star*, November 24, http://bit.ly/2uOzAHa.

treatment, and direct expropriation. Fair and equitable treatment and indirect expropriation claims are excluded.[21] In addition, for the first time in any US investment agreement or trade agreement investment chapter, claimants seeking ISDS under USMCA must demonstrate that they have first pursued proceedings under national courts or administrative tribunals and have either received a final decision, or 30 months have elapsed from the date such proceedings were initiated.[22]

The ISDS provisions have probably generated more opposition than any other USMCA provisions. For example, industry lawyers have criticized the exclusion of indirect expropriation:

> Most governments these days, maybe with the exception of a few I can think of, don't just issue a federal government decree saying they're going to expropriate your property. It's more sophisticated and it's more complicated than that. For heavily regulated industries it often is through regulation that they lose the value of their investment, often with a discriminatory element.[23]

Various observers in the United States and elsewhere have asked an obvious question: Does USMCA mean the death of ISDS, at least for agreements to which the United States is likely to become party? Analysts also wonder if the change represents a non-fatal but broader decline in ISDS. Globally, for instance, several Latin American countries have renounced the International Centre for Settlement of Investment Disputes (ICSID) Convention under which most ISDS proceedings are conducted, the EU Commission has developed an investment court/appellate body alternative, and opposition among

---

[21]   USMCA, Annex 14-D, Art. 14.D.3.
[22]   USMCA, Annex 14-D, Art. 14.D.5.
[23]   See "Industry Reps: Future Investment Rules Should Not Be Modeled on USMCA" (2018), World Trade Online, November 5, http://bit.ly/2G0RfSH.

citizens and legislators in EU member countries and the US continues to grow.[24]

Displeasure among attorneys, businesses and members of Congress over the weakened USMCA investment provisions goes beyond the agreement. The US Chamber of Commerce has strongly urged that the investment protection provisions (and some others) should not become precedents for future US trade agreements, arguing that USMCA "represents a notable step back" from NAFTA's Chapter 11.[25] These stakeholders will thus be unsatisfied with the treatment of investments in the United States' negotiating objectives for the United States-Japan Trade Agreement, which does not mention ISDS in the investment objectives section at all. Instead, it states: "Secure for U.S. investors in Japan important rights consistent with U.S. legal principles and practices, while ensuring that Japanese investors in the United States are not accorded greater substantive rights than domestic investors."[26] The same sparse language is used in the USTR's negotiating objectives for a proposed trade agreement with the EU.[27] In the phase one agreement with Japan these entreaties have been ignored.

In the text of the first stage trade agreement between the United States and Japan, neither host state obligations nor

---

[24] See Calliope Sudborough (2019), "What Is the ISDS Landscape Under the 'New NAFTA,'" Kluwer Arbitration Blog, January 9, http://bit.ly/2YM8OwZ.

[25] "Chamber: Elements of USMCA Should Not Be Viewed as Model for New FTAs" (2019), World Trade Online, January 9, http://bit.ly/2YQV2sX.

[26] "United States-Japan Trade Agreement (USJTA) Negotiations," December 2018, Office of the US Trade Representative, http://bit.ly/2FPP9Us, 6.

[27] "United States-European Union Negotiations," January 2019, Office of the US Trade Representative, http://bit.ly/2VrjcbG, 7.

ISDS are included in the text.[28] It is thus likely that if a trade agreement with the EU can be negotiated and put into force—which seems highly unlikely as of early 2020—it will exclude ISDS entirely, even if an investment chapter includes a list of host state obligations to foreign investors (e.g., national treatment, MFN treatment, and protection against performance requirements), as is the case with USMCA Chapter 14.

It has also been reported that in very preliminary discussions with UK officials about a free trade agreement, which took place in November 2018, US officials warned that the chances of having a successful discussion on ISDS would be significantly impaired if the UK were to propose a form of ICS (the EU's investment court/appellate body system).[29] Whether the absence of ISDS in any of these agreements would jeopardize congressional support is a premature question at present.

Also, while there may be a case for excluding ISDS from trade agreements with developed nations that maintain well-established and independent court systems, different considerations may arise with respect to protecting US investors in developing countries. Insofar as I am aware, USMCA is the first US trade agreement that affords differing treat-

---

[28]   US-Japan Trade Agreement, October 7, 2019, https://ustr.gov/countries-regions/japan-korea-apec/japan/us-japan-trade-agreement-negotiations/us-japan-trade-agreement-text. The agreement, annexes and side letters are limited to trade in agricultural goods (e.g., beef and rice) and certain manufactured products; for example, it does not address trade in autos and auto parts.

[29]   See Luke Eric Peterson (2019), "Analysis: Leaked Records of US-UK Discussions Between Negotiators, Offer Insights into Thinking on Investment Obligations and Dispute Settlement," IAREPORTER, November 28, www-iareporter-com.ezproxy1.library.arizona.edu/articles/analysis-leaked-records-of-us-uk-discussions-between-negotiators-offer-insights-into-thinking-on-investment-obligations-and-dispute-settlement/ (quoting Ambassador Lighthizer).

ment for developed and developing country parties. It has been suggested—probably naively—that the United States might strike a "quick hit" trade deal with Vietnam.[30] With Vietnam in particular, in the somewhat unlikely event that a trade agreement could be promptly negotiated, both parties would need to decide whether the current protections for US investors under the United States-Vietnam Bilateral Trade Agreement[31] would be terminated if and when the new agreement entered into force.

III   RESOLUTION OF "UNFAIR" TRADE DISPUTES

As discussed briefly in Chapter 1, the NAFTA Chapter 19 dispute settlement mechanism has been a non-negotiable "red line" for Canada since 1987.[32] The Chapter 19 binational panel process is an alternative to federal court review of anti-dumping and subsidies/countervailing duty determinations by the US Department of Commerce and the US International Trade Commission (and parallel agencies in Canada and Mexico). Under the United States-Canada Free Trade Agreement and again under NAFTA, administrative determinations in anti-dumping and countervailing duty cases—whether related to the amount of dumping, subsidies, or the existence of material injury—are reviewable by

---

[30]   "Pompeo: U.S. Could Strike a 'Quick Hit' Trade Deal with Vietnam" (2019), World Trade Online, March 5, http://bit.ly/2TYStl4.

[31]   Agreement Between the United States of America and the Socialist Republic of Vietnam on Trade Relations, July 13, 2000, Ch. IV, http://bit.ly/2I03DEG.

[32]   USMCA, Ch. 10, Sec. D, Art. 4. Chapter 19 was critical to Canada's acceptance of the United States-Canada Free Trade Agreement in 1987. See Alexander Panetta (2018), "NAFTA's Third-Party Arbitration System Was Canada's Big Prize ... Is It Worth Fighting For?" *The Star*, August 23, http://bit.ly/2K5W4hr.

binational panels composed of private citizens from the two countries involved. The panels are subject to the national unfair trade laws of the country that imposed the duties, but the process is international in that the panelists are nationals of two countries (i.e., the US and Canada) in a dispute involving the imposition of import duties onto either party.[33]

The maintenance of Chapter 19 procedures was apparently not a critical issue for Mexico in the USMCA negotiations (although the final provisions apply to Mexico as well as to Canada and the United States),[34] but it was politically essential for Canada. As Prime Minister Justin Trudeau said in early September 2018, "we will not sign a deal that is bad for Canadians and, quite frankly, not having a Chapter 19 to ensure that the rules [governing unfair trade rulings by administrative agencies] are followed would be bad for Canadians."[35] This statement reflected a long-held belief by Canada that US federal courts (such as the Court of International Trade and the Court of Appeals for the Federal Circuit) were not sufficiently independent from the executive branch (despite, in my view, little or no evidence of any bias).

It is safe to conclude that without US willingness to carry Chapter 19 provisions into USMCA with only minor changes,[36] Canada would not have agreed to be part of USMCA. The fact that the United States was willing to continue Chapter 19 provisions suggests perhaps—more than any other aspect of the negotiations with Canada—how important it was for the United States to assure that Canada became a USMCA party along with Mexico. Chapter 19 has never been popular with

---

[33]   NAFTA, Art. 1904.

[34]   USMCA, Annexes 10-B.1, 10-B.2, 10-B.3, 10-B.4 and 10-B.5, http://bit.ly/2CWnpgf.

[35]   See "Trudeau: Chapter 19, Cultural Exemptions Are NAFTA Red Lines for Canada" (2018), World Trade Online, September 4, http://bit.ly/2OOcXMo.

[36]   USMCA, Annexes 10-B.1, 10-B.2, 10-B.3, 10-B.4 and 10-B.5.

US officials or stakeholders. As I observed after an extensive review ten years ago,

> The panel process has been criticized (mostly by U.S. NGOs and others who have opposed NAFTA generally) in several respects. First, it has been attacked for putting decision-making power in the hands of individuals, including foreign nationals, without judicial experience, who are not accountable for their performance, who have not been appointed in accordance with Article III of the U.S. Constitution, and who may disregard the requirement that they behave as would local courts and apply U.S. law. The complexities and costs of a largely ad hoc system, which substitutes for what most believe is an acceptable national court system, have also been cited.[37]

For Canada, Chapter 19 has a long history rooted in a dispute over softwood lumber exports to the United States, which has generated multiple Chapter 19 reviews since the advent of the 1988 United States-Canada Free Trade Agreement[38] and again under NAFTA.[39] The dispute also generated one of three Chapter 19 "extraordinary challenges," a very limited review process in which Canada ultimately prevailed as it did in the

---

[37] David A. Gantz (2009), "The United States and Dispute Settlement Under the North American Free Trade Agreement: Ambivalence, Frustration and Occasional Defiance," in Cesare P.R. Romano (ed.), *The Sword and the Scales: The United States and International Courts and Tribunal*, New York: Cambridge University Press, pp. 356, 381.

[38] See *Certain Softwood Lumber Products from Canada*, Case nos. USA-CDA-1992-1904-01, USA-CDA-1992-1904-02, http://bit .ly/2IctBE3.

[39] See *Certain Softwood Lumber Products from Canada*, Case nos. USA-CDA-2002-1904-02, USA-CDA-2002-1904-03, USA-CDA-2002-1904-07, USA-CDA-2005-1904-01, USA-CDA-2006-1904-04, USA-CDA-2006-1904-05, http://bit.ly/2IctBE3.

bulk of the Chapter 19 binational panel disputes.[40] As Canada asserted after the USMCA negotiations were completed,

> Given the integrated nature of the North American economy, it is important to minimize the disruptions that can result from the imposition of trade remedies. This outcome ensures that trade remedies are applied in a fair, transparent, and responsible way while maintaining recourse, when necessary, to an impartial binational panel dispute settlement mechanism to review anti-dumping and countervailing duty measures imposed by CUSMA partners.[41]

At the same time, there is little evidence that Canada, despite insisting on the inclusion of a Chapter 19-style mechanism in USMCA, would have been unwilling to consider modifications that might have made Chapter 19 less controversial in the US and more effective. The timing of the negotiations, whereby Mexico and the United States concluded what was effectively a bilateral agreement in August 2018 and the US and Canada rushed to bring Canada into the accord by the end of September, effectively precluded a detailed review of Chapter 19.[42] Had the parties been afforded more time, it is at least possible that the limited review of binational panel determinations under NAFTA's extraordinary challenge procedures[43] could have been addressed and modified. Also,

---

[40]   See NAFTA, Art. 1904.13, Annex 1904.13; and *Softwood Lumber Products from Canada*, Case no. ECC-2004-1904-01USA, NAFTA Decisions and Reports, www.nafta-sec-alena.org/Home/Dispute-Settlement/Decisions-and-Reports.

[41]   Government of Canada (2018), "Trade Remedies and Related Dispute Settlement (Chapter 19) Summary," October, http://bit.ly/2Vp7WfU.

[42]   It was critical for Mexico to be able to sign USMCA before President López Obrador took office on December 1. President Trump, under the TPA, could not sign in less than 90 days after the text was made public.

[43]   NAFTA, Annex 1904.13.

the parallel remedies provided in the event of challenges to anti-dumping and countervailing duty orders available to private parties under Chapter 19 and to governments under the World Trade Organization's dispute settlement mechanism might have been discussed. (NAFTA and USMCA allow parties to choose between regional or WTO forums for most state-to-state disputes, but neither addresses parallelism with unfair trade disputes.[44]) The absence as of December 2019 of the WTO option, as discussed below, presumably makes this binational panel system under USMCA even more important to Canada and Mexico.

IV STATE-TO-STATE DISPUTE SETTLEMENT

A US Ambivalence

US efforts to undercut the WTO's appellate body are apparently due to dissatisfaction with both its procedures and substantive actions (the latter of which did not originate with the Trump Administration)[45] and the Trump Administration's commitment to "defending our national sovereignty over trade policy."[46] As of December 11, 2019, the appellate body ceased to function, since only one of the seven members remained active.[47] Some but not all of these complaints are applicable *mutatis mutandis* to other third-party dispute resolution mechanisms that affect the application of US trade laws

---

[44] NAFTA, Art. 2005.1; USMCA, Art. 31.3(1).

[45] See Kimberly Ann Elliott (2018), "Can the World Trade Organization Be Saved?" *World Politics Review*, October 16, http://bit.ly/2YMiffY.

[46] USTR (2017), "The President's Trade Policy Agenda," http://bit.ly/2WIGSs4, 3.

[47] See Jamey Keaten and Paul Wiseman (2019), "World Trade Without Rules? U.S. Shuts Down WTO Appeals Court," *Time*, December 10, https://time.com/5746978/wto-appeals-court/.

and policies, such as those in regional trade agreements. The United States-China "Phase One" trade agreement, concluded January 15, 2020, omits third-party dispute settlement including recourse to the WTO entirely, replacing it with a "bilateral evaluation and dispute resolution mechanism" that permits unilateral action by the United States in the event of alleged failure by China to comply with the agreement.[48]

Relatively little public discussion of US objections to NAFTA's Chapter 20 dispute settlement mechanism exists for what I believe are several obvious reasons. First, it has been possible for the United States (and the other parties) to indefinitely delay panel proceedings under Chapter 20 simply by refusing to appoint individuals to the Chapter 20 roster;[49] instead of panel members being more-or-less automatically appointed to adjudicate a dispute, each panel member is selected only after extensive bilateral consultations among the states party to the dispute. For example, in the most recently completed Chapter 20 proceeding, *Cross-Border Trucking Services*, 15 months passed between Mexico's first request for formation of the panel and when proceedings actually began.[50]

---

[48]   Economic and Trade Agreement Between the Government of the United States of America and the Government of the People's Republic of China, January 15, 2020, https://ustr.gov/sites/default/files/files/agreements/phase%20one%20agreement/Economic_And_Trade_Agreement_Between_The_United_States_And_China_Text.pdf, Ch. 7.

[49]   NAFTA, Arts 2008, 2009. On a few occasions NAFTA panelist rosters were designated but when they expired after three years they often were not replaced. USMCA provides in Article 31.8(1) that roster members once appointed remain in place until their successors are appointed, and that the initial roster of 30 persons must be in place as of the entry into force of USMCA. However, similar language in NAFTA (Article 2009.1) providing for appointment of roster members by January 1, 1994 (the date NAFTA entered into force) was apparently not complied with.

[50]   *In the Matter of Cross-Border Trucking Services*, USA-Mex-1998-2008-1, February 6, 2001, 6–7 (paras 21, 22),

Distrust from Mexico and Canada was strongly reinforced when the United States refused to cooperate for more than four years on the formation of a panel requested by Mexico to adjudicate related disputes over high-fructose corn syrup and US sugar quotas under NAFTA. Despite this history of US stonewalling, Mexico remained open to a new version of USMCA that was only moderately altered from NAFTA's Chapter 20 and thus is no guaranty that stonewalling will not occur in the future.[51]

Secondly, all three NAFTA parties appear to have generally preferred the WTO's dispute settlement process to NAFTA's for the review of trade disputes among them. They could be confident that WTO panels would be promptly appointed by the WTO secretariat, that panel and appellate body time limits for each stage of the dispute resolution process would be more or less observed, that other members could intervene in cases (often a benefit for Mexico and Canada that was not available in NAFTA dispute settlement), and that procedures to enforce rulings would be enforced.[52] Unfortunately, delays in WTO dispute settlements have increased in recent years, in part due to US refusal to appoint and reappoint appellate body members at the WTO.[53] The demise of the WTO dispute

---

NAFTA Decisions and Reports, www.nafta-sec-alena.org/Home/Dispute-Settlement/Decisions-and-Reports.

[51] See "Mexico's View of the Problems with the NAFTA Panel Appointment Process" (2018), *International Economic Law and Policy Blog*, October 12, http://bit.ly/2uR2tm5.

[52] See Understanding on the Rules and Procedures Governing the Settlement of Disputes, Annex 2 of the WTO Agreement, April 15, 1994, especially Arts 4, 6, 10, 11, 12, 16, 17, 19, 20, 22, http://bit.ly/2uR2x5j. In fairness, a significant majority of the nearly three dozen WTO actions involving NAFTA parties addressed anti-dumping and subsidies for unfair trade actions, where NAFTA jurisdiction is excluded. See NAFTA, Art. 2004; WTO, "Chronological List of Disputes Cases," March 2019, http://bit.ly/2TXpIoO.

[53] Elliott, "Can the World Trade Organization Be Saved?"

settlement mechanism makes effective regional mechanisms all the more important to Canada and Mexico in state-to-state dispute settlement as well as under the Chapter 19 mechanism in USMCA, but it was the Democratic Congress that forced the Trump Administration to improve the functioning of the USMCA state-to-state dispute settlement mechanism.

B   State-to-State Dispute Settlement Under USMCA

Mexico and Canada faced an unpleasant choice in the negotiations: they could either support a NAFTA-type mechanism in USMCA despite its imperfections or accept a mechanism that likely would have posed fewer restraints on the US than NAFTA Chapter 20. Faced with this dilemma, Mexico's negotiators beat back US efforts to formally grant veto power to parties that object to adverse panel decisions. As one of Mexico's negotiators noted, "Dispute resolution is for the small country. So, Mexico is particularly interested."[54] Simultaneously, the negotiator admitted that USMCA Chapter 31 does not address the root problem behind the delays in establishing panels (i.e., the United States' failure to agree to designate panel rosters in advance). However, he argued that this was a necessary compromise to avoid the US veto proposal.[55] In so doing, Mexico suggested—perhaps overly optimistically—that instances of blocked panels had been limited to a single case involving sugar, and "it's not something that will happen frequently, so we said okay."[56] As indicated earlier, the sugar case was not the only instance in which long delays in appointing panelists had occurred, but it may well have been the only one in which the United States acted in bad faith rather than simply exercising extraordinary care in choosing objective panelists.

---

[54]   "Mexico's View of the Problems."
[55]   Ibid.
[56]   Ibid.

The result initially was a USMCA state-to-state dispute settlement Chapter 31 that made few substantive changes compared to NAFTA and more closely resembles NAFTA than the TPP. A few possibly significant differences exist. For example, NAFTA states that "On receipt of the final report of a panel, the disputing parties shall agree on the resolution of the dispute, which normally shall conform with the determinations and recommendations of the panel, and shall notify their sections of the secretariat of any agreed resolution of any dispute."[57] USMCA simply mandated that "Within 45 days from receipt of a final report ... the disputing parties shall endeavor to agree on the resolution of the dispute."[58] USMCA provides more specific directions for the function of panels: "A panel's function is to make an objective assessment of the matter before it and to present a report that contains" findings of fact and determinations as to whether "the measure at issue is inconsistent with obligations in this agreement, (ii) a party has otherwise failed to carry out its obligations in this agreement, (iii) the measure at issue is causing nullification or impairment ... or (iv) any other determination requested in the terms of reference" as well as recommendations and reasons for the findings and determinations.[59] Also, reflecting the technological changes of the past 28 years, USMCA allows for electronic filing of documents.[60]

Still, in the event that a party wishes to challenge another party's application or interpretation of the agreement, USMCA, like NAFTA, provides for mandatory consultations and optional "good offices" (conciliation, mediation or other instances where a third party seeks to help the disputing parties resolve their differences) before resorting to arbitration.[61]

---

[57] NAFTA, Art. 2018(1).
[58] USMCA, Art. 31.18.
[59] USMCA, Art. 31.13(1).
[60] USMCA, Art. 31.12.
[61] USMCA, Arts 31.4, 31.5.

Roster appointment requirements were essentially unchanged from NAFTA as well, and five-person panels remain the rule.[62] Appointed panelists must "have expertise or experience in international law, international trade, other matters covered by this agreement, or the resolution of disputes arising under international trade agreements." Members must be selected objectively, be independent of the governments involved, and follow a code of conduct designed to avoid actual or apparent conflicts of interest.[63] Critically, under USMCA (as was the case with NAFTA), "The roster shall be appointed by *consensus* and remain in effect for a minimum of three years or until the parties constitute a new roster."[64] No appellate mechanism exists, and trade penalties (e.g., additional tariffs or quotas) are available if the losing party fails to implement the final report or otherwise "agree on the resolution of the dispute."[65]

Whether the Mexico negotiator's (in my view misplaced) optimism that parties (read "the United States") would refrain from blocking roster and panel appointments under USMCA remains to be seen, but as of December 2019 this became a less significant threat. Changes in the mechanism were demanded by the Democratic Congress (presumably because of their concerns over enforcement of the USMCA's labor and environmental obligations as discussed in Chapter 4) and accepted by the Trump Administration;[66] they were presumably welcomed by both Mexico and Canada.

The changes mandated by the Democratic Congress in the December 10, 2019 amendments focus primarily on appoint-

---

[62]   USMCA, Arts 31.6, 31.8, 31.9.

[63]   USMCA, Art. 31.8.2.

[64]   USMCA, Art. 31.8(1) (emphasis added).

[65]   USMCA, Art. 31.8.

[66]   USMCA Protocol of Amendment, December 10, 2019, https://ustr.gov/trade-agreements/free-trade-agreements/united-states-mexico-canada-agreement/protocol-amendments, para. 7 (now part of the consolidated USMCA text of December 13, 2019).

ment of roster members and selection of roster members
when a complaint is lodged, although they also add rules of
evidence designed to make the dispute settlement process
more predictable by adding rules of evidence to the rules of
procedure.[67] First, blocking of or failure to appoint roster
members should be significantly less frequent:

> The Parties shall establish, *by the date of entry into force of this
> Agreement*, and maintain a roster of up to 30 individuals who are
> willing to serve as panelists. Each Party shall designate up to 10
> individuals. The Parties shall endeavor to achieve consensus on
> the appointments. If the Parties are unable to achieve consensus
> by one month after the date of entry into force of this Agreement,
> the roster shall be comprised of the designated individuals. The
> roster shall remain in effect for a minimum of three years or until
> the Parties constitute a new roster. If a Party fails to designate its
> individuals to the roster, the Parties may still request the estab-
> lishment of panels under Article 31.6 (Establishment of a Panel).
> The Rules of Procedure, which shall be established by the date
> of entry into force of this Agreement, shall provide for how to
> compose a panel in such circumstances. Members of the roster
> may be reappointed. In the event that an individual is no longer
> able or willing to serve as a panelist, the relevant Party shall
> designate a replacement. The Parties shall endeavor to achieve
> consensus on the appointment. If the Parties are unable to achieve
> consensus by one month after the date the replacement is desig-
> nated, the individual shall be added to the roster.[68]

Unfortunately, USMCA still leaves to the yet-to-be-established
rules of procedure the steps to be taken if the party refuses to
designate its panelists; nor is it clear from the language quoted
above how long the appointed panelists are to serve on the
roster (except indicating that the minimum is three years and
a roster member serves until replaced).

Importantly, other revisions provide detailed procedures
for choosing the five panelists (in this quotation where there

---

[67] USMCA, Art. 31.11.2.
[68] USMCA, Art. 31.8.1.

are two disputing parties) and would presumably prevail in the event of a conflict of the USMCA text with the rules of procedure:

(a) The panel shall comprise five members, unless the disputing Parties agree to a panel comprised of three members.

(b) The disputing Parties shall endeavor to decide on the chair of the panel within 15 days of the delivery of the request for the establishment of the panel. If the disputing Parties are unable to decide on the chair within this period, the disputing Party chosen by lot shall select within five days as chair an individual who is not a citizen of that Party.

(c) If the responding Party refuses to participate in or fails to appear for the choosing by lot procedure, the complaining Party shall select an individual from the roster who is not a citizen of that Party ...

(d) Within 15 days of selection of the chair, each disputing Party shall select two panelists who are citizens of the other disputing Party.

(e) If a disputing Party fails to select its panelists within that period, those panelists shall be selected by lot from among the roster members who are citizens of the other disputing Party.

(f) If the responding Party refuses to participate in or fails to appear for the choosing by lot procedure, the complaining Party shall select two individuals from the roster who are citizens of the complaining Party ... [69]

Only time will tell whether this language, and the rules of procedure, will eliminate stonewalling, but the mechanism provides powerful incentives for parties to appoint their own rosters of potential panelists. It seems unlikely that any party would risk the selection of a panel chair by the complaining party without itself having any role in the selection process. Similarly, why would one party risk the selection of two panelists, who are citizens of another party, by that same party, rather than on its own behalf? (With the five-person

---

[69] USMCA, Art. 39.9.1.

panels, two of the panelists are each to be chosen from citizens of the *opposing* party. Thus, in a dispute between the
United States and Mexico, the United States is to choose
two Mexican citizens from the rosters, and Mexico is to
choose two US citizens, as was the case under NAFTA. It
is unclear why the USMCA negotiators chose to maintain
the five-panelist approach rather than following the CPTPP
and other mechanisms that have opted for three panelists.)
Still, the more sensible approach to addressing a situation
where the responding party refuses to appoint its panelists
or cooperate in the choice of the chairperson was apparently
never seriously considered. In USMCA, for example, when
the parties to an investment dispute are unable to agree on
the choice of arbitrators, the Secretary-General makes the
appointments.[70] It would have been preferable under Chapter
31 to designate an appointing authority such as the ICSID
Secretary-General, the Director-General of the WTO, or the
head of some similar body, to avoid lengthy disputes over
panel selections. Unfortunately, the Trump Administration is
not the only current or past US or foreign government that has
shied away from giving such responsibility to an independent
official.[71] An early test of whether the revised mechanism is
an improvement over NAFTA will be whether the United
States has appointed its roster by July 1, as required under the
agreement.

While neither NAFTA nor USMCA addresses alternative
dispute resolution, other than state-to-state dispute settlement,
in any detail, both provide for a mandatory advisory com-

---

[70] USMCA, Annex 14-D, Art. 14.D.6.2.

[71] Interestingly, the panel appointment process in Chapter 28 of
the CPTPP contemplates the use of an unspecified "independent third
party" under certain circumstances when the parties cannot agree on
the chairperson. However, the parties to the dispute must "jointly"
choose the independent third party! See CPTPP, Art. 28.9.2(5)(B).

mittee on private commercial disputes.[72] Some may consider this potentially significant, since the TPP calls for no similar advisory committee.[73] The "NAFTA 2022" committee has met periodically throughout the agreement's history.[74] Similar committees were contemplated in post-NAFTA FTAs negotiated by the US, but typically their formation was discretionary; to the best of my knowledge, none was ever formed.[75]

---

[72]   NAFTA, Art. 2022; USMCA, Art. 31.22.4.

[73]   TPP, Art. 28.23.

[74]   See NAFTA 2022 Committee, http://bit.ly/2VovcKG.

[75]   See, for example, Central America-United States-Dominican Free Trade Agreement (Dominican Republic, El Salvador, Guatemala, Honduras, Nicaragua, United States), August 5, 2015, http://bit.ly/2FPw4l3, Art. 20.22(4).

4. Labor rights and environmental protection

[The USMCA parties have resolved to:]
PROMOTE high levels of environmental protection, including through effective enforcement by each Party of its environmental laws, as well as through enhanced environmental cooperation, and further the aims of sustainable development, including through mutually supportive trade and environmental policies and practices; PROMOTE the protection and enforcement of labor rights, the improvement of working conditions, the strengthening of cooperation and the Parties' capacity on labor issues ...[1]

I   INTRODUCTION

The evolution of labor and environmental rights in US free trade agreements (FTAs) has been a nonlinear process over the last 26 years, beginning with the North American Free Trade Agreement (NAFTA) negotiations in 1991.[2] At that time, the inclusion of labor and environmental provisions in US FTAs was not a foregone conclusion; in fact, it was mostly an afterthought. Furthermore, no such provisions are found in the pre-NAFTA agreements with Israel and Canada.

---

[1]   United States-Mexico-Canada Agreement (USMCA), November 30, 2019 (not in force), Preamble, https://ustr.gov/trade-agreements/free-trade-agreements/united-states-mexico-canada-agreement/agreement-between.
[2]   The first US FTA, negotiated with Israel in 1985, was a relatively short document and contained no labor or environmental provisions. See David A. Gantz (2009), *Regional Trade Agreements: Law Policy and Practice*, Durham, NC: Carolina Academic Press, pp. 208–18.

However, the relationship between trade and labor was well established in the United States prior to NAFTA through nonreciprocal programs such as the Generalized System of Preferences,[3] the Caribbean Basin Initiative,[4] and the African Growth and Opportunity Act.[5] The time, therefore, was ripe for addressing labor and environmental issues in US Free Trade Agreements.

The two NAFTA "side" agreements on labor and on environment were considered necessary when President Bill Clinton succeeded President George H.W. Bush in January 1993, after NAFTA had been negotiated and signed by President Bush in December 1992, but before it had been submitted to Congress for approval. As a presidential candidate in October 1993, Clinton boldly endorsed NAFTA, but only on the condition that NAFTA's environmental and labor provisions be strengthened.[6] Clinton's decision was driven in part by concerns of members of Congress and other elected officials in the US that without labor and environmental provisions, working and living conditions on both sides of the border would deteriorate.[7]

Following NAFTA, labor and environmental provisions in US trade agreements evolved considerably due to strong congressional pressure reflected in various versions of Trade

---

[3]   See, for example, US legislation authorizing the GSP program, 19 U.S.C. Secs 2461 *et seq.*

[4]   19 U.S.C. Secs 2701–2707.

[5]   19 U.S.C. Secs 3701–3739 (2006).

[6]   Gerald F. Seib (2002), "Clinton Backs the North American Trade Pact, but Candidates' Stances on the Issue Aren't Clear," *Wall Street Journal*, October 5, A14.

[7]   See, for example, "NAFTA Effects: Claims and Arguments 1991–1994, 1996" (1996), Commission for Environmental Cooperation, www3.cec.org/islandora/en/item/1692-nafta-effects -potential-nafta-effects-claims-and-arguments-1991-1994-en.pdf (discussing various claims regarding the environmental effects of NAFTA).

Promotion Authority (TPA) legislation. This is particularly apparent in the inclusion of labor provisions in the body of subsequent free trade agreements such as those concluded with Australia, Chile and Singapore, among many others, and submission of labor and environmental disputes to the same state-to-state mechanism used for trade disputes.[8] Given how trade agreements are ratified in the United States—where passage in the House of Representatives typically requires at least 30 to 40 votes from the Democratic Party, which emphasizes labor rights and environmental protection issues—no president since Clinton has sought to conclude a regional trade agreement without including labor rights and environmental protection chapters.

As discussed in this chapter, USMCA in its final version provides important new mechanisms for improving the status of labor rights and levels of environmental protection in North America. As with other provisions, their success will depend largely on whether the parties have the political will to utilize them.

II   LABOR RIGHTS

A   NAFTA's NAALC and Subsequent FTAs

Many observers believe that NAFTA's poor coverage of labor was one of the agreement's most glaring weaknesses. NAFTA itself incorporates little coverage of labor issues except for references in the preamble to creating new employment opportunities, improving working conditions, and enhancing and enforcing basic workers' rights. NAFTA provides for

---

[8]   See David A. Gantz (2011), "Labor Rights and Environmental Protection Under NAFTA and Other US Free Trade Agreements," *University of Miami Inter-American Law Review*, **42**, 297.

temporary visitors for business purposes,[9] but it does not further deal with immigration-related matters.

When addressing NAFTA's perceived labor shortcomings and given the timing and the reluctance of all parties to reopening the discussions for a highly complex agreement that had already been negotiated and signed, the most practical solution was to negotiate parallel agreements. For example, the Clinton Administration's desire for broader labor coverage resulted in the North American Agreement on Labor Cooperation (NAALC).[10]

In the NAALC, each party retains the right to set and apply its own labor standards. Each party is also required to provide in its laws for unspecified "high labor standards"[11] and to enforce labor rights through specified procedures, including citizens to petition the authorities for redress.[12] Such public access was apparently intended to shed light on poor labor practices that otherwise would not have received much public attention. The NAALC parties also committed to encouraging freedom of association; the right to organize; the right to collective bargaining and to strike; the prohibition of forced labor; protection for child labor; minimum employment standards; the elimination of discrimination in employment; equal pay for men and women; the prevention of and compensation for occupational injuries and illnesses; and the protection of migrant workers.[13]

The NAALC initially provided for a Commission for Labor Cooperation (CLC) consisting of a council of ministers

---

[9]   North American Free Trade Agreement, United States-Canada-Mexico, December 15, 1992, Ch. 16.

[10]   North American Agreement on Labor Cooperation ("NAALC"), September 14, 1993, www.dol.gov/ilab/reports/pdf/naalc.htm.

[11]   NAALC, Art. 2.

[12]   NAALC, Art. 42.

[13]   NAALC, Annex 1.

and a secretariat.[14] Each NAFTA party established its own National Administrative Office (NAO) (now the Bureau of International Labor Affairs in the United States), which monitor the labor rights issues in North America. The primary functions of the IALB include "receiving complaints about non-enforcement of labor laws" by a NAFTA government.[15]

With regard to labor issues, the formal dispute settlement mechanism—which is solely available to the NAFTA governments—may be utilized only where there is a "persistent pattern of failure ... to effectively enforce enumerated labor standards."[16] Standards enforceable by arbitration are limited to occupational safety, health, child labor, or minimum wage technical labor standards.[17] In other words, denying the right to organize a union alone would not be subject to arbitration. After intergovernmental consultations are conducted, fact-finding and/or mediation by the CLC may occur. If issues are not resolved at this point, a party may request arbitration, a step requiring a two-thirds vote of the CLC for approval;[18] because of the two-thirds requirement, no arbitration has ever occurred under the NAALC. Moreover, the secretariat that was originally intended to pursue citizen complaints (which had some success in the early years), had for all practical purposes disappeared entirely by 2009, with its responsibilities absorbed by the three national labor offices, which were largely ineffective.[19]

Major innovations in US trade agreements concluded since NAFTA, including in the Trans-Pacific Partnership (TPP)

---

[14] NAALC, Arts 8–14.

[15] NAALC, Arts 15–16, esp. Art. 16.3.

[16] NAALC, Art. 27.1.

[17] NAALC, Art. 27.1.

[18] NAALC, Arts 28–29.

[19] Ruth Buchanan and Rusby Chaparro (2008), "International Institutions and Transnational Advocacy: The Case of the North American Agreement on Labor Cooperation," *UCLA Journal of International and Foreign Affairs*, **13**, 129, 157.

Agreement and now USMCA, have accepted the International Labor Organization (ILO) Declaration on Fundamental Principles and Rights at Work,[20] the elimination of sex-based discrimination,[21] and a mechanism for accepting citizen submissions regarding labor complaints through the establishment of contact points.[22]

However, the improvements in TPP did not deal effectively with one key issue, the requirement that "No Party shall fail to effectively enforce its labour laws through a sustained or recurring course of action or inaction in a manner affecting trade or investment between the Parties ..."[23] This linkage was primarily responsible for the refusal of a tribunal convened under the CAFTA-DR to find actionable violations of Guatemala's labor laws, with the panel concluding that the failure—which the panel recognized—was not done "in a manner affecting trade."[24] In USMCA, the scope of the "in a manner affecting trade" proviso is broadened:

> For greater certainty, a "course of action or inaction" is "in a manner affecting trade or investment between the Parties" if the course involves: (i) a person or industry that produces a good or supplies a service traded between the Parties or has an investment in the territory of the Party that has failed to comply with this obligation; or (ii) a person or industry that produces a good or

---

[20]   USMCA, Art. 23.3; such rights include freedom of association and the right to collective bargaining; elimination of forced or compulsory labor; abolition of child labor; and elimination of discrimination in employment. The Declaration is referenced in place of the various ILO agreements since the United States is not a party to any of them.

[21]   USMCA, Art. 23.9.

[22]   USMCA, Arts 23.11, 23.15; see TPP, Ch. 19.

[23]   TPP, Art. 19.5.1.

[24]   "Trade Dispute Panel Issues Ruling in US-Guatemala Labour Case" (2017), Bridges, July 6, www.ictsd.org/bridges-news/bridges/news/trade-dispute-panel-issues-ruling-in-us-guatemala-labour-law-case.

supplies a service that competes in the territory of a Party with a good or a service of another Party.[25]

As discussed below, additional changes incorporated in the final USMCA text extensively expand enforcement of USMCA's labor provisions, including, inter alia, a requirement that the responding government prove that a labor violation does not affect trade and investment, and establishing a new "facility-specific rapid response labor mechanism." The NAALC is formally terminated as of the date of entry into force of USMCA.[26]

B   Trump and López Obrador's Mutual Interest in Mexican Labor Law Reform

USMCA obligations relating to labor rights in Mexico support one of President Andrés Manuel López Obrador's (AMLO) major campaign promises, to reduce income inequality in Mexico. The USMCA provisions are also consistent with the Trump Administration's desire to make the production of goods in Mexico relatively less inexpensive, in this case by somewhat reducing the large differential between US and Mexican wage rates. As discussed in Chapter 3,[27] USMCA includes a requirement that a significant percentage of automobile and light truck content be produced in facilities where workers are paid at least $16 per hour. Taken together, these

[25] USMCA, Art. 23.5, fn. 9.

[26] Protocol Replacing the North American Free Trade Agreement with the Agreement Between the United States of America, the United Mexican States, and Canada, November 30, 2019, para. 3, https://ustr.gov/sites/default/files/files/agreements/FTA/USMCA/Text/USMCA_Protocol.pdf (to which USMCA is annexed).

[27] David A. Gantz (2019), "The United States-Mexico-Canada Agreement: Tariffs, Customs and Rules of Origin," Baker Institute, February 21, www.bakerinstitute.org/media/files/files/6ee1ade5/bi-report-022119-mex-usmca.pdf, 3.

factors assisted Mexican and US negotiators in fashioning strong, mutually acceptable labor reform provisions for Mexico.

C   USMCA Labor Provisions and Changes in Mexican Law

Many of the labor chapter's provisions reflect those of the Trans-Pacific Partnership and other free trade agreements negotiated by the United States including the NAALC side agreement as discussed earlier. However, a major innovation of USMCA is the Mexico-specific requirements in an annex to the labor rights chapter that are designed to facilitate the activities of independent unions and collective bargaining.[28] The key labor innovation in USMCA is an annex entitled "Worker Representation in Collective Bargaining in Mexico." It is evident from the language that AMLO endorsed this set of obligations during the negotiations:

> Mexico shall adopt and maintain the following provisions covered in this Annex, necessary for the effective recognition of the right to collective bargaining, given that *the incoming Mexican government has confirmed that each of these provisions is within the scope of the mandate provided to the incoming government by the people of Mexico in the recent elections.*[29]

The most significant labor obligations for Mexico are to guarantee the

> right of workers to engage in concerted activities for collective bargaining or protection and to organize, form, and join the union of their choice, and prohibit employer domination or interference in union activities, discrimination or coercion against workers for

---

[28]   USMCA, Annex 23-A.

[29]   USMCA, Annex 23-A, introductory paragraph (emphasis added).

union activity or support, and refusal to bargain collectively with the duly recognized union.[30]

Mexico's labor laws were modified and expanded in May 2019 to facilitate the implementation of the right to unionization through independent administrative bodies, including labor courts. In addition, the modified labor laws facilitate the registration of union elections and resolution of disputes, with a variety of safeguards for union organizing including the use of secret ballot votes subject to clear time limits and independent verification. Transparency obligations also exist, including a requirement that collective bargaining agreements be made available to affected workers.[31] The new labor laws were finally approved by Mexico's Congress at the end of April 2019,[32] although the Confederation of Mexican Workers (a group that favors the status quo of government-controlled labor unions) objected, presumably because of opposition to a new Federal Conciliation and Labor Registry.[33] USMCA effectively could not be introduced in the United States Congress until Democrats in both houses had an opportunity to review the new Mexican law thoroughly and assess whether

---

[30]   USMCA, Annex 23-A, para. 1.

[31]   USMCA, Annex 23-A, paras 3–7.

[32]   Eric Martin (2019), "Mexican Congress Passes Labor Law Tied to USMCA Trade Agreement," Bloomberg Law, April 29, www.bloomberg.com/news/articles/2019-04-29/mexican-congress -passes-labor-law-tied-to-usmca-trade-agreement; see also "Mexican Official: Labor Reform Legislation Slated to Pass by the End of April" (2019), World Trade Online, February 19, https://insidetrade .com/trade/mexican-official-labor-reform-legislation-slated-pass -end-april.

[33]   See "Mexico's Biggest Union to Challenge a Key Part of Labor Reform" (2019), Bloomberg Law, April 24, https://news .bloomberglaw.com/international-trade/mexicos-biggest-union-to -challenge-a-key-part-of-labor-reform.

it meets the USMCA requirements,[34] a process that effectively continued into fall 2019. For many Democratic members of Congress and union representatives, the issue was not the legislation itself but the prospects for effective enforcement.

The importance of such reforms as mandated by USMCA to Mexican workers is difficult to overemphasize. Data suggests that workers in Mexico receive a smaller share of the country's total economic output than workers in most other countries.[35] What passes for collective bargaining in Mexico is considered by many to be simply rubber-stamping, with workers under "protection contracts" often receiving little more than the minimum wages they would earn without labor contracts, and with union dues transferred directly from wage deductions to unions. In many instances, workers do not even know that such union contracts exist. In practice, workers in Mexico have not had the right to vote on unions, union representation, or labor contacts.[36] This should change under the new labor laws with the support of the AMLO Administration, despite opposition by some business groups that prize Mexico's low wages as a boon to exports. However, US unions and their supporters in Congress are deeply suspicious that Mexico's labor situation will not change without strong enforcement mechanisms invoked by the US government.

---

[34] See "Sources: Mexican Labor Legislation Unlikely to Pass by USMCA Deadline" (2018), December 13, World Trade Online, https://insidetrade.com/daily-news/sources-mexican-labor -legislation-unlikely-pass-usmca-deadline (noting the conditional support by key Democratic lawmakers).

[35] Nacha Cattan (2019), "Labor Reform Is Coming to Mexico, Where Low Pay Fuels Imports," Bloomberg Law, April 26, www .bloomberg.com/news/articles/2019-04-26/labor-reform-is-coming -to-mexico-where-low-pay-fuels-exports.

[36] Ibid.

D **Addressing Enforcement Concerns Through the USMCA Protocol**

Due to the weakness of NAFTA's labor provisions and many subsequent labor chapters in US trade agreements, Democratic members of Congress and their union allies demanded that better enforcement mechanisms be incorporated in USMCA to ensure that Mexico's government enforces the improved labor laws. "Mexico has yet to demonstrate that it has the resources and the infrastructure to follow-through on its promised reforms," AFL-CIO President Trumka (who later supported USMCA) said. "And trade without enforcement is a windfall for corporations and a disaster for workers, but we want to get to yes. But, if Mexico can't ensure workers' ability to bargain for higher wages through real unions, the entire deal is a non-starter."[37]

Ultimately, these labor concerns could only be resolved to the satisfaction of critics in the December 2019 amendments. This reflected House Speaker Nancy Pelosi's conviction, expressed in April 2019, that enforcement issues cannot effectively be addressed in the implementing legislation and would instead require renegotiating USMCA.[38]

The consolidated USMCA responds to these concerns through changes in procedures and burdens of proof for enforcement actions and comprehensive improvements in the USMCA enforcement mechanisms for labor rights. One of the difficulties of enforcement under prior post-NAFTA trade

---

[37] "AFL-CIO's Trumka to Lead USMCA-Focused Delegation to Mexico City Next Week" (2019), World Trade Online, August 29, https://insidetrade.com/daily-news/afl-cio%E2%80%99s-trumka-lead-usmca-focused-delegation-mexico-city-next-week.

[38] "Pelosi: USMCA Enforcement Issues Cannot Be Fixed in Implementing Bill" (2019), World Trade Online, April 2, https://insidetrade.com/daily-news/pelosi-usmca-enforcement-issues-cannot-be-fixed-implementing-bill.

agreements was a requirement that the labor violation affects trade or investment between the parties. USMCA in its final version establishes a presumption that labor violations affect trade or investment, leaving the difficult task of disproving this presumption to the respondent government.[39] The scope of a failure affecting trade or investment is clarified:

> A failure to comply … is "in a manner affecting trade or investment between the Parties" if it involves: (i) a person or industry that produces a good or supplies a service traded between the Parties or has an investment in the territory of the Party that has failed to comply with this obligation; or (ii) a person or industry that produces a good or supplies a service that competes in the territory of a Party with a good or a service of another Party …[40]

Given the extensive trade relationship between the United States and Mexico and Mexico's heavy dependence on exports to the United States, it seems unlikely that it could be shown for the vast majority of Mexican manufacturing enterprises that they do *not* affect trade or investment between the parties.

Other changes include the elimination of self-policing of forced or compulsory labor,[41] and the elimination of the requirement that violence against workers could only be addressed where there is "a sustained or recurring course of action" making individual incidents of violence actionable.[42] Monitoring is to be substantially improved through the establishment of US labor attachés in Mexico charged with monitoring Mexico's labor practices, along with establishment of benchmarks, periodic reporting to Congress and an interagency committee.[43] Improved enforcement and monitoring is

---

[39] USMCA, Art. 23.3, fns 4, 5.

[40] USMCA, Art. 23.3, fn. 4.

[41] USMCA, Art. 36.6.1.

[42] USMCA, Art. 23.7 (eliminating the earlier limitation).

[43] USMCA Implementation Act, December 13, 2019, H.R. 5430, 116th Congress, 1st Session, www.congress.gov/bill/116th -congress/house-bill/5430, Secs. 711–34.

to be enhanced by the creation of an interagency labor committee for monitoring and enforcement, including detailed specifications for a petition process and creation of hotline for reporting alleged violations along with a process for consultations on appointment and funding of rapid response labor panelists.[44] The implementing legislation also provides for establishment of up to five American labor attachés, to be stationed in Mexico at the American Embassy or at one of the nine American consulates, to investigate violations, and the establishment of an independent Mexico labor expert board.[45]

Mexican officials initially objected, asserting that these provisions, particularly those providing for the stationing of labor attachés in Mexico, had not been vetted with Mexico before the implementing legislation was submitted to the US Congress, were redundant in light of the rapid response labor mechanism, and were excessive in scope.[46] However, Mexican concerns were apparently assuaged when USTR Robert Lighthizer assured Mexican officials that the attachés would not be "labor inspectors," would work with their Mexican counterparts and members of civil society, and would abide by all Mexican laws. Lighthizer's letter also noted that the American Embassy in Mexico City and the Mexican Embassy in Washington both had many attachés from various US and Mexican agencies.[47]

---

[44] United States-Mexico-Canada Agreement Implementation Act, introduced December 13, 2019, Secs. 717–19, H.R. 5430, 116th Congress, 1st Session.

[45] Ibid., Secs. 721–3, 731–4.

[46] "Seade Headed to Washington to Discuss USMCA Bill Concerns" (2019), World Trade Online, December 15, https://insidetrade.com/trade/seade-headed-washington-discuss-usmca-bill-concerns.

[47] Letter from USTR Robert Lighthizer to Mexican Undersecretary Jesus Seade, December 16, 2019, https://ustr.gov/about-us/policy-offices/press-office/press-releases/2019/december/ustr-responds-mexico-usmca.

The most significant innovation in the USMCA amendments by far is the establishment in the USMCA state-to-state dispute settlement chapter, Chapter 31, of a "facility-specific rapid response labor mechanism."[48] The purpose of the mechanism and its ability to impose remedies is carefully defined; it is "to ensure remediation of a Denial of Rights, as defined in Article 31-A.2, for workers at a Covered Facility, not to restrict trade. Furthermore, the Parties have designed this Mechanism to ensure that remedies are lifted immediately once a Denial of Rights is remediated."[49] The focus is on "denial of rights," where the complainant party "has a good faith basis belief that workers at a Covered Facility (producing goods for trade or that compete with imported goods from the other Party) are being denied the right of free association and collective bargaining under laws necessary to fulfill the obligations of the other Party ..."[50] The mechanism contemplates the establishment by consensus of three lists of panelists with labor expertise, one for each party and one joint list, nominated by the time the agreement enters into force. The three joint list panelists will be persons who are neither US nor Mexican nationals. Rules of procedure will address composing panels if a party fails to designate its panelists.[51] The list is later to be expanded to five panelists for each list. Most of the other procedural aspects are like other state-to-state arbitration mechanisms.

The principal innovations also include the potential establishment of jurisdiction over individual Mexican enterprises ("Covered Facilities") and the speed at which the process is intended to take place (30 days after verification or 30 days after it is constituted if there is no verification). The mech-

---

[48]   USMCA, Annex 31-A (United States and Mexico), Annex 31-B (Canada and Mexico).

[49]   Ibid.

[50]   USMCA, Annex 31-A, Art. 31-A.2.

[51]   USMCA, Annex 31-A, Art. 31-A.3.

anism contemplates an initial review and remediation by the respondent party over a 45-day period; customs account settlements can be suspended by the complaining party in the interim. If the parties disagree on the results a panel may be requested.[52] Remedies for ultimate non-compliance by the Covered Facility may include suspension of preferential tariff treatment under USMCA or other (unspecified) penalties.[53]

The facility-specific rapid response labor mechanism can only be described as radical, going far beyond provisions contained in any earlier US FTA labor chapter or in the CPTPP. It holds the promise, if US and Mexican officials can effectively cooperate, of transforming the lives of many Mexican workers through the wages and benefits achievable with effective unionization and collective bargaining. It is not surprising that the added labor provisions, which reflect the influence of AFL-CIO President Richard Trumka, resulted in the endorsement of the modified USMCA by the AFL-CIO, the first time the organization has endorsed a US FTA in at least several decades.[54]

Experts have suggested that the shift in burden of proof and the establishment of an enterprise-specific enforcement mechanism, along with eliminating the need to show a "sustained or recurring course of action" where violence against workers is alleged, are among the most significant changes.[55]

---

[52]   USMCA, Annex 31-A, Arts 31-A.4, 31-A.5.

[53]   USMCA, Annex 31-A, Art. 31-A.10.

[54]   "AFL-CIO Endorses USMCA After Successfully Negotiating Improvement" (2019*)*, AFL-CIO, December 10, https://aflcio.org/pressreleases/afl-cio-endorses-usmca-after-successfully-negotiating-improvements.

[55]   See "Unpacking USMCA Labor Tweaks: Some Praise, Some Questions about a New Tool's Effectiveness" (2019), World Trade Online, December 16, https://insidetrade.com/daily-news/unpacking-usmca-labor-tweaks-some-praise-some-questions-about-new-tool%E2%80%99s-effectiveness?s=na (quoting Kathleen Clausen and Kimberly Elliot).

Many questions remain to be resolved in the future regarding the uses of the enforcement mechanism and the short (45-day) time frame contemplated for the review process. There are obvious risks, including the possibility that the mechanisms will be used as protectionist measures in the United States, as a basis for restricting specific Mexican exports to the United States. From an administrative point of view, unless the US Department of Labor's Bureau of International Labor Affairs (ILAB) is properly supported, enforcement may be more impressive on paper than in the real world. In the past the Trump Administration has not been a supporter of the ILAB, seeking earlier in 2019 to cut its budget by almost 80 percent.[56] The implementing legislation authorizes $210 million through 2023 for the ILAB to fund the labor attachés ($30 million) and related positions.[57]

More broadly, disagreements about implementation of the dispute settlement mechanism and the use of the labor attachés could result in serious disagreements between the two governments. Despite some skepticism on the part of Mexicans as to whether the mechanism will actually boost wages,[58] if good faith efforts are made on both sides (including within the United States) to use the tools to promote good labor practices in Mexico (rather than as protectionism and a source of conflict), almost every stakeholder will benefit; otherwise the skeptics will likely be right.

Finally, it is also uncertain as to how the mechanism might be applied to claims against the United States, where claims

[56]   Ben Penn, "New NAFTA's Labor Playbook Hinges on Agency Trump Tried to Gut" (2019), Bloomberg Law, December 20, https://news.bloomberglaw.com/daily-labor-report/new-naftas -labor-playbook-hinges-on-agency-trump-tried-to-gut.

[57]   Ibid.

[58]   See Sarah McGregor, "Mexicans Are Dubious Trump's Trade Deal Will Boost Wages" (2019), Bloomberg Law News, December 19, https://news.bloomberglaw.com/international-trade/mexicans -are-dubious-trumps-trade-deal-will-boost-their-wages.

are precluded based on a denial of rights for workers only if it takes place under an enforced order of the National Labor Relations Board.[59] The labor chapter does address briefly the dangers sometimes faced by migrant workers in the United States: "The Parties recognize the vulnerability of migrant workers with respect to labor protections. Accordingly, in implementing Article 23.3 [labor rights], each Party shall ensure that migrant workers are protected under its labor laws, whether they are nationals or non-nationals of the Party."[60]

The endorsement was reflected in the House vote approving USMCA by a vote of 385–41 on December 19, 2019, including 193 Democratic Party votes,[61] the most Democratic support for any trade agreement in memory.

E   Differences over Treatment of Labor and LGBTQ Rights (or Lack Thereof)

While the USMCA labor provisions for the most part are designed to address labor rights, one provision in the chapter has a much broader focus:

> The Parties recognize the goal of eliminating discrimination in employment and occupation and support the goal of promoting equality of women in the workplace. Accordingly, each Party shall implement policies that it considers appropriate to protect workers against employment discrimination on the basis of sex (including with regard to sexual harassment), pregnancy, sexual orientation, gender identity, and caregiving responsibilities; provide job protected leave for birth or adoption of

---

[59] USMCA, Annex 31-A, Art. 31A.2, fn. 1.

[60] USMCA, Art. 23.8.

[61] Jen Kirby (2019), "The USMCA Trade Deal Passes the House in a Rare Bipartisan Vote," Vox, December 19, www.vox .com/policy-and-politics/2019/12/19/21013178/usmca-trade-deal -passes-house-vote-approve-bipartisan-nafta-trump (noting that 193 Democrats supported the bill).

a child and care of family members; and protect against wage discrimination.[62]

This provision appeared in the October 1, 2018 initial draft of USMCA, apparently at the suggestion of Canada, because protection of LGBTQ rights, in the view of Prime Minister Trudeau, "represents Canadian Values."[63] However, this obligation was essentially eliminated with respect to the United States in the final text signed on November 30. In that version, a footnote was added:

> The United States' existing federal agency policies regarding the hiring of federal workers are sufficient to fulfill the obligations set forth in this Article. The Article thus requires no additional action on the part of the United States, including any amendments to Title VII of the Civil Rights Act of 1964, in order for the United States to be in compliance with the obligations set forth in this Article.[64]

Given that there is no US federal statute that protects workers from discrimination based on sexual orientation or gender identity, the statement in the footnote as quoted immediately above is patently false. The change was added at the request of the US Trade Representative in response to the complaints of some 46 Republican lawmakers who urged that "a trade agreement is not the place to set social policy and that the language conflicts with the administration's agency on sexual orientation and gender identity."[65] Still, the footnote likely

---

[62] USMCA, Art. 23.9.

[63] "Trudeau Defends Keeping LGBTQ Rights in USMCA as APEC Summit Wraps Up" (2018), Head Topics, November 18, https://headtopics.com/ca/trudeau-defends-keeping-lgbtq-rights-in-usmca-as-apec-summit-wraps-up-2582640.

[64] USMCA, Art. 23.9, fn. 13.

[65] Rosella Brevetti, Brenna Goth and Amy Guthrie (2018), "NAFTA 2.0 Gender, Labor Provisions at Issue Before Signing," Bloomberg Law, November 27, https://news.bloomberglaw.com/

protects the US from any actions by Canada or Mexico challenging US compliance with the provision, and thus preserves the ability of the US federal government and the states to continue to allow employment discrimination based on a person's LGBTQ status.

III PROTECTION OF THE ENVIRONMENT

The USMCA environmental chapter also incorporates major improvements over the North American Agreement on Environmental Cooperation (NAAEC)[66] approved by Congress in 1993. Most of these were reflected in post-NAFTA FTA environmental chapters, including the TPP.[67] Innovations since NAFTA include the environmental provisions in the body of USMCA, which state that the trade dispute settlement provisions are also applicable to environmental (and labor) disputes. USMCA affirms the parties' commitments to their previous multilateral environmental agreements (but they agreed not to ratify any additional ones). USMCA also affirms existing and makes new commitments in the areas of ozone layer protection, ship pollution, air quality and marine litter.[68] The relationship between trade and biodiversity is recognized,

---

international-trade/nafta-20-gender-labor-provisions-at-issue-before -signing.

[66] North American Agreement on Environmental Cooperation (NAAEC), September 14, 1993, www.cec.org/sites/default/files/ naaec.pdf.

[67] See Trans-Pacific Partnership, incorporated in the Comprehensive and Progressive Trans-Pacific Partnership, March 8, 2018, https://international.gc.ca/trade-commerce/trade-agreements -accords-commerciaux/agr-acc/cptpp-ptpgp/text-texte/cptpp-ptpgp .aspx?lang=eng; TPP text, chap. 20, https://international.gc.ca/trade -commerce/trade-agreements-accords-commerciaux/agr-acc/tpp -ptp/text-texte/toc-tdm.aspx?lang=eng.

[68] USMCA, Arts 24.8–24.12.

along with the problem of invasive alien species, the protection of marine wild capture fisheries, the need for effective sustainable fisheries management, the conservation of marine species, and addressing fishers' subsidies that lead to over-fishing.[69] One of the most important aspects of USMCA is the decision to preserve the major aspects of the NAAEC's Commission on Environmental Cooperation, its secretariat, and the Joint Public Advisory Committee[70] established under the NAAEC but not replicated under any subsequent US FTA prior to USMCA. However, the USMCA December 13 amendments effectively restored some of the environmental protections first set out in the 2007 "Bipartisan Trade Deal"[71] and incorporated in US FTAs with Colombia, Panama and Peru.

A   Background: The NAAEC

The NAAEC's objectives include protecting and improving the environment; promoting sustainable development; and increasing party cooperation for conserving, protecting and enhancing the environment. Other objectives are supporting NAFTA's environmental goals; avoiding trade distortions or new trade barriers; strengthening cooperation to develop and improve environmental rules and regulations; and enhancing compliance with environmental laws and regulations. Finally, the long list of aspirations has a major focus on promoting transparency and public participation in the development of

---

[69]   USMCA, Arts 24.15–24.19.

[70]   Agreement on Environmental Cooperation Among the Governments of the United States of America, the United Mexican States and Canada, December 18, 2018, www.international.gc.ca/trade-commerce/assets/pdfs/agreements-accords/cusma-aceum/cusma-ECA.pdf.

[71]   Bipartisan Trade Deal, USTR, May 2007, https://ustr.gov › uploads › factsheets › 2007 › asset_upload_file127_11319.

environmental laws and regulations; promoting economically efficient environmental measures; and promoting pollution prevention policies and practices.[72] It was intended to be accomplished in part through each party's obligation to enforce its environmental laws and regulations, to provide private citizen access to procedures for publicizing and examination of alleged violations of the agreement, and to encourage procedural due process for national administrative and judicial proceedings.[73]

The NAAEC was also designed to provide a mechanism for requiring the NAFTA parties to enforce their internal environmental laws and regulations. Each party, while maintaining the right to establish its "own levels of environmental protection," is to "ensure that its laws and regulations provide for high levels of environmental protection and … strive to continue to improve those laws and regulations."[74] The latter commitment is not realistically enforceable, because the NAAEC sets no substantive environmental standards other than to call upon each party to create laws to protect the environment.[75] Thus, nothing prevents a party from weakening its environmental laws and then neglecting to strongly enforce them.

The NAAEC also created the Commission for Environmental Cooperation (CEC), consisting of a Council on Environmental Cooperation and a semi-autonomous secretariat,[76] as well as a Joint Public Advisory Committee (JPAC) with four public members for each party.[77] The secretariat continues to perform a useful function in public outreach and conducts research on

---

[72]   NAAEC, Art. 1.
[73]   NAAEC, Arts 5–7.
[74]   NAAEC, Art. 3.
[75]   Ibid.
[76]   NAAEC, Arts 8–9.
[77]   NAAEC, Art. 16.

such matters as climate change, ecosystems and pollutants, with reports issued on each.[78]

Located in Montreal, Canada, the CEC is authorized to review private citizen complaints about the failure to enforce environmental laws, and it has the investigatory powers and authority to seek expert advice and issue reports.[79] The secretariat has the authority to develop a "factual record" relating to the alleged violations of the agreement (something less than a full report) when the submission so warrants.[80] Where the investigation demonstrates that a NAFTA party has a "persistent pattern of failure ... to effectively enforce its environmental laws," a process of binding consultation and dispute resolution through an arbitral process is in theory made available.[81] This process is open only to the government parties.[82] For the US and Mexico, an adverse arbitral decision that the party does not comply with could result in trade sanctions. For Canada, in lieu of a trade benefit suspension, a fine may be assessed and enforced in the federal court.[83] The process is clearly designed to encourage voluntary compliance; suspension of trade benefits is the last resort, occurring only after a complex and lengthy procedure that can be initiated only with the agreement of two of the three national representatives on the CEC.

---

[78] See Commission for Environmental Cooperation, "Our Work, 2017," www.cec.org/about-us/jpac/jpac-members.

[79] NAAEC, Arts 14–15.

[80] NAAEC, Art. 15.

[81] NAAEC, Art. 36.

[82] NAAEC, Art. 24 (providing that a panel may be convened by the Council "on the written request of any consulting Party ...").

[83] NAAEC, Art. 36A.

B   Post-NAFTA Environmental Provisions

Dissatisfaction with the NAAEC, particularly among Democrats in Congress, was almost immediate. The significant post-NAFTA FTAs fall into several groups: the 2003–04 agreements with Australia, Chile, Singapore, the United States-Central America-Dominican Republic Free Trade Agreement and several others;[84] the 2006–07 FTAs with Colombia, Panama, Peru, and South Korea; and the 2016 12-nation TPP. The first two groups were guided by the 2002 Trade Promotion Authority (TPA), while the finalization of the TPP in 2016 reflected the 2015 TPA. The most significant changes with environmental provisions in the post-NAFTA FTAs, all now reflected in most respects in USMCA, were to ensure that a) the environmental provisions would be included in the body of the agreement and b) alleged violations would be subject to the same procedures and trade sanctions as violations of trade-related provisions of the free trade agreements.

More recently, first with the treatment of tropical hardwoods in the FTA with Peru in 2006[85] and the treatment of environmental and fishery issues in the TPP, environmental provisions effectively became a necessary part of any US regional trade agreement requiring congressional approval. In addition, the negotiating objectives of the 2015 Trade Promotion Authority included similar environmental provisions with which the Trump Administration has sought to comply.[86] However, certain aspects of those provisions in the

---

[84]   Bahrain, Morocco and Oman.

[85]   See Peru Environmental Cooperation Agreement [US-Peru], July 26, 2006, https://ustr.gov/sites/default/files/Peru %20Environmental%20Cooperation%20Agreement.pdf.

[86]   Bipartisan Congressional Trade Priorities and Accountability Act of 2015, P.L..114-26, 114th Cong., section 102(b)(10), 129 Stat. 319 (June 29, 2015), www.congress.gov/114/plaws/publ26/PLAW -114publ26.pdf.

2007 Bipartisan Trade Deal agreements were not fully carried over into the TPP or the original USMCA.

C   USMCA's Treatment of Environmental Issues

The general negotiating guidelines for the USMCA's environmental chapter also included rules that eliminate the weakening of environmental laws; incorporate obligations accepted by the parties under multilateral environmental agreements; commit to public advisory committees; create a senior-level environmental committee (presumably referring to the Council for Environmental Cooperation created under the NAAEC); incorporate measures to combat illegal fishing, prohibit fisheries subsidies, and promote sustainable fisheries management and conservation;[87] protect and conserve indigenous ecosystems (including measures to combat wildlife and timber tracking); and encourage cooperative activities designed to facilitate implementation of environmental commitments.[88]

The simplest way for the USMCA negotiators to incorporate these obligations, as the US Summary of Objectives suggests, was to borrow much of the language from the recently negotiated TPP's Chapter 20. The many advantages of this approach included (1) broader coverage of environmental issues such as fisheries and wildlife trafficking compared to NAFTA and subsequent US FTAs; (2) provisions to make environmental violations subject to the state-to-state dispute settlement mechanism; (3) incorporation of the basic approach to environmental obligations found in earlier US FTAs; and (4) a committee of high-level representatives, which, if

---

[87]   TPP, Arts 20.13–20.17.

[88]   Office of the US Trade Representative (2017), "Summary of Objectives for the NAFTA Renegotiation," July 17, https://ustr .gov/sites/default/files/files/Press/Releases/NAFTAObjectives.pdf, 13–14.

implemented, could provide a useful oversight function for compliance with the environmental obligations. However, this approach was not satisfactory to the Democratic Congress, which insisted on several additional changes.

First, as with the labor chapter of USMCA, the burden of proof is shifted with regard to demonstrating that an environmental failure "is in a manner affecting trade or investment between the Parties." With the changes, it is presumed that a failure meets this requirement, with the burden shifting to the respondent government to show otherwise.[89] Also in changes parallel to those in the labor chapter, affecting trade or investment means that the person or industry accused of the alleged failure either engages in goods or services trade with the complaining Party, or the goods or services produced in the responding Party compete in the responding Party's market with goods or services imported from the complaining Party.[90]

The other major change resulting from amendments relates to a series of multilateral environmental agreements to which the USMCA parties are party. Here, each party is obligated to "adopt, maintain and implement laws, regulations and all other measures to fulfill its respective obligations" under the MEAs. The list of MEAs includes the Convention on International Trade in Endangered Species; the Montreal Protocol to Protect the Ozone Layer, the 1978 Ship Pollution Convention; the Ramsar Convention on Wetlands; the Convention on Conservation of Antarctic Marine Living Resources; the International Whaling Convention; and the Convention establishing the Inter-American Tropical Tuna Commission.[91] Other conventions may be added to the list in the future if the parties agree.

---

[89]   USMCA, Art. 24.4, fn. 5.
[90]   USMCA, Art. 24.8, fns 6 and 7.
[91]   USMCA, Art. 24.8.4.

The "Initial Provisions and General Definitions" of USMCA were also modified to provide that where there is a conflict between provisions of USMCA and any of the same eight conventions, those conventions shall prevail.[92] This conflict approach originated with NAFTA, but the list of MEAs in NAFTA was much shorter.[93] Those who might consider that resolving potential conflicts between MEAs and trade agreements is straightforward should keep in mind that the WTO's Committee on Trade and the Environment, organized in 1995, has yet to produce any rules for potential conflicts between MEAs and the WTO covered agreements.[94]

As with labor, an interagency committee for environmental monitoring and enforcement is created in the implementing legislation, with details as to its functions, including reporting.[95]

The environmental chapter addresses respect for sustainable development; an obligation on each party to effectively enforce its own environmental laws (but without any obligations as to the content of those laws); transparency and opportunities for individuals to ask questions or request the investigation of alleged violations of environmental laws; fair, equitable, and transparent judicial or administrative procedures for the enforcement of environmental laws; protection of the ozone layer; and additional marine pollution and air quality issues.[96] In addition, the USMCA text covers corporate social responsibility, voluntary mechanisms to enhance environmental performance, biodiversity protections, sustainable

---

[92]   USMCA, Art. 1.3.

[93]   NAFTA, Art. 104.

[94]   See WTO, Decision on Trade and Environment, April 15, 1994, www.wto.org/english/docs_e/legal_e/56-dtenv_e.htm.

[95]   United States-Mexico-Canada Agreement Implementation Act, introduced December 13, 2019, Secs. 811–17, H.R. 5430, 116th Congress, 1st Session.

[96]   USMCA, Arts 24.2–24.11.

forest management, and trade in environmental goods and services (the latter responds to unsuccessful multilateral efforts to reduce tariffs on trade in environmental goods).[97] The Amendments tighten somewhat the disciplines in USMCA relating to protection of the ozone layer and protection of the marine environment, from ship pollution in both cases, establishing presumptions that a party's failure to comply is related to trade or investment between the parties and providing parallel definitions.[98]

The general satisfaction by members of industry with the original environment chapter in USMCA (not shared with many Democrats in Congress) is reflected in the conclusion of the Trade and Environmental Policy Advisory Committee Report, which states that the September 30, 2018 draft of the agreement:

> Largely meets the environmental objectives established by Congress in the Bipartisan Trade Act of 2015. It also includes several welcome new environmental initiatives, for example, to reduce marine litter, a prohibition on commercial whaling, enhanced language on IUU and sustainable fisheries management, and sustainable forest management, which will contribute to better environmental management in North America and beyond.[99]

Like many observers, the TPA advisory committee strongly supported provisions of the chapter designed to eliminate fishery subsidies that distort trade, as well as provisions requiring transparency for such programs. The committee also supported provisions that address illegal, unreported

---

[97] USMCA, Arts 24.12–24.24.

[98] USMCA, Arts 24.9, 24.10.

[99] Trade and Environmental Policy Advisory Committee Report, September 27, 2018, https://ustr.gov/sites/default/files/files/agreements/FTA/AdvisoryCommitteeReports/Trade%20and%20Environment%20Policy%20Advisory%20Committee%20%28TEPAC%29.pdf, 2.

and unregulated fisheries; discuss marine wild capture fisheries; support sustainable fisheries management; promote the conservation of marine species; and act on marine litter (an addition that goes beyond the TPP).[100] As with many earlier post-NAFTA agreements, provisions to restrict trade in plants, animals, and illegally logged wood products, and to address invasive species, were also welcomed.[101] The advisory committee was however disappointed with the environmental chapter's failure to address climate change and global warming, particularly in the lack of "provisions that incentivize trade and investment in areas like infrastructure investment and support for renewable energy supplies that promote constructive climate policies."[102] The majority of the nine Democratic members of the US Senate who voted against USMCA gave the absence of treatment of climate change as a primary reason for their opposition.[103]

While some observers feared that the negotiators would fail to incorporate major structural and administrative features of the NAAEC, this fortunately did not happen. Rather, USMCA preserves most of the best features, including: (1) a quasi-independent secretariat to receive citizen complaints and undertake valuable research and reports; (2) an internationalized citizen complaint procedure; and (3) a joint public advisory committee.[104] The "Agreement on Environmental

---

[100]   Ibid., 7–9.

[101]   Ibid., 9–10.

[102]   Ibid., 10–11.

[103]   These included Senators Chuck Schumer (D-NY), Edward Markey (D-MA), Corey Booker (D-NJ), Kamila Harris (D-CA), Sheldon Whitehouse (D-RI) and Jack Reed (D-RI). Sylvia Lane (2020), "Here Are the 10 Senators Who Voted Against Trump's North American Trade Deal," The Hill, January 16, https://thehill.com/policy/finance/478636-here-are-the-10-senators-who-voted-against-trumps-north-american-trade-deal.

[104]   2018 Agreement on Environmental Cooperation Among the Governments of the United States of America, United Mexican

Cooperation" explicitly continues the NAAEC's CEC, including its council, secretariat and JPAC.[105] Also, as with NAFTA, "any person of a Party may file a submission asserting that a Party is failing to effectively enforce its environmental laws. Such submissions shall be filed with the Secretariat of the Commission for Environmental Cooperation (CEC Secretariat)" with procedures like those in the NAAEC up to and including ministerial-level consultations.[106]

Environmental disputes in USMCA are subject to the same state-to-state mechanism that applies to trade disputes.[107] Under NAFTA, state-to-state dispute settlement did not function well due to mechanisms that permitted any of the three parties to delay the proceedings through chronic failure to appoint standing rosters of panelists.[108] The improved panel selection process discussed in Chapter 3 should make state-to-state dispute resolution, including of disputes relating to environmental issues, more effective than it was under NAFTA.

One of the shortcomings of many post-NAFTA US FTAs was the absence of an environmental secretariat and a commission for environmental cooperation. In this respect the continuation of the NAFTA CEC and secretariat in USMCA is a significant improvement over the sparse use of secretariats in other post-NAFTA agreements. Of course, these administrative mechanisms will be useful only if the three

---

States and Canada, December 2018, www.epa.gov/international -cooperation/2018-agreement-environmental-cooperation-among -governments-united-states.

[105] Ibid., Art. 2.

[106] USMCA, Arts 24.27–27.31.

[107] USMCA, Art. 24.32.

[108] NAFTA, Ch. 20, Art. 2009. The most recent NAFTA Chapter 20 panel report was issued on February 6, 2001. See *In the Matter of Cross-Border Trucking Services*, USA-MEX-98-2008-1, February 6, 2001, www.nafta-sec-alena.org/Home/Dispute-Settlement/Decis ions-and-Reports. See also Chapter 3, section III of this volume.

USMCA parties together make a good faith effort to support the USMCA secretariat and its "factual record" investigations financially and otherwise, a result that will be made more likely if interested members of Congress and environmental NGOs encourage such efforts through provisions in the USMCA implementing legislation.

The preservation of the JPAC concept is also in my view particularly important. For example, in November 2017, the JPAC recommended that the Council on Environmental Cooperation focus its limited resources on "environmental cooperation instead of punitive actions"; reaffirming the parties' commitment to the secretariat; continuing to encourage public participation in the CEC's activities; and continuing to support the secretariat's research on trade and the environment.[109] The JPAC gently urged continuation of the citizen complaint procedures:

> The CEC should continue to provide opportunities for the public to raise concerns about enforcement of environmental laws while providing a mechanism to ensure that issues and concerns are addressed by federal, state or provincial governments, as appropriate.[110]

The fact that the USMCA negotiators and the advisory committee appear to have paid attention to these recommendations gives cause for some optimism. It may be hoped that the USMCA environmental provisions and the provisions of the Agreement on Environmental Cooperation will be more successful, particularly with the USMCA amendments, than those of NAFTA and the NAAEC in meeting the objectives

---

[109] JPAC Expert Forum on the North American Agreement on Environmental Cooperation (NAAEC) (2017), "Assessing the Past, Looking Towards the Future," Advice to Council no. 17-05, www .cec.org/sites/default/files/documents/jpac_advice_council/jpac -advice17-05.pdf.

[110] Ibid., 5.

of TPA, as well as those in Congress and the public who are concerned with environmental protection. The prospect of greater success in these respects appears to have encouraged some members of Congress who otherwise would not have supported the USMCA to do so.

IV   NORTH AMERICAN DEVELOPMENT BANK

A relatively obscure institution designed to fund border infra-structure projects along the United States-Mexican border, the North American Development Bank (NADBank), was created in 1993 to deal with the anticipated increases in border pollution resulting from increased industrial development along the border, including the movement of workers from the interior to the border area in Mexico and then chronic issues involving sewage and industrial waste.[111] The NADBank has operated effectively for some 25 years. It has financed a total of about $3.13 billion to support financing for the development and implementing of water and more recently energy infrastructure projects and leveraging another $9.64 billion in private and government lending.[112] It also provides technical assistance for projects, often necessary for the small border communities that lack the expertise to undertake such projects on their own. NADBank has never been controversial and was not an issue in the NAFTA renegotiations. It is not mentioned in USMCA but the US implementing legislation provides for

---

[111] See Tiffany Stecker (2019), "'New NAFTA' Offers Money for Border Sewage Fixes (1)," *Bloomberg News*, December 16, https://news.bloombergenvironment.com/environment-and-energy/new-nafta-offers-money-for-border-sewage-fixes; NADBank, "About the North American Development Bank," www.nadb.org/about/overview.

[112] North American Development Bank, "Our Impact," www.nadb.org/our-impact.

a long overdue increase in paid-in capital of $225 million, bringing the aggregate callable capital to $1.75 billion.[113] The legislation also authorizes an additional $300 million to fund Environmental Protection Agency grants designed to support sewer system upgrades in the border region.[114] The legislation indicates that the Secretary of the Treasury is to:

> direct the representatives of the United States to the Board of Directors of the Bank to use the voice and vote of the United States to give preference to the financing of projects related to environmental infrastructure relating to water pollution, wastewater treatment, water conservation, municipal solid waste, stormwater drainage, non-point pollution, and related matters.[115]

Such instruction would help to assure that the important work of the NADBank will continue in the future.

---

[113] United States-Mexico-Canada Agreement Implementation Act, Secs 831–4.

[114] Ibid., Sec. 821.

[115] Ibid., Sec. 832(a).

5. Energy production and policies

I INTRODUCTION

Energy is one of Mexico's largest exports, ranking behind only motor vehicles and machinery in dollar terms.[1] However, production has steadily decreased in recent years, from an average of about 3.4 million barrels per day (bpd) in the early 2000s to about 1.7 million bpd by November 2018.[2] Foreign (and other private) investment in the energy sector was restricted to the Mexican state until 2013–14. Then, with a series of more than 21 legislative changes and three amendments to Mexico's Constitution,[3] led by the Peña-Nieto Administration and the Institutional Revolutionary Party (PRI), but supported as well by the National Action Party (PAN) and the Party of the Democratic Revolution (PRD, President Andrés Manuel López Obrador's former party), the reforms were intended in significant part to support the

---

[1] Daniel Workman (2019), "Mexico's Top Ten Exports," WTEx, January 4, www.worldstopexports.com/mexicos-top-exports/.

[2] Tsvetana Paraskova (2019), "Can Mexico Stop Its Oil Production?" Yahoo Finance, January 24, https://finance.yahoo.com/news/mexico-stop-oil-production-decline-220000322.html.

[3] See Diana Villiers Negroponte (2018), "Mexico's Energy Reforms Become Law," Brookings, August 14, www.brookings.edu/articles/mexicos-energy-reforms-become-law/.

enactment of financial, education, telecommunications and fiscal reforms.[4]

The success of the López Obrador presidency may well depend on his energy policies, including his treatment of the bloated, inefficient state-owned oil company, Pemex, and the ability to continue to attract additional foreign investment in the hydrocarbons sector. Because energy exports are a major source of foreign exchange for Mexico, maintaining and increasing energy export earnings are critical to generating the revenues that AMLO will require to carry out many of his domestic reforms, including those designed to improve the lives of Mexico's poor.

The focus of this chapter is on the challenges posed by the energy reforms undertaken by the previous administration; the limitations that the United States-Mexico-Canada Agreement (USMCA)[5] imposes on changes in Mexico's energy policies (such as restricting foreign investment in the sector); other USMCA provisions that could affect energy; and a critique of AMLO's early energy-related policy decisions. Also included is a summary of the changes in the legal treatment of the United States-Canada energy relations under USMCA as compared to Chapter 6 of NAFTA. The chapter ends with a short conclusion.

---

[4]   See Manuel Rueda (2012), "Peña Nieto Makes Big Promises to Mexico," ABC News, December 1, https://abcnews.go.com/ABC _Univision/News/pea-nieto-makes-big-promises-mexico/story?id= 17857633.

[5]   Agreement Between the United States of America, the United Mexican States, and Canada, November 30, 2018 (not yet in force), Appendix to Annex 4-B, http://bit.ly/2YSXFL9.

II MEXICO'S ENERGY REFORMS AND AMLO'S CHALLENGES

Key elements of the reforms overwhelmingly approved by Mexico's Congress included:

- maintaining state ownership of subsoil hydrocarbons resources, but allowing private companies to take ownership of those resources once they are extracted and to book reserves for accounting purposes;
- creating four types of contracts for exploration and production: service contracts (companies are paid for activities done on behalf of the state), profit-sharing contracts, production sharing contracts, and licenses (enabling a company to obtain ownership of the oil or gas at the wellhead after it has paid taxes);
- opening the refining, transport, storage, natural gas processing and petrochemicals sectors to private investment;
- transforming Pemex into a productive state enterprise with an autonomous budget and a board of directors that does not include union representatives;
- strengthening four federal entities with regulatory roles in the hydrocarbons industry (the Ministries of Energy and Finance, the National Hydrocarbons Commission or CNH, and the Energy Regulatory Commission) and creating a National Agency for Industrial Safety and Environmental Protection; and
- establishing a sovereign wealth fund, the Mexican Petroleum Fund for Stabilization and Development, to be managed by the Central Bank.[6]

---

[6]   Mexico's energy reforms were approved by the Mexican Chamber of Deputies on December 11, 2013 (95–28) and the Senate on August 5, 2014. See Veronica Cantu, Mauricio Garza, Martin Quintero and Jaime A. Trevino (2014), "Mexican Energy Reform: The New Enacted Hydrocarbons Law", J.A. Trevino Abogados,

Because actual exploration and development have been hampered by fluctuating oil prices in recent years,[7] the prospects for Mexico in the medium and long term are generally mixed. Because of low prices, only two of the original 14 blocs found bidders in 2015.[8] Less than three years later, in January and March 2018, more than 70 different firms made more than $100 billion in new oil investment commitments, important revenue for a government that seeks sweeping social changes.[9] However, whether an increase in oil production, an influx of capital to Pemex, and reforms to foreign investment in Mexico's energy sector can all be achieved during AMLO's sexenio remains uncertain due to factors both within and beyond his control, as discussed in this chapter.

The challenge in my view is highly significant. The statutory and constitutional energy reforms engineered by former President Enrique Peña-Nieto, if and only if they are supported by AMLO, offer Mexico an opportunity to re-energize its declining petroleum sector by encouraging foreign oil companies, including but not limited to those located in the United States, to continue to invest and explore—which activities have often been postponed since ten leases were awarded

August 7, www.jatabogados.com/publications/articles/The_Mexican
_Energy_Reform_-_The_New_Enacted_Hydrocarbons_Law
.pdf. See also Clare Ribando Selke, Michael Ratner, M. Angeles
Villarreal and Phillip Brown (2015), "Mexico's Oil and Gas Sector:
Background, Reform Efforts, and Implications for the United States,"
Congressional Research Service, September 28, https://fas.org/sgp/
crs/row/R43313.pdf, 4.

[7]   See International Energy Agency (2016), "Mexico Energy
Outlook,"   www.iea.org/publications/freepublications/publication/
MexicoEnergyOutlookExecutivesummary_WEB_UK.pdf.

[8]   Selke et al., "Mexico's Oil and Gas Sector," 7.

[9]   See Craig Guthrie (2018), "AMLO and the Realities of
Mexico's Oil Reform," *Petroleum Economist*, July 9, www
.petroleum-economist.com/articles/politics-economics/south-central
-america/2018/amlo-and-the-realities-of-mexicos-oil-reform.

in 2017,[10] initially because of relatively low world oil prices but later because of uncertainties as to what AMLO's energy policies would entail. This could encourage investment in Mexico's oil sector to go forward, even though world oil prices have fluctuated in recent years from above $75 per barrel to as low as $41 per barrel.[11]

Yet, despite the legal constraints discussed below, it is still possible, if unlikely, that AMLO, who distrusts the energy overhaul[12] and has a supermajority in the Mexican Congress, could seek to roll back the Peña-Nieto Administration's energy reforms. (If this occurs, the leases awarded in the past to US or Canadian enterprises could be subject to challenge under the dispute settlement provisions of NAFTA Chapter 11 for up to three years after USMCA enters into force.) Dealing with Pemex's institutional problems, including a $108 billion debt, will also affect future oil and gas production.

Many of the domestic promises that AMLO made during his campaign and is now seeking to implement, including those related to improving education and combatting endemic corruption and violence, are largely dependent on AMLO's ability to encourage investment in and gain revenue from the hydrocarbons sector, which would permit Mexico to increase its oil and gas exports in the future. Even though the major impact of such investment is not likely to be felt directly during AMLO's sexenio, income from new leases alone could soon provide some of the funding for AMLO's

---

[10] "Ten Blocks Awarded Under Mexico's Round 2.1 Lease Sale" (2017), *Offshore*, June 20, www.offshore-mag.com/articles/2017/06/ten-blocks-awarded-under-mexico-second-round-lease-sale.html.

[11] See "Average Annual OPEC Crude Oil Price from 1960–2018," Statista, www.statista.com/statistics/262858/change-in-opec-crude-oil-prices-since-1960/. They are currently much lower.

[12] Nacha Cattan and Eric Martin (2018), "Mexico's AMLO Takes Office with Attack on Energy Overhaul," Bloomberg, December 1, www.bloomberg.com/news/articles/2018-12-01/lopez-obrador-takes-the-reins-in-mexico-vowing-a-transformation.

promised reforms. Thus, if the AMLO Administration fails to encourage and protect new investment in the petroleum sector, his sexenio will likely be a failure, and could result in a level of social and political instability that Mexico has not seen in many decades.

III   USMCA LEGAL CONSTRAINTS ON MEXICO'S ENERGY POLICIES

Despite the liberalization of the petroleum sector beginning in 2013 by the Peña-Nieto Administration, USMCA Chapter 8, in language apparently insisted upon by AMLO's representatives in the negotiations, specifies that:

> 2. In the case of Mexico, and without prejudice to their rights and remedies available under this agreement, the United States and Canada recognize that:
>   (a) Mexico reserves its sovereign right to reform its Constitution and its domestic legislation; and
>   (b) The Mexican State has the direct, inalienable, and imprescriptible ownership of all hydrocarbons in the subsoil of the national territory, including the continental shelf and the exclusive economic zone located outside the territorial sea and adjacent thereto, in strata or deposits, regardless of their physical conditions pursuant to Mexico's Constitution.[13]

Does this mean that the López Obrador Administration could roll back the 2013 reforms to Mexico's energy law permitting foreign investment in the sector? Not really, because there are other constraints in USMCA on AMLO's treatment of energy beyond those included in Chapter 8, even though the legal structure of Mexico's obligations is complex. The United States' view is that the Chapter 8 language essentially states the obvious: any sovereign state retains the right to change its

---

[13]   USMCA, Ch. 8.2.

constitution and laws, even if such changes may incur international responsibility to treaty partners. In other words, under USMCA, AMLO's legal authority over Mexico's petroleum laws and policies is constrained.

Mexico did not make any specific reservations affecting investment in the energy sector to its USMCA obligations beyond the stating-the-obvious language in Chapter 8. However, Mexico agrees in USMCA to a type of "most-favored-nation" clause, agreeing to afford to other parties (as well as service providers and state-owned enterprises) treatment regarding energy that is no more restrictive than treatment Mexico grants to parties to other trade agreements Mexico has concluded. The key USMCA provision is as follows:

Article 32.11: Specific Provision on Cross-Border Trade in Services, Investment, and State-Owned Enterprises and Designated Monopolies for Mexico
With respect to the obligations in Chapter 14 (Investment), Chapter 15 (Cross-Border Trade in Services), and Chapter 22 (State-Owned Enterprises and Designated Monopolies), Mexico reserves the right to adopt or maintain a measure with respect to a sector or sub-sector 32-12 for which Mexico has not taken a specific reservation in its Schedules to Annexes I, II, and IV of this agreement, *only to the extent consistent with the least restrictive measures that Mexico may adopt or maintain under the terms of applicable reservations and exceptions to parallel obligations in other trade and investment agreements that Mexico has ratified prior to entry into force of this agreement, including the WTO agreement,* without regard to whether those other agreements have entered into force.[14]

---

[14] USMCA, Art. 32.11 (emphasis added). The reference is obviously to the Trans-Pacific Partnership/Comprehensive and Progressive Trans-Pacific Partnership, since at the time the USMCA negotiations were concluded, Mexico had ratified that agreement, but it had not entered into force.

Under this clause, Mexico must afford treatment to the United States and to *US* investors in sectors covered in the three chapters of USMCA listed above that is no less favorable than treatment Mexico has offered in parallel trade and investment agreements. This is a clear reference to the Comprehensive and Progressive Trans-Pacific Partnership Agreement (CPTPP), which was signed by Mexico in March 2018 and went into force for Mexico and six of the other ten CPTPP parties on December 30, 2018.[15] It would have been preferable in my view for a reference to Chapter 8 to be included in the list in Article 32.11, but if Article 14 (investment protection) is included it probably does not matter.

In the CPTPP/TPP, Mexico listed several specific energy-related reservations.[16] Those reservations permit foreign investment in the sector under the conditions set out in the 2013 legislation enacted by the Peña-Nieto Administration, barring any less favorable treatment. Thus, under the proviso quoted above, incorporating the energy reservations agreed to by Mexico in the CPTPP, the López Obrador Administration (and any subsequent Mexican governments) may not make the rules under which foreign investment is permitted in the energy sector any *more* restrictive than those set out in the CPTPP annexes.

---

[15] CPTPP [Australia, Brunei, Canada, Chile, Colombia, Malaysia, Mexico, New Zealand, Peru, Singapore and Vietnam], March 8, 2018, incorporating by reference and with minor changes to the TPP Text, https://international.gc.ca/trade-commerce/trade -agreements-accords-commerciaux/agr-acc/cptpp-ptpgp/text-texte/ index.aspx?lang=eng. (The original TPP annexes, including those for Mexico, are not altered.) Brunei, Chile, Malaysia and Peru have not ratified CPTPP as of June 2020.

[16] Trans-Pacific Partnership [Australia, Bahrain, Canada, Chile, Japan, Malaysia, Mexico, New Zealand, Peru, Singapore, United States and Vietnam], February 4, 2016 (superseded), Annex I Mexico 17–26, https://ustr.gov/trade-agreements/free-trade-agreements/ trans-pacific-partnership/tpp-full-text.

To reiterate, the Peña-Nieto energy reforms are directly incorporated into CPTPP Annex I Mexico 17 through Annex I Mexico 27 (page numbers in each case). The effect of this is to make them binding obligations toward the other ten CPTPP parties: Mexico can liberalize the restrictions on foreign investment contained in the Peña-Nieto reforms and Annex I without violating either the CPTPP or USMCA (incorporated through Article 32.11), but it cannot make the rules more restrictive. In other words, the *minimum* level of treatment of foreign investment in Mexico's energy sector is established through these annexes. And through the operation of USMCA Article 32.11, these are the *most* restrictive measures Mexico may take in its relations with the United States under USMCA (and with Canada, although because Canada is a CPTPP party, it directly has the protections outlined under Annex I of that agreement). Article 32.11 was thus included at the behest of US negotiators to protect US energy sector investors in Mexico, now and in the future. Thus, US investments in the energy sector, as long as they are made through concession agreements or other government contracts, are protected under these provisions and the provisions of USMCA Chapter 14 discussed in Part IV of this chapter.

This analysis was confirmed by the Office of the US Trade Representative (USTR).[17] In an interview with USTR officials, it was stated that members of Mexico's USMCA negotiating team, including AMLO's representatives, fully understand the commitments incorporated through these provisions. While the legal case seems solid to me, I have some uneasiness that when the analysis is widely publicized—as is inevitable when hearings on USMCA are held in the US House and Senate and in the Mexican Congress—some backlash may occur in Mexico. Still, one can easily understand

---

[17] Assistant USTR C.J. Mahoney and several of his colleagues, in discussion with the author.

why AMLO, whose representatives participated in negotiations several months prior to his inauguration, did not want to include a straightforward commitment in USMCA Chapter 8 precluding any rollback of the Peña-Nieto energy reforms, even if he had no intention of doing so at that time. If AMLO had misgivings about permitting further foreign investment in the energy sector in the future, he need only do what he has already done—that is, establish a three-year moratorium on new leases, as discussed below.

The USTR appears to have been equally effective in considering the views of the members of the industry advisory committee and explaining the approach as summarized above. The committee noted in its report that "In combination, we believe that Chapter 8 and Chapter 32/Article 11 and the horizontal provisions of the rest of the USMCA all work together to commit Mexico, Canada, and the U.S. to energy markets that are open to trade with each other and open to investment from each other."[18]

IV   INVESTOR PROTECTION IN MEXICO'S HYDROCARBONS SECTOR

As discussed in Chapter 3 of this volume, USMCA's Chapter 14 on investment protections reduces protection for investors in most sectors compared to NAFTA's Chapter 11. Changes include eliminating claims for violations of fair and equitable treatment and for pre-investment discrimination, as well as imposing an exhaustion of local remedies requirement before an investor may seek international arbitration. However,

---

[18]   Addendum to the Report of the Advisory Committee on Energy and Energy Services, October 25, 2019, https://ustr.gov/sites/default/files/files/agreements/FTA/AdvisoryCommitteeReports/ITAC_6_REPORT-Energy_and_Energy_Services_Addendum.pdf.

Chapter 11-like protection[19] is maintained entirely for several sectors that were apparently deemed sensitive and for which both the Mexican and US governments and US stakeholders wished to assure investor protections for contracts or other agreements with the Mexican government. These include oil and gas and electric power production.[20] Thus, for the energy sector, investor–state dispute settlement (ISDS) protection not only includes national treatment, most-favored-nation treatment, and protection against direct expropriation, but also guarantees of fair and equitable treatment and protections against indirect expropriation.[21] In addition, the exhaustion of local remedies requirement does not apply to energy.

A major objective of this coverage, which was accepted by the then-incoming AMLO Administration as well as the Trump and Peña-Nieto Administrations, is to give American petroleum and natural gas investors a strong sense of confidence in Mexico. It provides investors assurance that should a dispute arise—for example, between the investor and Pemex under an exploration contract or lease—the investor would have the recourse normally expected under investment chapters such as NAFTA Chapter 11 and the 35 bilateral investment treaties Mexico has concluded with other third parties ranging from the United Kingdom to China.[22]

For Canadian investment in Mexico's oil (or other energy) sectors, the two parties and their affected stakeholders could also rely on Chapter 9 of the CPTPP, with certain limitations

---

[19] Enforcement of such protections would be subject to certain updates between 1994 and 2017 to the US investment chapter, reflecting, inter alia, Chapter 9 of the TPP.

[20] USMCA, Annex 14-E.

[21] Ibid.

[22] See "Mexico: Bilateral Investment Treaties," UNCTAD, Investment Policy Hub, http://investmentpolicyhub.unctad.org/IIA/CountryBits/136. Many, if not most of these treaties almost certainly exclude investment in Mexico's energy sector, but not in most of the other sectors covered by USMCA Chapter 14.

on the scope of coverage of investment agreements under the original Article 9.1 of the CPTPP.[23] However, it appears that ISDS under Chapter 9 of the CPTPP would *not* be available to Canadian investors that had concluded "investment agreements" with Mexican entities such as Pemex unless those agreements specifically provided for ISDS. (Subsidiaries of Canadian energy firms operating in the United States, or in third countries where bilateral investment treaties with Mexico were in force, would be protected.)

It is notable that the Energy Sector Advisory Committee expressed disappointment at the reduced breadth of ISDS in USMCA:

> The existing NAFTA agreement included a full suite of ISDS investor provisions that protected current and future United States investment in Canada and Mexico. It allowed the United States energy industry to mitigate the risks associated with large scale, capital intensive, and long-term projects. The new renegotiated agreement with Mexico has scaled back those ISDS provisions considerably. While it is greatly appreciated that the major importance of the trade agreement with Mexico and potentially Canada, ISDS protections for the oil & gas, infrastructure, energy generation, and telecommunications sectors has been recognized and added to the new agreement, we would further recommend that a more inclusive list of energy sources receive the full suite of protections to help mitigate investment risk.[24]

---

[23]   CPTPP, Art. 2, Annex, para. 2, which deletes the definition of "investment agreement" from the revised CPTPP.

[24]   Report of the Industry Trade Advisory Committee on Energy and Energy Services, September 27, 2018, https://ustr.gov/sites/default/files/files/agreements/FTA/AdvisoryCommitteeReports/ITAC%206%20REPORT%20-%20Energy%20and%20Energy%20Services.pdf, 4.

V   APPLICABILITY OF USMCA CHAPTER 11 TO ENERGY

A decision by the AMLO Administration to roll back the 2013 energy reforms would not in itself be a violation of the USMCA's technical barriers to trade (TBT) provisions, which by nature are procedural rather than substantive. Chapter 11 "applies to the preparation, adoption, and application of standards, technical regulations, and conformity assessment procedures, including any amendments, of central level of government bodies, which may affect trade in goods between the parties." Changes in technical regulations require that preference be given to international standards and that parties provide a written explanation of any other standard used, with an obligatory exchange of information, consultation, and a high level of transparency. The preference is always toward conformity with international standards and avoidance of regulations that unduly restrict trade, with the other parties to the agreement maintaining the right to seek a less-trade-restrictive method to fulfill the regulation's objective, including one based on an international standard.

The TBT chapter thus has only limited applicability to oil and gas issues. For example, if Mexico (or the United States) proposed a regulation requiring that gasoline contain 15 percent ethanol (instead of the current 10 percent standard), the other party could invoke the TBT procedures. However, in the unlikely event that Mexico would roll back the current petroleum laws, the TBT agreement would only be a legal hurdle procedurally. The TBT's most valuable provisions are those related to consultation and transparency, giving each party the opportunity to discourage another party from issuing regulations that restrict trade.

VI   AMLO'S QUESTIONABLE HYDROCARBONS POLICIES

Several actions by the populist AMLO Administration during its first year have raised questions about the nature of AMLO's foreign investment and administrative policies, including but not limited to petroleum production. Perhaps most significantly, the then-incoming AMLO government announced in late November 2018 that Mexico would suspend further bidding for oil and gas exploration leases until 2021.[25] The reasons for this decision are not entirely clear, but it appears that the Administration wishes to have time to review existing leases for evidence of corruption or other irregularities and, more generally, that it prefers the government rather than private enterprise to dominate petroleum development. Regardless of any justification, the result could be to significantly reduce or eliminate income from the sale of leases during the first half of AMLO's sexenio, forgoing a significant source of potential revenue to finance his ambitious reforms and to fulfill campaign pledges.

As of the beginning of 2020, the shock and disappointment of President-elect AMLO's decision to abandon the $13 billion new Mexico City airport project in October following a so-called referendum[26] had not yet fully dissipated, even though it appeared that at least $1.8 billion of the $6 billion in bonds issued to fund the project would be bought back from investors at par plus accrued interest.[27]

---

[25]   "Mexico E&P Auctions on Hold Until 2021: Report" (2018), The Oil and Gas Year (blog), November 21, www.theoilandgasyear.com/news/mexico-ep-auctions-on-hold-until-2021-report/.

[26]   Cattan and Martin, "Mexico's AMLO Takes Office with Attack on Energy Overhaul."

[27]   Justin Villamil, Nacha Cattan and Andrea Navarro (2018), "Mexico Peso Rallies as AMLO Resolves Airport Bond Dispute,"

The energy sector in the medium and longer term may also be affected by uncertainties surrounding AMLO's commitment to spend some \$8 billion on a gasoline refinery ("Dos Bocas") along with the administration's efforts to reduce gasoline imports from the United States by about 28 percent from 2018 levels.[28] The refinery decision has created additional skepticism for investors due to the administration's decision in early May 2019 to abandon the effort to solicit financing from private companies that had qualified for the initial bidding process (such as Bechtel, Techint and WorleyParsons). Instead, AMLO indicated that Pemex would undertake the construction on its own using Mexican instead of international design firms.[29] Whether this step results in cost savings, or a loss due to Pemex's lack of competence, remains to be seen. Observers note that upgrades to Mexico's gasoline refineries promised in the early 2000s have never been completed, and that the country's existing refineries are operating at only about one-third of their capacity.[30]

A more general concern is AMLO's less-than-rational commitment to an entity—Pemex—that has been plagued by corruption for decades and is in serious financial straits, being said to be the world's most indebted oil company with total debt of about \$108 billion.[31] He has provided Pemex with \$1.3

Bloomberg, December 19, www.bloomberg.com/news/articles/2018-12-19/mexcat-bondholders-accept-1-8-billion-airport-buyback-offer.

[28]   Robbie Whelan and Rebecca Elliott (2019), "Mexico Reduces U.S. Gasoline Imports," *The Wall Street Journal*, January 11, www.wsj.com/articles/mexico-reduces-u-s-gasoline-imports-11547249440.

[29]   Amy Stillman and Carlos M. Rodriguez (2019), "Investors Raise Concerns as AMLO Hands Refinery Project to Pemex," Bloomberg, May 9, www.bloomberg.com/news/articles/2019-05-09/mexico-scraps-tender-for-8-billion-refinery-pemex-to-take-lead.

[30]   Ibid.

[31]   Eric Martin and Justin Villamil (2019), "AMLO Risks His Own Fall as He Tries to Pull Pemex Back from the Brink,"

billion in new tax breaks over six years, causing some observers to warn that the fragility of Pemex's economic situation could affect the federal government's ability to borrow more broadly.[32] This level of confidence has repeatedly been proved unjustified. Early claims by Pemex that it was reversing the years of production declines proved inaccurate. Output in 2019 was expected to fall by about 7.6 percent from the 2018 level, to about 1.77 million barrels per day, well below the 1.85 million bpd forecast in the 2020 budget.[33]

In December 2019 AMLO demonstrated that actions relating to foreign investors in pursuit of "energy nationalism" were not confined to the early months of the administration. It was announced by the Comisión Federal de Electricidad (CFE), the state-owned electricity monopoly, that it planned to restrict private participation in the energy market through increasing transmission costs for renewable energy sources. (CFE has a near monopoly on energy production and on the national transmission lines.) The transmission fees for such producers would be increased above their current subsidized rates, likely making such energy production uneconomical in the future[34] given that wind and solar energy production normally takes place far from electricity consumers. Even though only 6 percent of Mexican energy production is from renewables such as solar and wind, the cost is said to be less than

---

Bloomberg, March 20, www.bloomberg.com/news/articles/2019-03-20/amlo-risks-a-fall-as-he-tries-to-pull-pemex-back-from-the-brink.

[32]   Ibid.

[33]   Jude Webber (2020), "Mexico's Pemex in Deep Water as Debt Outlook Worsens," *Financial Times*, January 8, www.ft.com/content/5d45694e-221f-11ea-b8a1-584213ee7b2b?shareType=nongift.

[34]   Jude Webber (2019), "Mexico Plans Crackdown on Private Electricity Market," *Financial Times*, December 21, www.ft.com/content/c7e4d878-21f4-11ea-b8a1-584213ee7b2b?shareType=nongift.

half of that for gas-fired or thermal power plants. One former official has criticized the proposal, suggesting that "The main objective is to strengthen CFE by weakening all features of the market and erasing the independence of [national grid operator] Cenace [National Energy Control Center] and [the regulator] CRE ... regardless of the impact on consumers and costs."[35] Like Pemex, CFE's profits are declining; the enterprise carries some $19 billion in debt[36] and corruption allegations have surfaced.[37] The reported measures would affect hundreds of contractors with various power generators including Iberdrola SA, Acciona SA and Enel SpA, among others (44 in all).[38]

If these unilateral administrative changes in the rules of the game are implemented, one result will be further lack of foreign investor confidence in Mexico, which previously had been ranked as the second most desirable Latin American country for renewable energy investment.[39] With an estimated $8.6 billion in private investments in the renewable energy sector, the new transmission charges could generate various

---

[35] Ibid.

[36] Ibid.

[37] See Eric Martin and Amy Stillman (2019), "Mexico's Investigator Finds No Wrongdoing by CFE Chief Bartlett," Bloomberg, December 19, www.bloomberg.com/news/articles/2019-12-20/mexico-investigator-finds-no-wrongdoing-by-cfe-chief-bartlett (suggesting widespread skepticism at the finding by independent observers).

[38] See Amy Stillman (2019), "Mexico's Renewable Power Suppliers Face Risks Under Grid Proposal," Bloomberg, December 22, www.bloomberg.com/news/articles/2019-12-22/mexico-s-cfe-mulls-cutting-discounts-in-blow-to-renewable-sector; Fernando Perez Lozada, "Change of Clean Energy Rules in Mexico: Potential Impact for Investors," Kluwer Arbitration Blog, January 13, http://arbitrationblog.kluwerarbitration.com/2020/01/13/change-of-clean-energy-rules-in-mexico-potential-impact-for-investors/.

[39] Lozada, "Change of Clean Energy Rules."

national legal actions based on *amparo* jurisdiction,[40] as well a series of investor–state disputes against CFE and the government, or, later, under one or more of Mexico's bilateral investment treaties or under the USMCA's Chapter 14. Under USMCA, power generation is one of the few sectors where actions based on indirect takings will still be permitted, assuming the investors are from the United States.[41] CFE's apparent objective is to set limits on the amount of renewable energy permitted in the national grid,[42] at a time when most other countries are trying to increase production of electric power through renewables. The idea of curbing renewable development in a country where petroleum production is decreasing, national gas is widely flared because of a lack of pipeline capacity and much of the country experiences sunny days and/or windy days the majority of the year appears to me to be extremely unwise for all of these reasons.

A further cause for investor uncertainty is the inclusion in Mexico's 2020 budget of the assumption that Pemex will be able to increase oil production to 1.951 million bpd from the July 2019 level of 1.671 million bpd, a level that has not been achieved since 1982. The optimistic forecast assumed that Pemex would be able to stabilize its production declines with the assistance of an additional \$4.4 billion capital infusion from the government.[43] Without the revenue from such

---

[40]   Lozada, "Change of Clean Energy Rules."

[41]   See USMCA, Ch. 14; NAFTA, Ch. 11; Chapter 3 of this book. Enel, an Italian power company, would enjoy similar protection under the Italy-Mexico Bilateral Investment Treaty, June 30, 1999, https://investmentpolicy.unctad.org/international-investment -agreements/countries/136/mexico.

[42]   Jude Webber, "Mexico Plans Crackdown."

[43]   Amy Stillman, Nacha Cattan and Eric Martin (2019), "Mexican Budget Assumes Oil Output Surge Not Seen Since 1982," Bloomberg.com, September 9, www.bloomberg.com/news/articles/ 2019-09-09/mexico-s-budget-assumes-an-oil-output-surge-not-seen -since-1982.

volume increases other areas of government spending could be jeopardized. Production in 1/2020 was 1.748 million bpd.

VII THE UNITED STATES-CANADA RELATIONSHIP ON ENERGY ISSUES UNDER USMCA

While NAFTA Chapter 6 specified few obligations for Mexico, it imposed restrictions on potential limitations on energy trade between the United States and Canada. This included a ban preventing Canada from reducing exports to the United States below the portion of total domestic demand in the past three years.[44] In other words, Canada could not reduce petroleum exports to the United States unless it also reduced domestic consumption of Canadian oil. The ability of these two parties to invoke national security grounds to limit petroleum exports or imports was also circumscribed.[45]

Although the United States has in the past 25 years become the world's largest oil producer,[46] its energy relationship with Canada was sufficiently important to both parties that they concluded a side letter/agreement to USMCA on energy. However, that agreement departs significantly from NAFTA Chapter 6. The USMCA agreement begins by observing that:

> The parties recognize the importance of enhancing the integration of North American energy markets based on market principles, including open trade and investment among the parties, to support North American energy competitiveness, security, and independ-

---

[44] North American Free Trade Agreement [US-Mex.-Can.], December 8, 1993, Art. 605, www.nafta-sec- alena.org/Home/Texts -of-the-Agreement/North-American-Free-Trade-Agreement.

[45] NAFTA, Art. 606.

[46] Douglas A. McIntire (2019), "US to Be World's Largest Oil Producer in 2019," 24/7 Wall St., January 18, https://247wallst.com/ energy-economy/2019/01/18/us-to-be-worlds-largest-oil-producer -in-2019/.

ence. The parties shall endeavor to promote North American energy cooperation, including with respect to energy security and efficiency, standards, joint analysis, and the development of common approaches.[47]

The text covers such issues maintaining regulatory oversight through authorities separate from those that regulate the industry itself, and also encourages regulatory transparency and procedures for gaining access to electronic transmission facilities and pipeline networks.[48] The latter presumably reflects concerns both in Canada and with the Trump Administration in the United States over the permitting process and court actions, which delayed the Keystone XL pipeline for many years, including at the present time.[49]

VIII   CONCLUSION

The Peña-Nieto era energy reforms offer the AMLO Administration an opportunity to lay the groundwork for an increase in Mexico's hydrocarbons production in the future, even if the current decline in the country's production and exports probably could not be remedied between now and 2024, when AMLO's term ends. USMCA may also help preserve foreign investor confidence by making the traditional ISDS protections available in the event of hydrocarbon-related disputes with the Mexican government or Pemex. Still, there is no assurance after AMLO's first 18 months in office that wise energy policies will be pursued. Actions by the

---

[47]   USMCA, Canada and US side agreement on energy, November 30, 2018, https://ustr.gov/sites/default/files/files/agreements/FTA/USMCA/Text/CA-US_Side_Letter_on_Energy.pdf.

[48]   Ibid., Arts 4, 5.

[49]   See Lisa Friedman and Coral Davenport (2018), "Judge Blocks Disputed Keystone XL Pipeline in Setback for Trump," *The New York Times*, November 9, www.nytimes.com/2018/11/09/climate/judge-blocks-keystone-pipeline.html.

administration—particularly AMLO's strong support for Pemex, tasking Pemex to construct a new oil refinery, the moratorium on further lease auctions and threatened restrictions on clean energy providers—raise serious questions as to whether current policies will stem or exacerbate hydrocarbon production declines at a time when support for renewable energy seems poised to disappear and world petroleum prices have precipitously fallen.

6. Textiles, apparel and agriculture

I   INTRODUCTION

The changes in the United States-Mexico-Canada Agreement (USMCA) for the textiles, apparel and agriculture sectors are relatively minor, although they reflect somewhat greater protectionism, particularly with textiles and apparel. In terms of the agriculture industry, USMCA modestly liberalizes US dairy market access to Canada, and US wine growers receive greater access to Canadian markets. Wine and cheese exporters to Mexico also receive significant protection from limitations on the use of common geographical indications[1] in Mexico as a result of Mexican negotiations with the European Union (EU) on a revised free trade agreement.[2] In USMCA, Mexican fruit and vegetable producers also benefit from beating back US efforts to make it easier to restrict such imports under US anti-dumping laws,[3] although the benefits

---

[1]   According to the World Intellectual Property Organization, "A geographical indication (GI) is a sign used on products that have a specific geographical origin and possess qualities or a reputation that are due to that origin," WIPO, www.wipo.int/geo_indications/en/.

[2]   See EU Commission (2018), "EU and Mexico Reach New Agreement on Trade," April 21, https://trade.ec.europa.eu/doclib/press/index.cfm?id=1830.

[3]   Under the Tariff Act of 1930, 19 U.S.C. Secs 1671–1677n, as amended, US industries may petition the government for relief in the form of additional tariffs from imports that are sold in the US at less

for tomato exporters were largely nullified by subsequent Commerce Department restrictions.

For North American agricultural producers, particularly those in the US and Mexico, the provisions of USMCA are overshadowed, at least through early 2020, by the risk that the Trump Administration will impose penalty tariffs on Mexican imports. This risk was reflected in the administration's threat to impose additional tariffs on all imports from Mexico to force greater cooperation in stemming the flow of illegal immigrants from Central America to the US.[4] The tariffs have not been applied as of this writing, and the risk was increasingly discounted by Mexico for unspecified reasons, probably because Mexico has responded positively to American pressures to take more effective steps to discourage migrants from Central America from crossing Mexico's southern border and the belief that further US sanctions would jeopardize US Congressional approval of USMCA.[5] Similarly, USMCA by no means insulates Mexican produce suppliers from "unfair" trade actions brought by the US, as discussed below.

This chapter summarizes the most significant textile, apparel and agricultural provisions of USMCA, focusing on the changes compared to NAFTA. Geographical indications and agricultural biotechnology are also addressed even though they are further affected by USMCA's intellectual property rules.

---

than fair value ("dumped"), if the sales can be shown to cause material injury to domestic producers of the same product.

[4] Irina Ivanova (2019), "What Does the U.S. Import from Mexico? A Whole Lot," CBS News, June 1, www.cbsnews.com/news/what-does-the-us-import-from-mexico-a-whole-lot/.

[5] See "Mexican Official: Threat of U.S. Tariffs 'More and More Distant'" (2019), World Trade Online, September 10, https://insidetrade.com/trade/mexican-official-threat-us-tariffs-more-and-more-distant.

II   TEXTILES AND APPAREL

Despite the relatively small volume of apparel production in the US (constituting about 3 percent of the US market),[6] the textile and apparel industry remains one of the most protected sectors, along with steel. The textile and apparel sector received extensive protection under NAFTA, with a "yarn forward" rule that stated that in order to be treated as originating in North America and receive tariff-free trading benefits, the formation of yarn, weaving or knitting of fabric, and cutting and sewing of a garment must occur in North America.[7] Typically, this meant that apparel and other textile goods used fabric produced in the US, while the sewing and other required steps for garment and textile production took place in Mexico. For example, an El Paso, Texas, mattress manufacturer purchased fabric, zippers, and threads in the US and conducted the first round of design, cutting, and stitching in El Paso. The enterprise then sent the materials to a sister plant in Ciudad Juárez, Mexico, for further assembly, after which the finished mattress was shipped back to El Paso for distribution in the US.[8]

If anything, protections for the US textile industry increased under USMCA. In USMCA, reliance on low-cost fabrics from Asia is discouraged, and duties on non-originating yarn and fabric ("tariff preferential levels" or TPLs) are limited to 10 percent by volume of North American garments to qualify

---

[6]   See Robert Farley (2016), "Yes, Donald Trump, Some Clothes Are Made in the USA," Huffpost, May 11, www.huffingtonpost.com/entry/donald-trump-clothes-usa_us_5733508ce4b096e9f0935956.

[7]   NAFTA, Annex 3-B.

[8]   See Colin Eaton (2018), "Businesses Along Texas Border Fear 'Going Belly Up' Without NAFTA," *Houston Chronicle*, February 9, www.houstonchronicle.com/business/article/In-Texas-border-econ omy-fears-of-going-belly-12564578.php.

for duty-free treatment.[9] In addition, other changes under USMCA require that sewing thread, pocketing fabric, narrow elastic bands and coated fabric used in the production of apparel be made in North America in order for those products to be treated as originating and thus subject to duty-free treatment.[10]

In addition to the substantive restrictions on the use of non-originating fabrics, the record-keeping requirements mandated by USMCA's additional documentation rules are likely to further increase the costs and complexities of apparel manufacturing in North America. Spokespersons for the industry have suggested that such increased costs are likely to discourage North American producers from taking advantage of the potential tariff benefits of USMCA, leading to greater outsourcing of apparel manufacturing to lower-wage countries in Asia. This would lead to a potential reduction in sales of fabrics and thread in the US. As the apparel members of the US advisory committee asserted:

> If fewer apparel companies source under the terms of this Agreement, they will buy fewer U.S. textiles, which will hurt U.S. fabric and yarn exports and manufacturing as well. The possibility that Mexico may become even less important to the U.S. apparel industry, and consequently lead to lower demand of U.S. textiles, is particularly concerning since about half of all U.S. yarn and fabric exports go to NAFTA countries for conversion into finished products like apparel.[11]

Given that about half of all US-manufactured yarn and fabric is exported to NAFTA countries for apparel manufacturing,

---

[9]   USMCA, Ch. 6, esp. Art. 6.1.

[10]   USMCA, notes to HTSUS Chs 61–2.

[11]   Report of the Industry Trade Advisory Committee on Textiles and Clothing, September 27, 2018, https://ustr.gov/sites/default/files/files/agreements/FTA/AdvisoryCommitteeReports/ITAC%2011%20REPORT%20-%20Textiles%20and%20Clothing.pdf, 6.

demand for these products would decrease if the production of apparel decreases further in the region.[12] Of course, US producers of thread, coated fabrics and the like applauded the USMCA changes because of the positive impact they may have on US sales of such products.[13]

III   AGRICULTURE

A   Agriculture Under NAFTA

One of the most significant market-opening aspects of NAFTA was the elimination of virtually all quotas and tariffs on agricultural trade between the US and Mexico, and most restrictions on trade between the US and Canada. As a result, Canada and Mexico became, even before the US-China trade war, the largest and third-largest export markets for the United States, respectively. US agricultural exports to Canada were worth $23 billion in 2016 and included prepared food, fresh vegetables, fresh fruit, snack foods and non-alcoholic beverages. US imports from Canada amounted to $22 billion.[14]

The elimination of Mexican tariffs and quotas on imports of corn and hard beans in particular was one of the most

---

[12]   "Stakeholders: USMCA Rules Could Undercut Benefits for the Apparel Industry" (2018), World Trade Online, November 20, https://insidetrade.com/daily-news/stakeholders-usmca-rules-could -undercut-benefits-apparel-industry.

[13]   Ibid.

[14]   Office of the United States Trade Representative (USTR), "U.S.-Canada Trade Facts," https://ustr.gov/countries-regions/ americas/mexico. A comprehensive analysis of the effects of NAFTA's termination on regional agricultural trade is beyond the scope of this report but is available through the Congressional Research Service. See Renee Johnson (2017), "Potential Effects of a U.S. NAFTA Withdrawal: Agricultural Markets," Congressional Research Service, November 13, https://fas.org/sgp/crs/row/R45018 .pdf.

controversial aspects of NAFTA given the adverse effects on small corn farmers in Mexico, who were not able to compete with lower-cost, highly mechanized, and well-financed farms in the US. The result was, as apparently intended by the negotiators, to facilitate capital-intensive and highly competitive US grain and meat exports to Mexico, while at the same time encouraging Mexican exports of labor-intensive fruits and vegetables to the US.

US agricultural exports to Mexico have been worth about $18 billion annually in areas such as wheat, hops, other grains, corn, soy, beef, chicken and pork. Imports from Mexico totalcd $23 billion in 2016 and included mostly fresh fruit and vegetables, as well as wine and beer, processed foods and processed fruits and vegetables.[15] Most US export goods are fungible, with Brazil, Argentina, Canada and Australia all eager to export more to Mexico. In this respect, it is notable that during the initial USMCA negotiations, at a time when President Donald Trump was threatening to terminate NAFTA unilaterally, Mexico's government made initial inquiries into shifting some grain and corn purchases from US exporters to Brazil and Argentina, even though transport costs would have been higher because of the greater distances involved. In the short term, Mexican consumers would have been harmed through higher food prices, partly as a result of peso devaluation but also through increases in animal feed costs. With the USMCA, Mexico's government is now in a position to avoid such price increases, even if some effort continues to establish new agricultural supply chains with South American suppliers in the event that USMCA does not come into force.

Because NAFTA and USMCA include zero tariffs on most agricultural products exported to Mexico, US exports of farm products to Mexico have a huge tariff advantage.

---

[15] USTR, "U.S.-Mexico Trade Facts," https://ustr.gov/countries -regions/americas/mexico.

Under World Trade Organization (WTO) rules, which apply currently to Argentina and Brazil and would apply to US exports after NAFTA, wheat is subject to a 15 percent tariff, beef is subject to a 25 percent tariff and chicken is subject to a 75 percent tariff.[16]

Mexico exports labor-intensive farm produce to the US, such as tomatoes, avocados, peppers, grapes, cucumbers, melons, berries, onions, avocados and cantaloupes, which account for 44 percent of total US imports.[17] Most such fruits and vegetables currently enter duty-free; the most-favored-nation (MFN) tariffs applicable to US imports from non-free trade agreement countries are high for some types of produce (e.g., 12.8–29.8 percent for cantaloupes depending on the season), while for others they are much lower (e.g., 2.8–3.9 cents/kg for tomatoes).[18]

Tomatoes are a significant export to the US from Mexico. Under NAFTA and USMCA they are not subject to tariffs or quotas. If such tariffs had been increased under USMCA or with the termination of NAFTA, the increased costs as a result of tariffs would have presumably been passed on to consumers, or consumers would have had fewer choices, particularly in the off season. Sufficient alternative sources for tomatoes or other produce imported from Mexico probably do not exist in the US, especially in the winter, due to the increasing shortage of legal farm workers and water shortages in Arizona and California, among other factors. However, independently of NAFTA and USMCA, the US industry sought and ultimately

---

[16]   Ana Swanson and Kevin Granville (2017), "What Would Happen if the U.S. Withdrew from NAFTA," *New York Times*, October 12, www.nytimes.com/2017/10/12/business/economy/what -would-happen-if-the-us-withdrew-from-nafta.html.

[17]   Renee Johnson (2016), "The U.S. Trade Situation for Fruit and Vegetable Products," Congressional Research Service, December 1, https://fas.org/sgp/crs/misc/RL34468.pdf.

[18]   See Harmonized Tariff Schedule of the United States, USITC Pub. 4750 (2018).

received more extensive so-called unfair trade protection. The tomato anti-dumping dispute and agreement are discussed separately below.

Beyond produce, grains, and animal products, processed foods and beverages constitute a very significant portion of total NAFTA trade. As the Agricultural Technical Advisory Committee for Trade observed in its report,

> U.S. processed food and beverage exports to the world exceeded $43 billion in 2017, accounting for roughly one third of all U.S. agricultural exports. Nearly half of these exports are destined for Mexico and Canada. Canada is by far the largest market for U.S. food and beverage exports, with exports to Canada valued at $12.8 billion in 2017. NAFTA has provided significant economic opportunities to the sector and allowed for the creation of a truly integrated North American market.

As the Committee clearly stated in its comments on priorities and negotiating objectives when the Administration announced its intent to modernize NAFTA, the many beneficial aspects of this trilateral agreement should be preserved and no outcome of the current renegotiation should decrease market access or weaken integration in North America.[19]

B   Agriculture Under USMCA

USMCA does not make any major changes to agricultural trade within North America other than US-Canadian dairy trade. It therefore preserves most agricultural trade within the region, including trade in processed foods. Some of NAFTA's original restrictions remain in USMCA, including those on imports of dairy products, wheat, and some meat products in

---

[19]   Agricultural Technical Advisory Committee for Trade in Processed Foods, September 27, 2018, https://ustr.gov/trade -agreements/free-trade-agreements/united-states-mexico-canada -agreement/advisory-committee.

Canada. In terms of Mexico under USMCA, most agricultural products remain duty- and quota-free.

US agricultural exports to Mexico, in 2018 the third-largest market behind Canada and China, are focused on corn, wheat, soy, beef, pork and chicken, all of which are efficiently grown under highly mechanized conditions in the US. The US also exports dairy products, apples, pears and grapes to Mexico.[20] In 2017, US agricultural exports to Mexico totaled $19.5 billion, while imports from Mexico amounted to $25.5 billion.[21]

As noted earlier, US food imports from Mexico are concentrated in labor-intensive products. In 2017, the US imported $6.7 billion of vegetables including tomatoes and avocados, and $5.3 billion of fruits and nuts, including melons and berries.[22] It was thus important to Mexican as well as US agricultural producers that the duty-free trade in agricultural products established in NAFTA was carried over into USMCA.

C   Reduction of Canadian Dairy and Other Barriers

Dairy is important to the US, not because of the dollar volume of trade (below 1 percent of total US-Canada trade), but because Canadian restraints on dairy imports became a major issue in the USMCA negotiations between the US and Canada on which Trump repeatedly focused. The industry concerns in the US, particularly in key milk-producing states such as Wisconsin, result from a situation where there is "a dairy glut that's so bad it's led some American farmers to spill milk."[23]

---

[20]   "Mexico Country Commercial Guide" (2018), Export.gov, October 12, www.export.gov/article?id=Mexico-Agriculture.

[21]   Ibid.

[22]   Ivanova, "What Does the U.S. Import from Mexico?"

[23]   Jeff Daniels (2017), "US Dairy Glut Leads to Problem of Spilled Milk in Some Markets, as NAFTA Brings Other Worries,"

Converting milk into milk powder or milk protein, which do not spoil and are used in many processed food products, potentially helps dairy producers address milk surpluses. Thus, the opportunity to increase milk (or milk protein) exports to Canada under USMCA became an important issue for US negotiators.

The impasse was resolved only at the last minute, a significant Canadian concession that permitted Canada to become a signatory of the agreement.[24] According to the Agricultural Technical Advisory Committee,

> USMCA delivers additional export market access for US dairy products across a diverse range of product categories. This expansion of access to the very tightly constrained Canadian market is welcome and will create new opportunities for the US dairy industry in Canada's trade-restrictive market. As the agreement is implemented, it will be critical to monitor Canada's TRQ administration practices to ensure that procedures are not wielded to dampen TRQ fill-rates.[25]

Under the Trans-Pacific Partnership, Canada had agreed to permit US dairy farmers to supply approximately 3.25 percent of the Canadian dairy market through their exports to Canada; the level of access is increased to approximately 3.6 percent under USMCA. Furthermore, one major aspect of the Canadian dairy supply management scheme the US consid-

---

CNBC, September 22, www.cnbc.com/2017/09/22/dairy-glut-in-us -leads-to-problem-of-spilled-milk.html.

[24] See Katie Lobosco (2018), "Canada Opened Its Dairy Market. But by How Much?" CNN Politics, October 2, www.cnn.com/2018/ 10/02/politics/usmca-canada-dairy/index.html.

[25] Agricultural Technical Advisory Committee for Trade in Animals and Animal Products, Addendum, October 25, 2018, https://ustr.gov/sites/default/files/files/agreements/FTA/ AdvisoryCommitteeReports/Agricultural_Technical_Advisory _Committee_%28ATAC%29%2CAnimals_and_Animals_Products _Addendum.pdf, 1.

ered highly detrimental to its exports, the "Class 7" milk category that applies to imports of milk powder and milk protein, will be discontinued.[26] It is estimated that this change will be worth about $600 million to the US dairy industry in increased milk powder and protein exports to Canada. In exchange for Canadian acceptance of US milk proteins, US import barriers for processed peanut and sugar products will be liberalized to a modest degree.[27] Mexican trade with the US was not affected by these changes to dairy trade.

Canada also agreed to "grade imports of United States wheat in a manner no less favorable than it accords Canadian wheat, and to not require a country of origin statement on its quality grade or inspection certificate" and "strong rules to ensure tariff-rate quotas are administered fairly and transparently to ensure the ability of traders to fully use them."[28] The full impact of changes in Canada's highly restrictive grain management system will likely require several years to determine.

D   Preservation of (Most) Mexican Access to the US Winter Vegetable Market

Under NAFTA, produce imported from Mexico into the US was duty- and quota-free. Among the initial US proposals for changes to NAFTA, the Trump Administration—under pressure from Florida tomato growers—demanded that Mexico

---

[26]   USMCA, Annex 3-B.

[27]   See Lobosco, "Canada Opened Its Dairy Market"; Gary Hufbauer and Steven Globerman (2018), "The United States-Mexico-Canada Agreement: Overview and Outlook, *Fraser Research Bulletin*, November, https://piie.com/system/files/documents/hufbauer201811-usmca.pdf, 7.

[28]   USTR (2018), "United States-Mexico-Canada Fact Sheet: Strengthening North American Trade in Agriculture," October, https://ustr.gov/trade-agreements/free-trade-agreements/united-states-mexico-canada-agreement/fact-sheets/strengthening.

accept new "unfair" trade remedies that could have significantly restricted access to Mexico's markets for US fruits and vegetables, with a particular emphasis on tomatoes.[29] US growers had effectively argued that competition from Mexico was "unfair" because Mexico enjoyed unfair comparative advantages in lower labor costs, lower humidity, and a more favorable winter climate.[30] Mexican officials were able to reject the proposed changes, and no such provisions are included in the final text of USMCA.

However, this issue did not disappear with the signing of USMCA on November 30, 2018. Florida Senator Marco Rubio objected to the absence of tomato import restraints in USMCA because it effectively preserves the status quo. He subsequently threatened to oppose USMCA's approval by Congress.[31] Other stakeholders, including produce importers in the US, welcomed rejection of new limits on Mexican source produce: "In terms of tariff treatment, (the agreement) is generally open for fresh produce and that's good."[32] Mexico's negotiating success was particularly welcomed by Arizona-based traders, who benefit from a large volume of

---

[29] Caitlin Dewey (2017), "How a Group of Florida Tomato Growers Could Help Derail NAFTA," *The Washington Post*, October 16, www.washingtonpost.com/business/economy/how-a -group-of-florida-tomato-growers-could-help-derail-nafta/2017/10/ 16/e1ec5438-b27c-11e7-a908-a3470754bbb9_story.html?utm_term =.88330100e6bc.

[30] Ibid.

[31] Sean Higgins (2018), "Rubio Says USMCA Would Force US to Rely on Mexican Winter Vegetables, 'Unacceptable,'" *Washington Examiner*, November 30, www.washingtonexaminer .com/policy/economy/marco-rubio-says-usmca-would-force-us-to -rely-on-mexican-winter-vegetables-unacceptable.

[32] See Tom Karst (2018), "Industry Cheers News NAFTA," *The Packer*, October 4, www.thepacker.com/article/industry-cheers-new -nafta.

Mexican fruit and vegetable imports through the Nogales port of entry.[33]

However, this sense of relief was short lived, at least for Mexican tomato exports to the United States. In retrospect, Mexican growers and US importers probably should have anticipated that trade frictions over US tomato exports would continue given the long history of the dispute, with the current anti-dumping action dating from 1996.[34] On May 7, 2019, the US Department of Commerce terminated an agreement that had resulted in the suspension of duties on tomato imports since 2013. The result of cancelling this agreement, the latest action in a trade dispute between the US and Mexico that has lasted for three decades, was the imposition of preliminary duties of 17.6 percent on tomato imports and the resumption of the anti-dumping investigation that had been suspended in 2013.[35]

In addition, Mexican growers sought an injunction from the Court of International Trade against resuming the anti-dumping investigation on the grounds that the Department of Commerce failed to follow proper procedures in ending the suspension agreement. This injunction was denied, and the court further opined that the growers were unlikely to prevail due to the merits of this case: "The court finds that the stated basis for Commerce's withdrawal from the 2013 Suspension Agreement is the voluntary withdrawal provision with 90 days' notice, and that Commerce did not withdraw from the

[33] Ibid.

[34] See "Fresh Tomatoes from Mexico: Suspension of Antidumping Duty Investigation" (2019), International Trade Administration, September 24, www.federalregister.gov/documents/2019/09/24/2019-20813/fresh-tomatoes-from-mexico-suspension-of-antidumping-duty-investigation.

[35] "U.S.-Mexico Tomato Suspension Agreement Terminated, Imports to Face 17.5% Duties" (2019), Western Growers, May 9,   www.wga.com/blog/us-mexico-tomato-suspension-agreement-terminated-imports-face-175-duties.

2013 Suspension Agreement due to a perceived violation of the 2013 Suspension Agreement."[36]

Because of the high stakes, it seemed likely that Mexican growers and the US Department of Commerce would eventually conclude a new suspension agreement, incorporating higher base prices for imported tomatoes and other provisions, favorable to US growers. Ultimately, this occurred in late August 2019, with both parties agreeing to new reference prices for tomatoes of $0.31–$0.59 per pound, with organic tomatoes priced 40 percent higher. These prices, which went into effect on September 19, 2019, are an increase from the $0.25–$0.59 per pound under the earlier suspension agreement.[37] The new five-year suspension agreement also includes an inspection mechanism applicable to some 66.4–92 percent of entering tomatoes.[38] While imports of Mexican tomatoes will continue without tariffs, some US importers have criticized the agreement on the grounds that the increased inspection requirements could lead to increased administrative costs and a backup at the border, which is risky for perishable products.[39]

The current trade action does not address tomato imports from Canada, which represent the second-largest source of

[36] See "Judge Denies Mexican Tomato Growers' Request for Duty Relief" (2019), World Trade Online, June 27, https://insidetrade.com/daily-news/judge-denies-mexican-tomato-growers'-request-duty-relief.

[37] Jude Webber (2019), "U.S. and Mexico Resolve Tomato Spat," *Financial Times*, August 21, www.ft.com/content/70e1cdd8-c420-11e9-a8e9-296ca66511c9; see also Cathy Siegner (2019), "US Faces Potential Tomato Shortage, Price Hikes from Tariffs," FoodDive, May 31, www.fooddive.com/news/us-faces-potential-tomato-shortage-price-hikes-from-tariffs/555884/.

[38] Webber, "U.S. and Mexico Resolve Tomato Spat."

[39] Katie Lobosco (2019), "Trump's New Produce Deal with Mexico Could Hit Tomato Prices," CNN, August 26, www.cnn.com/2019/08/26/politics/mexico-us-tomato-agreement/index.html.

tomatoes sold in the US.[40] Other vegetable and fruit imports from Mexico and Canada have not yet been affected by unfair trade actions.

E   Wine, Spirits and Geographical Indications

USMCA also provides for various administrative procedures permitting review of "geographical indications" agreed to by Mexico in other trade agreements. Such geographical indications include many that have been accepted by the US, such as bourbon, Scotch whisky, and champagne, which are terms that can only be used under WTO rules when the products are produced in Kentucky, Scotland, and the champagne region of France, respectively. However, there has been an ongoing debate between the US, which has resisted the use of additional geographical designations, and the EU, which typically seeks additions to the protected list in new trade agreements. A key example is the term "chardonnay," which the EU argues should be used only for wine produced in France even though chardonnay has been produced and labeled for decades in many other jurisdictions, including California and Australia.

Avoiding new geographical indications is particularly important to American cheese and wine exporters who fear pressure from the EU will restrict the Mexican market for products that the US believes to be generic rather than specific to geographic location (e.g., Gouda or Edam cheese from the Netherlands, feta cheese from Greece, and chardonnay from France). Among other steps designed to prevent US product exports to Mexico from being restricted due to Mexico's geographical indication rules, USMCA requires government

---

[40]   Zhengfei Guan, Trina Biswas and Feng Wu (2017), *The U.S. Tomato Industry: An Overview of Production and Trade*, Gainesville, FL: Institute of Food and Agricultural Sciences Extension, University of Florida, pp. 7–8, https://gcrec.ifas.ufl.edu/media/gcrecifasufledu/images/zhengfei/FE---US-tomato.pdf.

analysis by Mexico before it imposes any new geographical indications. In particular, the criteria for determining when a product is generic or specific to a particular region must be determined.[41] These procedural requirements were included in USMCA because the EU and Mexico are currently in negotiations for a revised free trade agreement, and the EU and Canada concluded the Comprehensive Economic and Trade Agreement (CETA) in September 2017. Both agreements incorporated enhanced geographical indication protection for exported EU products. The USMCA provisions also explicitly protect a list of US cheeses marketed in Mexico.[42] However, as the Agricultural Policy Advisory Committee noted,

> The US–Mexico Trade Agreement includes a number of elements that further transparency and due process in the GI arena. However, it stops short of fully preserving American agriculture's market access opportunities. For instance, exports of products with common food names which have been produced by the United States for decades, such as parmesan, will face restrictions moving forward. Therefore, important work remains to be undertaken … in order to preserve the maximum range of market access opportunities possible for American agriculture.[43]

F   Intellectual Property Related to Agriculture

Modern agricultural trade depends in part on preservation of intellectual property (IP), particularly in research and development and agricultural biotechnology, areas in which the US is a world leader. USMCA's IP provisions in these fields

---

[41]   USTR (2018), "U.S.-Mexico Trade Agreement, Report of the Agricultural Policy Advisory Committee," September 27,   https://ustr.gov/sites/default/files/files/agreements/FTA/AdvisoryCommitteeReports/Agriculture%20Policy%20Advisory%20Committee.pdf.

[42]   Ibid.

[43]   Ibid.

have been strongly supported by the industry, and the advisory committee has made the following observations:

> The APAC applauds the ground-breaking achievements in the US–Mexico Trade Agreement which can serve as a template for future trade agreements. For the first time, a trade agreement specifically addresses agricultural biotechnology critical to the foundation of the future of American agriculture … In addition, the APAC notes positively of the explicit inclusion of enhanced protections for other IP elements such as trademarks, patents (including the recognition of patented plant varieties) and trade secrets.[44]

Among the relevant provisions in USMCA are those designed to encourage agricultural innovation and trade in biotechnology,[45] and those protecting proprietary formulas for pre-packaged foods and food additives.[46] USMCA also includes provisions for agricultural biotechnology, which is defined as: "technologies, including modern biotechnology, used for the deliberate manipulation of an organism to introduce, remove, or modify one or more heritable characteristics of a product for agriculture and aquaculture use and that are not technologies used in traditional breeding and selection."[47] The agricultural biotechnology provisions reflect a commitment by the parties,

> Confirm[ing] the importance of encouraging agricultural innovation and facilitating trade in products of agricultural biotechnology, while fulfilling legitimate objectives, including by promoting transparency and cooperation, and exchanging information related to the trade in products of agricultural biotechnology.[48]

---

44   Ibid.
45   USMCA, Art. 3.14.
46   USMCA, Annex 3-D.
47   USMCA, Art. 3.12.
48   USMCA, Art. 3.14.1.

G   Seasonal Agricultural Workers

In contrast to other agriculture-related concerns, the availability of seasonal workers to provide agricultural labor in the US is not addressed in USMCA. The US agricultural industry had hoped, probably unrealistically, that USMCA would make some provision for seasonal farm workers, but this was not to be the case in either USMCA's labor chapter or elsewhere in the agreement. As the advisory committee report noted,

> American agriculture is disappointed that this negotiating opportunity did not achieve consensus on facilitating the cross-border flow of seasonal and select year-long workers. The current H2A [*sic*] to a program is both difficult and expensive to navigate. It is not user-friendly and does not work for year-round occupations like dairying. The result for America's farmers, ranchers and processors is a shortfall of labor available to participate in both seasonal and year-round agricultural jobs.[49]

IV   CONCLUSION

In terms of changes in USMCA, US importers of apparel and materials used in apparel production did not achieve their objectives, but it is too soon to tell whether impact of the changes overall will be significant. The US has been highly protective of its textile and apparel sector in NAFTA and all subsequent trade agreements,[50] so it is not surprising that such actions continued under USMCA.

In agriculture, the major takeaway is likely a broad feeling of relief for US and Mexican traders of agricultural products. In terms of the more severe tomato import restrictions, it would be inaccurate to blame USMCA. One simply needs to

---

[49] USTR, "U.S.-Mexico Trade Agreement."
[50] See USTR (2017), "Summary of the TPP Textile and Apparel," https://ustr.gov/trade-agreements/free-trade-agreements/trans-pacific-partnership/tpp-full-text, 4.

understand that (a) about half of the tomatoes grown in the US are grown in Florida,[51] and (b) Florida's 29 electoral votes are important in the upcoming 2020 presidential election. This issue is likely to be a continuing challenge to US importers of Mexican produce.

Despite these tomato restrictions, the largely free agricultural trade that is vital to all three NAFTA parties, and to the interests of their consumers, was largely untouched in USMCA. While some Canadian restrictions remain, US dairy farmers modestly increased access to the highly regulated Canadian market for milk solids. It thus seems highly likely that under USMCA, as under NAFTA, Canada and Mexico will be among the largest markets for US agricultural exports. Given the threats to continued US agricultural exports to China as a result of the continuing trade frictions that may or may not be resolved by the "Phase One" agreement concluded in January 2020 calling for substantially increased Chinese imports of US agricultural goods,[52] the more tangible USMCA results provide one of the brighter spots for American agriculture today.

---

[51]   Webber, "U.S. and Mexico Resolve Tomato Spat."

[52]   See Economic and Trade Agreement Between the Government of the United States of America and the Government of the People's Republic of China, January 15, 2020, https://ustr.gov/sites/default/files/files/agreements/phase%20one%20agreement/Economic_And_Trade_Agreement_Between_The_United_States_And_China_Text.pdf, Ch. 3; see Josh Zubbrun and Anthony DeBarros (2020), "U.S. and China Face a Steep Climb to Meet Trade Goals," *Wall Street Journal*, January 16, www.wsj.com/articles/trade-deal-sets-aggressive-targets-for-chinese-purchases-11579176229 (noting that China would have to increase its US source agricultural imports from their 2017 levels to about $40 billion worth annually).

7. Intellectual property, services and digital trade

I   INTRODUCTION

One of the changes taking place in the US economy today is the increasing interrelationship among goods, services and intellectual property (IP). While it is not the purpose of this discussion to analyze this relationship in any detail, it is worth noting that the United States-Mexico-Canada Agreement (USMCA), as with other regional trade agreements, beginning with the North American Free Trade Agreement (NAFTA), has recognized the importance of all three sectors to the US economy and to encouraging US trade. Increasingly, issues relating to the digital economy, which incorporate aspects of both IP and services, are critical to fostering global trade.

It is difficult to overemphasize the importance of IP and services to the US economy. According to the US Department of Commerce and the US Patent and Trademark Office, "IP-intensive industries support at least 45 million U.S. jobs and contribute more than $6 trillion dollars to, or 38.2 percent of, US gross domestic product (GDP)."[1] Some 81 US industries are identified as relying extensively on patents, copyright or trademark protections, including software publishers, sound recording, auto and video equipment producers, cable

---

[1]   US Patent and Trademark Office (2016), "Intellectual Property and the U.S. Economy," September 26, www.uspto.gov/learning-and -resources/ip-motion/intellectual-property-and-us-economy.

and subscription programming, performing arts companies, and radio and television broadcasting.[2] Total merchandise exports of IP-intensive industries amounted to $842 billion in 2014, with licensing rights worth $115.2 billion in 2012.[3] As a recent report noted,

> Intellectual property (IP) protection affects commerce throughout the economy by: providing incentives to invent and create; protecting innovators from unauthorized copying; facilitating vertical specialization in technology markets; creating a platform for financial investments in innovation; supporting startup liquidity and growth through mergers, acquisitions, and IPOs; making licensing-based technology business models possible; and, enabling a more efficient market for technology transfer and trading in technology and ideas.[4]

As the Commerce Department further observes,

> The services sector is an important part of the U.S. economy. According to [the Census Bureau's Bureau of Economic Analysis], in 2009 services accounted for 79.6 percent of U.S. private-sector gross domestic product (GDP), or $9.81 trillion. Services jobs accounted for more than 80 percent of U.S. private-sector employment, or 89.7 million jobs.[5]

What is particularly important for this discussion is that the US has long enjoyed a trade surplus in services. In 2009, US exports of services totaled $502 billion, with a surplus of $132 billion, a larger surplus in services than any other country.[6] In 2016, the US enjoyed a services trade surplus with Canada

---

[2]   Ibid.

[3]   Ibid.

[4]   Ibid.

[5]   John Ward (2010), "The Services Sector: How Best to Measure It," International Trade Administration, US Dept. of Commerce, https://2016.trade.gov/publications/ita-newsletter/1010/services -sector-how-best-to-measure-it.asp.

[6]   Ibid.

and Mexico amounting to a combined $31 billion, compared to an $86.8 billion goods deficit with those countries. The United States also enjoyed surpluses each year between 2004 and 2015.[7]

Thus, even if most of the chapters of USMCA, like NAFTA, address various aspects of trade in goods, some are focused directly on IP and services, and many of the innovations in USMCA, such as the chapters on telecommunications, competition law, small and medium-sized industries, and state-owned enterprises, encompass trade in services as well as goods and depend on the parties' respect for rules protecting IP.

Because of its relationship to IP and services, this report includes discussion of the new USMCA chapter on digital trade, which, among other things, prohibits localization requirements for data storage and bans tariffs on goods that are delivered digitally. The chapter also briefly addresses the possible impact of the reduced protection for US investment in Canada and Mexico (discussed in detail in an earlier report) on the IP and services sectors.

II   INTELLECTUAL PROPERTY

Chapter 17 of NAFTA was negotiated like the rest of NAFTA in 1991–92, several years before the World Trade Organization's (WTO) Agreement on Trade-Related Aspects of Intellectual Property (TRIPS)[8] entered into force on January

---

[7]   Jennifer Powell (2018), "Services in the NAFTA," US International Trade Commission, Office of Industries, Working Paper ID-056, www.usitc.gov/publications/332/working_papers/id _18_056_services_in_the_nafta.htm, 1.

[8]   Agreement on Trade-Related Aspects of Intellectual Property, Annex 1C of the WTO Agreement, April 15, 1994 (as amended January 23, 2017), www.wto.org/english/docs_e/legal_e/31bis_trips _01_e.htm.

1, 1995. At the time, a draft of TRIPS was available, but no one, including the NAFTA negotiators, could be sure that the Uruguay Round negotiations would be successfully concluded.[9] The similarities of NAFTA Chapter 17 and TRIPS are greater than the differences,[10] but both are severely out of date given that they were negotiated at a time when the Internet was in its infancy and trade secrets were given little attention internationally, to refer to just a few elements. Under such circumstances, the Trans-Pacific Partnership (TPP, now the Comprehensive and Progressive TPP, or CPTPP), and later USMCA, provided valuable opportunities to modernize the IP relationships among the NAFTA and USMCA partners, in many cases reflecting innovations taking place in US trade agreements concluded well after NAFTA entered into force.[11] Much of USMCA's IP chapter is taken from TPP with relatively minor changes. However, significant additions, deletions and changes are reflected in the December 2019 amendments.[12] Both are discussed herein.

---

[9]   See WTO, "Understanding the WTO: Basics—The Uruguay Round," www.wto.org/english/thewto_e/whatis_e/tif_e/fact5_e.htm (providing a brief history of the Uruguay Round and noting that "it took seven and a half years, almost twice the original schedule").

[10]   See, for example, Joel R. Reidenberg (1993), "Trade, TRIPS and NAFTA," *Fordham Intellectual Property, Media and Entertainment Law Journal*, **4**(1), 283–6, https://ir.lawnet.fordham.edu/iplj/vol4/iss1/17/.

[11]   For example, in the United States-Peru Trade Promotion Agreement, patent terms could be adjusted where issuance of a patent had been delayed, and test data for pharmaceutical products was required to be kept confidential for at least five years, presumably to discourage generic drug manufacturers. See United States-Peru Trade Promotion Agreement, Art. 16.10.2, April 12, 2006, https://ustr.gov/trade-agreements/free-trade-agreements/peru-tpa/final-text.

[12]   Protocol of Amendment to the United States-Mexico-Agreement, December 11, 2019, https://ustr.gov/trade-agreements/free-trade-agreements/united-states-mexico-canada-agreement/protocol

The IP chapter in USMCA mentioned above encompasses 64 pages including annexes, so it is impractical in a book of this length to cover all aspects, particularly given the significant changes in some areas. However, agriculture-related IP issues, such as geographic indications, are discussed in Chapter 6.

Overall, USMCA's IP chapter is thus a combination of concepts that were included in NAFTA more than 25 years ago, innovations since 1994 found in many other US Free Trade Agreements (FTAs), more recent changes embodied in the TPP, and a few that are USMCA-specific.

A   Committee on IP Rights

Among the highlights of the USMCA changes are the establishment of a Committee on Intellectual Property Rights (IPRC).[13] A certain skepticism of new committees is warranted, given the general reluctance of the parties to schedule meetings.[14] Still, it seems reasonable to hope that given the significance of the subject matter and the committee's obligations to exchange information, strengthen border enforcement of IP rights, consider issues relating to trade secrets and procedural fairness in patent litigation, and act as a mediator in disputes over geographical indications,[15] the mechanism will be utilized frequently. Observers have suggested that the new provisions on trade secrets are among those that "could increase the importance of the Committee moving forward."[16]

-amendments. Citations are, unless context requires otherwise, to the consolidated USMCA text.

[13]   USMCA, Art. 20.14.

[14]   This IPR Committee is not required to meet until a year after entry into force of USMCA. USMCA, Art. 20.14.4.

[15]   USMCA, Art. 20.14.2–3.

[16]   Nicoleas Mayne (2018), "Changes to NAFTA's Intellectual Property Provisions in the USMCA," IP Law Trends, October

B   Extended Copyright and Trademark Protection

Reflecting again changes in US trade policy since NAFTA was negotiated, USMCA provides for a requirement that the USMCA parties afford protection for copyright of at least 70 years after the author's death, a period that is, for example, beyond the 50 years under Canadian law. If the life of a natural person is not the basis for measurement (e.g., for an enterprise such as Disney), the term must be at least 75 years from when the work was first published or 70 years after the end of the year of creation.[17] This compares to only 70 years under NAFTA.[18]

Protection of trademarks exceeds that found in NAFTA but is consistent with the TPP requirements. Initial registration shall be for a term of at least ten years, and parties must maintain an electronic system for applications for and maintenance of trademarks.[19]

C   Enforcement in the Digital Environment

It may well be that one of the most important innovations for American copyright and trademark owners is the requirement that IP enforcement procedures must be made available for the digital environment when infringement takes place. This includes an obligation to provide "enforcement procedures that permit effective and expeditious action by right holders against copyright infringement covered under this Chapter that occurs in the online environment."[20] Circumvention of "effective technological measures" (e.g., any copying

---

25,   www.iplawtrends.com/changes-to-naftas-intellectual-property -provisions-in-the-usmca/.

[17]   USMCA, Art. 20.63.

[18]   NAFTA, Art. 1705.4.

[19]   USMCA, Arts 20.25, 20.23; see TPP, Arts 18.26, 18.24.

[20]   USMCA, Art. 20.89.

measures) are explicitly made subject to criminal penalties in most circumstances.[21] Detailed requirements for enforcement are also specified. Each party's national law is to provide "legal incentives for Internet Service Providers to cooperate with copyright owners to deter the unauthorized storage and transmission of copyrighted materials or, in the alternative, to take other action to deter the unauthorized storage and transmission of copyrighted materials." These laws are also meant to protect Internet Service Providers by "precluding monetary relief against Internet Service Providers for copyright infringements that they do not control, initiate or direct, and that take place."[22] It is evident that the drafters sought and presumably achieved a balance of interests in this controversial area.

D   Enhanced Protection of Trade Secrets

Extensive protection of trade secrets was not a major element of NAFTA although it was addressed.[23] Subsequent agreements have recognized the importance of protecting trade secrets in a high technology society. Patent protection is extensive once a patent has been granted, but in order to obtain a patent, the person seeking the patent must disclose extensive information regarding the invention to demonstrate that it is novel, non-obvious, and has utility, information that becomes public once the patent is granted.[24] Thus, if an enterprise wishes to keep secret its proprietary technology for making a product, it may decide to rely on trade secret protection, protection that depends on keeping the process confidential through restricting knowledge of it to those who

---

[21]   USMCA, Art. 20.67.

[22]   USMCA, Art. 20.89.1.

[23]   NAFTA, Art. 1711.

[24]   See "What Can Be Patented?" Legal Zoom, www.legalzoom .com/knowledge/patent/topic/what-is-patentable.

need to know and concluding confidentiality agreements with employees.[25] Intangible assets, including trade secrets, are protected in the United States under both state and federal law,[26] but such protection may be less effective elsewhere.

The trade secret provisions are based on the TPP but go somewhat further, particularly to protect against trade secret theft by state-owned enterprises. Among these innovations are a restriction on national laws limiting the term of protection for trade secrets, requirements that judges adjudicating trade secret matters do not disclose confidential information, and prohibitions against a party discouraging or impeding voluntary licensing of trade secrets.[27] Criminal penalties for willful misappropriation of a trade secret are required under national law.[28]

E   Patent Terms for Pharmaceutical Products

USMCA initially followed an approach taken in US FTAs, at least since 2006, whereby a patent term can be extended when issuance has been delayed. It also includes provisions requiring that pharmaceutical companies' test data be treated as

---

[25] See Steven D. Gordon (2018), "Trade Secrets and Non-Disclosure Agreements," Holland & Knight, December 17, www.hklaw.com/en/insights/publications/2018/12/trade-secrets-and -nondisclosure-agreements?utm_source=Mondaq&utm_medium= syndication&utm_campaign=View-Original (explaining the use of non-disclosure agreements with key employees).

[26] "Protecting Trade Secrets," FindLaw, https://smallbusiness .findlaw.com/intellectual-property/protecting-trade-secrets.html.

[27] USMCA, Arts 20.1.1, 20.1.5, 20.1.7. See also Nathaniel Lipkus and Jamie Maddox (2018), "A Need-to-Know Guide on IP in the U.S.-Mexico-Canada Agreement," Osler, October 2, www .osler.com/en/resources/cross-border/2018/a-need-to-know-guide -on-ip-in-the-u-s-mexico-canada-agreement (an excellent summary of USMCA's IP innovations).

[28] USMCA, Art. 20.72.

confidential for at least five years,[29] presumably to discourage rapid entry of generic competitors into the market. These provisions were not uniform and gave the parties somewhat more flexibility in certain FTAs, such as the agreement with Peru.[30]

However, the December 2019 amendments, in a major achievement for those Democrats who have chafed at the extensive protection given to pharmaceutical enterprises for their branded drugs against generic competition, make significant changes. In particular, the availability of patent term extensions when unreasonable delays result in an effective shorting of the legal patent term has been modestly curtailed. The new provisions limit the extension to five years and permit generic competitors to sell or import a competing product for "purposes related to generating information to meet requirements for marketing approval for the product."[31] Other changes make it easier for a potential competitor to access the branded drug's previously undisclosed test data, and authorize a USMCA party to provide incentives for persons who successfully challenge the validity of a patent or demonstrate non-infringement and to disclose publicly information regarding the patent and patent terms that have been granted.[32] The USMCA provision that permitted patents to be available for new uses of a known product was also removed.[33] These modifications were characterized by the House Committee on Ways and Means as ensuring fair com-

---

[29]   USMCA, Arts 20.46, 20.48.

[30]   United States-Peru Trade Promotion Agreement, April 12, 2006, Art. 16.10, https://ustr.gov/trade-agreements/free-trade-agreements/peru-tpa/final-text. See Nancy Pelosi Statement on the USMCA Protocol of Amendment, "Prescriptions Drugs," December 10, 2019 (noting that the changes reflect key principles that had been included in trade agreements with Peru, Panama and Colombia).

[31]   USMCA, Arts 20.46, note 40, and 20.47.

[32]   USMCA, Arts 20.48, note 42, and 20.50.2.

[33]   USMCA, Art. 20.36.2 was deleted by USMCA Protocol, para. 3-A.

petition and "maintaining the balance between competition and incentives for innovation" reflected in US law but not in USMCA. This was accomplished, according to the release, by incorporating, inter alia, a "revised regulatory review provision to clarify the circumstances in which generic and biosimilar companies may use a patented invention so that they can obtain marketing approval on day one of patent expiration" and "revised data protection provision to incorporate limitations in U.S. law that foster generic competition."[34]

Most controversially in the original USMCA intellectual property chapter, the parties were to be required to afford data protection to biologic drugs for at least ten years.[35] The agreed term under TPP, as in Canadian law, was only eight years,[36] although under USMCA, Canada had five years to implement the new requirements.[37] The ten-year term became controversial in the US as well as Canada, even though current US law provides for 11 years, because some members of Congress were concerned that incorporating a ten-year term in the Agreement would make it more difficult for a future Congress to reduce protection for biologic drugs.[38] The negotiations between the Trump Administration and the Democratic Congress resulted in the deletion of the Article requiring such protection for biologic drugs.[39] Some objections were lodged

---

[34]   House Committee on Ways and Means (2019), "Improvements to the USMCA," December 10, https://waysandmeans.house.gov › documents › USMCA win factsheet, 3.

[35]   USMCA, Art. 20.49.

[36]   TPP, Art. 18.51.

[37]   Mayne, "Changes to NAFTA's Intellectual Property Provisions in the USMCA."

[38]   See "Blumenauer, Stakeholders Elevate Push for USMCA Biologic Drug Changes" (2019), World Trade Online, May 10, https://insidetrade.com/daily-news/blumenauer-stakeholders-elevate -push-usmca-biologics-changes (discussing Democratic objections to the ten-year period).

[39]   USMCA, Art. 20.49 was deleted by the Protocol, para. 3-E.

by Republican members,[40] but did not result in significant Republican opposition to the compromise.

F   Enforcement Generally

Enforcement of IP rights has been a major concern of US rights holders and the US government since well before NAFTA. In this respect USMCA becomes the cutting edge. As the United States Trade Representative (USTR) observed after conclusion of the negotiations,

> For the first time, a trade agreement will require *all* the following:
>
> - Ex officio authority for law enforcement officials to stop sus-pected counterfeit or pirated goods at every phase of entering, exiting, and transiting through the territory of any Party.
> - Express recognition that IP enforcement procedures must be available for the digital environment for trademark and copyright or related rights infringement.
> - Meaningful criminal procedures and penalties for unauthor-ized camcording of movies, which is a significant source of pirated movies online.
> - Civil and criminal penalties for satellite and cable signal theft.
> - Broad protection against trade secret theft, including against state-owned enterprises.[41]

These obligations are the subject of detailed requirements in the text, including situations where criminal penalties rather

---

[40]   "GOP Lawmakers Lament Proposed Scale-Back of Biologics Protection in USMCA" (2019), World Trade Online, December 4, https://insidetrade.com/daily-news/gop-lawmakers-lament-proposed -scale-back-biologics-protections-usmca.

[41]   USTR, "United States-Mexico-Canada Trade Fact Sheet: Modernizing NAFTA into a 21st Century Trade Agreement: Intellectual Property," https://ustr.gov/trade-agreements/free-trade -agreements/united-states-mexico-canada-agreement/fact-sheets/ modernizing.

than civil penalties must be provided.[42] Among the more important for the US are "Border measures," whereby "Each Party shall provide for applications to suspend the release of, or to detain, suspected counterfeit or confusingly similar trademark or pirated copyright goods that are imported into the territory of the Party."[43] This language undoubtedly reflects continuing frustration with the reluctance of Canada (rather than Mexico) to develop mechanisms to interdict counterfeit goods at the border, particularly with regard to shipments from Asia that find their way across the US border after arrival at the Port of Vancouver.[44] USMCA also strengthens provisions for statutory damages for infringement. It specifies that the damages amount be both fully compensatory and sufficient to serve as a deterrent.[45]

Canada resisted US demands in one significant area:

> One item which Canada did not concede relates to ISP liability. Article [20.89] requires legal remedies for instances of copyright infringement occurring online and safe harbours to limit the liability of internet service providers (ISPs). The language of this provision was tightened to limit when ISPs can benefit from safe harbours, requiring the service provider to adopt and reasonably implement certain policies and standard technical measures including a "notice-and-takedown" system, in addition to not receiving a direct financial benefit from infringing activities … [An annex to the IP chapter is intended to clarify that Canada

---

[42]   USMCA, Sec. J.

[43]   USMCA, Art. 20.84.1.

[44]   One Canadian law firm, commenting on the slowness of the amendment of Canadian IP legislation in 2015, noted that the delays "should come as no surprise to those familiar with the long-standing concerns expressed by many of Canada's trading partners over its intellectual property rights protection regime, or more precisely, lack thereof." See "Canada Begins Border Enforcement for Counterfeits" (2015), Bennett Jones (blog), January 15, www.bennettjones .com/Blogs-Section/Canada-Begins-Border-Enforcement-for -Counterfeits.

[45]   USMCA, Art. 20.25(6).

is exempt from the provision's application based on its current "notice-and-notice" system and other safeguards in Canadian copyright law.][46]

G   Conclusion

If one considers the enormous changes in the scope and coverage of IP in regional trade agreements to which the US, Mexico and Canada have become parties, particularly the TPP and the more than a dozen US FTAs concluded since 2003,[47] the USMCA provisions primarily reflect the latest iteration of that evolutionary process, with a minor rollback reflecting the administration's need for Democratic congressional support for approval of USMCA. Modernization of the WTO's TRIPS Agreement is impossible because of the demise of the Doha Development Round of multilateral trade negotiations,[48] and most non-US regional trade agreements, including those negotiated by the European Union (EU), contain only much more modest, largely unenforceable IP provisions.[49] Under

---

[46] Lipkus and Maddox, "A Need-to-Know Guide." See USMCA, Annex 20-A, Annex to Sec. J.

[47] These include FTAs, inter alia, with Australia, Singapore, Chile, South Korea, Central America and the Dominican Republic, Colombia, Panama, Peru, Bahrain, Jordan and Morocco, all of which include some version of "TRIPS-Plus" content, particularly with regard to the extension of patent terms as a result of delays in approval of pharmaceutical products and protection of confidential test data. See, for example, Tom Bollyky (2015), "Intellectual Property in Free Trade Agreements," Council on Foreign Relations, December 11, https://sites.nationalacademies.org › documents › webpage › pga_170567, 11.

[48] See Editorial Board (2016), "Global Trade After the Failure of the Doha Round," *New York Times*, January 1, www.nytimes.com/2016/01/01/opinion/global-trade-after-the-failure-of-the-doha-round.html.

[49] Bollyky, "Intellectual Property in Free Trade Agreements," 13.

such circumstances, the only apparent route to modernizing international intellectual property rules has been through regional trade agreements such as USMCA and the TPP/ CPTPP, although the balance in the area of branded versus generic drugs is still in flux.

III   SERVICES

A   Treatment of Services Generally

NAFTA incorporated three services chapters: Chapter 12, addressing cross-border services; Chapter 13, addressing (not very effectively) telecommunications services; and Chapter 14, addressing financial services. At the time, these were far-reaching provisions, going well beyond what was ulti-mately incorporated in the WTO's General Agreement on Trade in Services,[50] particularly regarding market access for financial services in Mexico. Mexico agreed to allow Canada and the US access to its financial services markets (banking, brokerage and insurance) over specified periods of time, with limits placed both on the percentage of ownership in each domestic bank and other financial institution permitted and in terms of the overall foreign participation in the Mexican financial system, with a multi-year phase-in in most cases.[51] However, the Mexican financial crisis beginning in December 1994 made most of the phase-in provisions irrelevant; the new (as of December 1, 1994) Ernesto Zedillo Administration decided that increased liquidity was essential to permit the Mexican economy to recover and waived the NAFTA restric-tions on foreign investment in the banking sector (not simply for Canada and the US, but generally), resulting, inter alia,

---

[50]   General Agreement on Trade in Services, Annex 1-B to the WTO Agreement, April 15, 1994, www.wto.org/english/docs_e/ legal_e/26-gats_01_e.htm.

[51]   NAFTA, Annex VII, VII-M-I to V-M-22.

in most domestic banking assets being acquired by foreign interests over a period of several years.[52]

The cross-border services chapter in NAFTA was also relatively comprehensive for its time, including various professional services, the highly controversial cross-border trucking services, and investment market-opening measures, among many others. Still, it is accurate overall to suggest that the changes to the cross-border services and financial services provisions in USMCA compared to NAFTA are relatively minor, although they may be significant for some providers in certain instances. In contrast, NAFTA's largely ineffective telecommunications chapter has been substantially expanded and improved in USMCA.

B Cross-Border Services and the Cultural Exceptions

With cross-border services, despite the relatively extensive market access requirements under the original NAFTA, coverage has not changed in some sectors. For example, air services are excluded except for maintenance, including line maintenance and specialty air services, as is government procurement.[53] The general obligations relating to national treatment, most-favored-nation (MFN) treatment, and market access from NAFTA are preserved.[54]

For professionals, a challenge for cross-border services regulation is recognition by the other party of the educational

---

[52] See Heiner Schultz (2006), "Foreign Banks in Mexico: New Conquistadors or Agents of Change?" April 22, https:// pdfs.semanticscholar.org/9c4c/3285001ce95fdc7561da 53ae29f04e1136d6.pdf (noting that after the 1994 financial crisis foreign banks acquired more than 80 percent of Mexican domestic banking assets).

[53] USMCA, Arts 15.2.4, 15.2.3(b).

[54] USMCA, Arts 15.3, 15.4, 15.5.

and licensing qualifications of the foreign person providing services, whether in medicine, accounting, engineering, law, or other disciplines. NAFTA went further in some disciplines (e.g., engineering services) than in others (e.g., legal services).

For example, lawyers licensed in Canada and the US are subject to national treatment in Mexico.[55] This means that a US lawyer who is a citizen of the US may be authorized to practice in Mexico, but only if she has the education required of Mexican nationals and a *cédula* issued by the Mexican government after the candidate has completed the requisite level of Mexican higher education. In other words, there is no recognition of a US law degree or bar membership in Mexico. Under USMCA, a party has the option of recognizing the education, experiences, or licenses granted by another party, but it is not required to do so.[56] Mutual recognition of professional qualifications is encouraged in USMCA through hortatory provisions designed to encourage relevant bodies (such as the three national bar associations) "to establish dialogues with the relevant bodies of the other Parties, with a view to facilitating trade in professional services."[57] At least with legal services, similar language in NAFTA did not produce significant results, and there is probably little likelihood that it will do so under USMCA. In all NAFTA parties, foreign legal consultants are recognized, whereby a lawyer qualified for practice in one country may provide legal services related to the law of the country in which he or she is authorized to practice or relating to international law in the country of another party.[58] Guidelines are provided in USMCA for

---

[55]   NAFTA, Annex I-M-46.

[56]   USMCA, Art. 15.9.1.

[57]   USMCA, Annex 15-C, para. 2.

[58]   NAFTA, Annex VI—Miscellaneous commitments; see www .sice.oas.org/Trade/NAFTA/anx6.asp.

"mutual recognition agreements" or similar arrangements for professional services.[59]

Reflecting the somewhat greater importance given to small and medium-sized enterprises (SMEs) in USMCA than in NAFTA,[60] the chapter provides a modest obligation: "With a view to enhancing commercial opportunities in services for SMEs, and further to Chapter 25 (Small and Medium-Sized Enterprises), each Party shall endeavor to support the development of SME trade in services and SME-enabling business models, such as direct selling services, including through measures that facilitate SME access to resources or protect individuals from fraudulent practices."[61]

One unusual innovation of the USMCA cross-border services chapter mandates changes in Canadian broadcast rules designed to permit the National Football League (NFL) to sell licenses to Bell Media, a Canadian enterprise, effectively a limitation on Canada's "cultural industries" exception discussed below. With the change, the NFL can license the Super Bowl to Bell Media, which in turn will permit licensing the content to Canadian TV stations. These TV stations will then be permitted to substitute Canadian advertising for the advertising viewed by US audiences.[62] This is an obvious commercial benefit for the NFL, and probably for Canadian TV stations, although it will deprive some Canadians who would otherwise enjoy viewing American Super Bowl advertisements—which, in the view of many, including myself, are often more interesting that the football games—of such opportunities.[63]

---

[59] USMCA, Annex 15-C, App. 1.

[60] See USMCA, Ch. 25.

[61] USMCA, Art. 15.10.

[62] USMCA, Annex 15-D.

[63] Probably not a serious problem, since at least 75 percent of the Canadian population live within about 90 miles of the US border, probably close enough to the US border to watch the Super Bowl over TV stations in Buffalo or Seattle. See "Canada—Close

Canada has long enjoyed a "cultural industries" exception to some trade obligations under NAFTA.[64] A similar exemption applies to Canada under USMCA,[65] with some limitations, although programming services, as noted immediately above, remain covered. The term "cultural industries" applies to publication of books, magazines, periodicals or newspapers whether in print or electronic form; film and video recordings; audio and music recordings; and radio, television and cable transmissions intended for the general public. Certain exceptions apply to Canadian measures, except customs duties and programming services.[66] Also, a party (e.g., the United States) may take measures of "equivalent commercial effect" if the actions by Canada are otherwise inconsistent with USMCA obligations.[67] As discussed in Chapter 1, preserving cultural industries was a "redline" issue; without its inclusion in USMCA, Canada might well have refused to accede.

For the first time, Mexico also benefits from "cultural exceptions." Some actions with regard to cultural industries are permitted for Mexico and the United States even if prohibited for Canada. The US and Mexico recognize "that states have the sovereign right to preserve, develop and implement their cultural policies, to support their cultural industries for the purpose of strengthening the diversity of cultural expressions, and to preserve their cultural identity."[68] The Mexico-specific provisions preserve a list of exceptions to market access national treatment, some of which were included in the NAFTA annexes. In USMCA, the exceptions

---

to the Border" (2008), Twelve Mile Circle, February 12, www .howderfamily.com/blog/canada-close-to-the-border/.

[64]   NAFTA, Annex 2106 (incorporating certain provisions of the US-Canada FTA).

[65]   USMCA, Art. 32.6.

[66]   Ibid.

[67]   USMCA, Art. 32.6.4.

[68]   USMCA, Annex 15-E.

deal mostly with radio and TV broadcasting, newspaper publishing, cinema services and audiovisual services.[69] It seems doubtful that the restrictions on radio and TV broadcasting will be considered objectionable to most potential US suppliers, although, unlike Canada, the majority of the Mexican population does not live within 90 miles or so of the US border. However, restrictions on cinema services may be considered more objectionable, and there is some irony in the restriction given the fact that dozens of movies made by American producers have been filmed in Mexico.[70]

One of the most contentious aspects of NAFTA's cross-border services chapter was reciprocal obligations on the part of Mexico and the US to permit each other's trucks to carry international cargoes from one country to the other, after a multi-year phase-in period.[71] For a variety of reasons, which are well beyond the scope of this book, beginning in 1995 the US refused to comply with the NAFTA requirements, allegedly on the basis of safety concerns but, in the opinion of some, largely for political reasons.[72] The matter was one of a few that were the subject of a decision rendered by a Chapter 20 dispute settlement panel in 2001.[73] However, the dispute

---

[69]   USMCA, Annex 15-E.

[70]   See "Famous Movies from Mexico," Ranker, www.ranker .com/list/movies-from-mexico/reference (listing 100 such movies).

[71]   NAFTA, Annex I, I-M-63, I-M-64; I-M-67. I-M-68, I-U-18, I-U-19 and I-U-20. (Cross-border trucking services were not an issue as between the US and Canada.)

[72]   For a full discussion of the issues up to 2001, see *In the Matter of Cross-Border Trucking Services*, Secretariat File no. USA-MEX-98-2008-01, Final Report of the Panel, February 6, 2001, paras 35–100, www.nafta-sec-alena.org/Home/Dispute-Settlement/ Decisions-and-Reports. Disclosure: I was one of the five members of the Chapter 20 panel.

[73]   *In the Matter of Cross-Border Trucking Services*.

over Mexican truck access continued in one form or another until 2019.[74]

USMCA significantly modifies the NAFTA obligations. In effect, it permits the US to continue the existing practices of permitting approved Mexican trucking enterprises to operate in the US, but also allows the US to terminate such practices:

> [T]he United States reserves the right to adopt or maintain limitations on grants of authority for persons of Mexico to provide cross-border long-haul truck services in the territory of the United States outside the border commercial zones if the United States determines that limitations are required to address material harm or the threat of material harm to U.S. suppliers, operators, or drivers. The United States may only adopt such limitations on existing grants of authority if it determines that a change in circumstances warrants the limitation and if the limitation is required to address material harm. The Parties shall meet no later than five years after the entry into force of this agreement to exchange views on the operation of this entry.[75]

Procedures are established for reviewing the cross-border services practices; elimination of them is not automatic but requires, inter alia, an investigation and determination by the International Trade Commission.[76] There is little public evidence to indicate that the Mexican negotiators fought hard to preserve the NAFTA rights, presumably because the eco-

---

[74]   See James Jaillet (2018), "NAFTA Replacement Would Give U.S. the Ability to Limit Cross-Border Trucking Program," *Overdrive*, October 1, www.overdriveonline.com/usmca-the-new -nafta-would-give-u-s-the-ability-to-limit-cross-border-trucking -program/ (noting that as of late 2018 only 41 Mexican carriers have Department of Transportation authority to operate out of the commercial—12-mile—border zone in the United States).

[75]   USMCA, Annex II-U-7.

[76]   See USMCA Implementation Act, H.R. 5430, December 13, 2019, 116th Cong., 1st Session, www.congress .gov/bill/116th-congress/house-bill/5430/text#toc-H73D0 1E68344741998F1F91CA8B3E3628, Sec. 322.

nomic impact of Mexican truck access was not substantial.[77] Interestingly, Mexico did not impose a reciprocal limitation.

C   Financial Services

USTR suggests that the major achievements of USMCA compared to earlier trade agreements such as NAFTA in this sector are certain "core obligations" including:

- national treatment, to ensure that US financial service suppliers receive the same treatment as local suppliers;
- most-favored-nation treatment, to ensure that US financial service suppliers receive the same treatment as those from other countries;
- market access, which prohibits imposition of certain quantitative and numerical restrictions that would limit the business of US financial services suppliers.[78]

Other observers have offered a more mixed evaluation:

The USMCA ensures that the three member Parties will maintain a heightened level of openness in the financial services sector. At the same time, the USMCA appears to do nothing to further open the sector to competition. The continued ability to restrict access to cross-border financial services and perpetuate government favoritism is a drag on innovation and cost efficiency.[79]

---

[77] Major disincentives to such cross-border operations include the prohibition of Mexican carriers from hauling loads from one US city to another; only international cargoes are allowed. Insurance requirements for carriers operating in the United States can also be expensive to meet.

[78] USTR, "United States-Mexico-Canada Trade Fact Sheet: Modernizing NAFTA." See USMCA, particularly Arts 17.3–17.6.

[79] Tori K. Whiting and Gabriella Beaumont-Smith (2019), "Backgrounder: An Analysis of the United States-Mexico-Canada Agreement," Heritage Foundation, January 28, www.heritage.org/trade/report/analysis-the-united-states-mexico-canada-agreement, 33.

USMCA is explicitly forward-looking in establishing a standstill prohibiting restrictions on cross-border trade that were not in place as of January 1, 1994 (or with national treatment)[80] and by requiring all parties to allow market access for other parties to any newly established financial services, subject only to the proviso that the host party allows its domestic financial services providers to engage in the new types of services.[81] Where public entities in the NAFTA parties operate payment and clearing systems, financial institutions of other NAFTA parties must be granted access, except with respect to another party's lender of last resort facilities.[82]

The USMCA parties also made significant efforts to strike a reasonable balance among privacy, business decisions of financial institutions, and the need of financial regulators for information. Thus, "No Party shall prevent a covered person from transferring information, including personal information, into and out of the Party's territory by electronic or other means when this activity is for the conduct of business within the scope of the license, authorization, or registration of that covered person," subject to the right of any Party to "protect personal data, personal privacy and the confidentiality of individual records and accounts, provided that such measures are not used to circumvent this Article."[83]

Not surprisingly, the financial services chapter does not apply to measures adopted or maintained with respect to a party's government procurement of financial services or subsidies provided by a party with regard to cross-border

---

[80]   USMCA, Art. 17.6.

[81]   USMCA, Art. 17.7.

[82]   USMCA, Art. 17.15. For a useful summary of USMCA's financial services chapter highlights, see Daniel A. Leslie (2018), "The USMCA—Impact on the Financial Services Sector," Norton Rose Fulbright, October, www.nortonrosefulbright.com/en-us/knowledge/publications/5dde68a0/the-usmca--impact-on-the-financial-services-sector.

[83]   USMCA, Art. 17.17.

supply of financial services by another party.[84] The chapter also includes a proviso that the parties will seek to develop regulatory procedures to expedite the offering of insurance services by licensed suppliers.[85]

Several other chapters of USMCA could have a significant impact on financial services. For example, limitations on currency manipulations (discussed in Chapter 10), a first for US trade agreements, could obviously affect banking operations in North America.[86]

D   Telecommunications Services

In retrospect, NAFTA's telecommunications services chapter, Chapter 13, was of only limited utility. The provisions sought to assure liberalization of telecommunications services (at the time primarily telephone and value-added services) through non-discrimination (among the NAFTA parties and in comparison to other countries through MFN requirements), open access to and use of public networks, and support for freer flow of information.[87] Telecommunications services under NAFTA were also affected by technical barriers to trade (discussed in Chapter 8) and by the cross-border services discussed above, which, provided that telecommunications and most other services were afforded non-discriminatory treatment, benefitted from the absence of commercial presence requirements and

---

[84]   USMCA, Arts 17.2.4, 17.2.5. Government procurement of financial services as between the United States and Mexico is governed by USMCA Ch. 13. Financial services relating to government procurement as between the United States and Canada are governed only by the WTO's Government Procurement Agreement.

[85]   USMCA, Art. 17.16.

[86]   See USMCA, Ch. 33.

[87]   See Geneva E. Stephens (1997), "Telecommunications Under the NAFTA and Its Effect on Canada's Telecommunications Industry," *Law and Business Review of the Americas*, **3**(1), 93, 96.

from the professional licensing and certification procedures stipulated in that chapter.[88]

In NAFTA, the most important innovations included guarantees of access and use of public telecommunications networks or services by nationals of another party, including broadcasters and cable system operators.[89] These access and usage rights included the purchasing or leasing of equipment to interface with the public network, interconnections, attachments to the public network, and the performance of related operating functions, all designed to assure that US telecommunications companies could participate effectively in the growing Mexican market.[90] During the years immediately after NAFTA entered into force, one of the primary disputes between the US and Mexico arose over the connection fees charged by Mexican telephone networks (primarily the Mexican near-monopoly, Telmex, owned by billionaire Carlos Slim) to US long-distance carriers such as AT&T, including fees for the millions of calls to Mexico originating each year in the US. The carriers and the US believed these fees were unreasonable because they exceeded cost-oriented rates, and the US also objected to Mexico's alleged failure to prevent anti-competitive practices by major telecoms suppliers (for example, Telmex). After extended and unsuccessful consultations, the US chose to challenge the allegedly unreasonable interconnection fees, not in NAFTA but before the WTO, where the US ultimately prevailed on the key issues.[91]

---

[88]   NAFTA, Arts 1202, 1203, 1205, 1210.

[89]   NAFTA, Arts 1301–1302.

[90]   NAFTA, Art. 1302.2.

[91]   See *Mexico—Measures Affecting Telecommunications Services*, DS204, April 2, 2004, adopted June 1, 2004, https://docs .wto.org/dol2fe/Pages/FE_Search/FE_S_S009-DP.aspx?language =E&CatalogueIdList=48485&CurrentCatalogueIdIndex=0& FullTextHash=&HasEnglishRecord=True&HasFrenchRecord=True &HasSpanishRecord=True. See also the WTO's summary, www .wto.org/english/tratop_e/dispu_e/cases_e/ds204_e.htm.

The case suggests that NAFTA's Chapter 13 failed to meet US expectations in terms of liberalizing the Mexican telecommunications market.

In USMCA, much of the NAFTA's Chapter 13 remains. However, several significant changes have occurred to discourage dominant telecommunications firms in Mexico from trying to exclude international telecommunications firms from the Mexican market. Some observers have suggested that the US negotiators were concerned with efforts of Movil SAB, the dominant mobile network, also owned by Carlos Slim, to restrict competition. AT&T reportedly has been investing heavily in the Mexican wireless market in recent years and expanding its wireless infrastructure.[92] After Mexico's Supreme Court overturned the country's legal restrictions designed to prevent Movil from excluding competitors, USMCA negotiators adopted general restrictions on such anticompetitive practices in the telecommunications markets of all three NAFTA parties.[93]

The various competitive safeguards in USMCA are designed to preclude anticompetitive practices such as cross-subsidization between different types of service providers (e.g., cell phone service and land line service) and the failure of the local carriers to provide technical information about facilities needed for competitors to provide services.[94] Access to a network must be offered on an "unbundled" basis so suppliers can, inter alia, rent telecommunications infrastructure rather than having to build their own infrastructure.[95] Interconnection criteria with major suppliers are specified in detail and fees must be reasonable.[96] Such cri-

---

[92] See Whiting and Beaumont-Smith, "Backgrounder," 35.
[93] Ibid.
[94] USMCA, Art. 18.6.
[95] USMCA, Art. 18.8.
[96] USMCA, Art. 18.9.

teria reflect the requirements of the (post-NAFTA) 1996 US Telecommunications Act.[97]

Reflecting the greater concern with state-owned enterprises elsewhere in USMCA compared to NAFTA,[98] and perhaps reflecting the desire of the United States to deal effectively with a potential problem in future trade agreements with certain countries, this chapter provides that "No Party shall accord more favorable treatment to a supplier of telecommunications services in its territory than that accorded to a like service supplier of another Party on the basis that the supplier receiving more favorable treatment is owned or controlled by the central level of government of the Party."[99] A (luke-warm) effort to address the high cost of roaming services in some jurisdictions is also included, with the requirement that "The Parties shall endeavor to cooperate on promoting transparent and reasonable rates for international mobile roaming services that can help promote the growth of trade between the Parties and enhance consumer welfare."[100] In my limited travel experience in Canada, reasonable roaming rates are more likely to be achieved by agreements between major Canadian wireless services providers such as Bell Canada and Rogers and their US counterparts—Verizon, AT&T, T-Mobile and Sprint.

IV   DIGITAL TRADE

For obvious reasons, NAFTA did not incorporate a chapter on digital trade. In this book, it seems appropriate to consider digital trade in the same chapter as IP and services because of the close interrelationships (for example, copyright law cuts across several of these sectors).

---

[97]   Telecommunications Act of 1996, S. 652, 104th Cong. (1996), https://transition.fcc.gov/Reports/tcom1996.txt.
[98]   See USMCA Ch. 22.
[99]   USMCA, Art. 18.18.
[100]   USMCA, Art. 18.25.1.

In USMCA, the digital trade chapter was one of the most important modernizing elements adapted from the TPP. USTR, with considerable justification, boasts that "The new Digital Trade chapter contains the strongest disciplines on digital trade of any international agreement [as of October 2018], providing a firm foundation for the expansion of trade and investment in the innovative products and services where the United States has a competitive advantage."[101] This language is a clear and welcome recognition of the enormous importance of the global sale of digital products produced in the US. Note also the relationship between the promotion of openness of digital trade in this USMCA chapter and the promotion of simplified procedures for exports of small shipments by US enterprises such as Amazon, as required in USMCA, Chapter 7. Enterprises such as Amazon are creatures of the Internet, but most of the goods ordered from Amazon must still be shipped from bricks-and-mortar warehouses using standard shipping services, whether the packages are destined for customers in the US, Canada, or Mexico.

Some of the obligations reflect unsuccessful efforts made for several decades in other forums, such as the WTO, to prevent the application of customs duties or other discriminatory measures to such products as e-books, videos, music, computer software, video games and the like.[102] Similarly, cross-border transfers of electronic information are not to be prohibited or restricted for business purposes, with exceptions for non-discriminatory public policy objectives that are not arbitrary, unjustifiable discrimination, or a disguised restriction on trade.[103] One of the most important obligations is a ban on data localization, that is parties requiring a person

---

[101] USTR, "United States-Mexico-Canada Fact Sheet."

[102] USMCA, Art. 19.3. The provision does not preclude Mexico from imposing value added taxes on such products, or Canada from imposing provincial or national sales taxes.

[103] USMCA, Art. 19.11. See GATT 1994, Art. XX.

subject to the chapter "to use or locate computing facilities in the Party's territory as a condition for conducting business in that territory" or "require the transfer of, or access to, a source code of software owned by a person of another Party ... as a condition for the import, distribution, sale or use of that software."[104]

Other obligations reflect more basic non-discrimination[105] and the modern need for legal frameworks governing electronic transactions, electronic authentication and electronic signatures.[106] The chapter also recognizes the need to protect consumers from fraudulent or deceptive commercial activities.[107]

Certainly, one of the most controversial areas of digital trade today is protection of personal consumer information (or lack of effective protection). The USMCA language may be more important for what it does *not* do.[108] It does include a laundry list of key principles, ensuring compliance with protective measures:

> The Parties recognize that ... key principles include limitation on collection; choice; data quality; purpose specification; use limitation; security safeguards; transparency; individual participation; and accountability. The Parties also recognize the importance of ensuring compliance with measures to protect personal information and ensuring that any restrictions on cross-border flows of personal information are necessary and proportionate to the risks presented.[109]

As others have observed, there is no mandatory minimum level of protections and no ban on the parties relying on vol-

---

[104] USMCA, Arts 19.12, 19.16.

[105] USMCA, Art. 19.4.

[106] USMCA, Arts 19.5, 19.6.

[107] USMCA, Art. 19.7 (cross-referencing USMCA, Art. 21.4.2 on consumer protection).

[108] USMCA, Art. 19.8.

[109] USMCA, Art. 19.8.3.

untary undertakings by enterprises to protect privacy.[110] Many Americans are among those who would generally be reluctant to rely on voluntary undertakings given the frequency of massive personal data breaches in recent years, including those where Marriott, Equifax, eBay, Yahoo and Target were the offenders.[111]

Consequently, USMCA seeks to protect consumers, whereby "The Parties recognize the importance of adopting and maintaining transparent and effective measures to protect consumers from fraudulent or deceptive commercial activities."[112] Parties are also required to maintain consumer protection laws designed to prohibit fraudulent and deceptive commercial activities and to cooperate with each other to enhance consumer welfare.[113]

However, interactive computer service providers, those with a "system or service that provides or enables electronic access by multiple users to a computer service," are not to be treated as information content providers in determining liabilities for harm related to information storage or processing, or when the supplier acts in good faith.[114] In theory, this "safe harbor" would permit service suppliers to tailor content to users, thereby increasing the quality of the services for consumers.[115]

An annex to the digital services chapter imposes special requirements on Mexico. It provides a three-year grace period for Mexico's obligations relating to interactive computer services and confirms that those requirements are subject to

---

[110] Whiting and Beaumont-Smith, "Backgrounder," 37.

[111] See Taylor Armerding (2018), "The 18 Biggest Data Breaches of the 21st Century," CSO, December 20, www.csoonline.com/article/2130877/the-biggest-data-breaches-of-the-21st-century.html.

[112] USMCA, Art. 19.7.1.

[113] USMCA, Arts 19.7.2, 19.7.3.

[114] USMCA, Arts 19.1, 19.17.

[115] Whiting and Beaumont-Smith, "Backgrounder," 38.

USMCA's general exceptions.[116] Mexican compliance is also required to be both effective and consistent with Mexico's Constitution (and implies the need for new legislation),[117] but Mexico maintains, under the scope of "public morals," that its legislation is designed, inter alia, to protect against online sex trafficking and sexual exploitation of minors.[118]

Largely hortatory language provides that the parties will "endeavor" to build their national capacities for incident response and strengthen mechanisms for cooperation, with the caveat that "risk-based approaches may be more effective than prescriptive regulation."[119] The parties also agree to promote open access to government-generated public data and "endeavor to cooperate to identify ways in which each Party can expand access to and use of government information, including data that the Party has made public, with a view to enhancing and generating business opportunities, especially for SMEs."[120]

Interestingly, the USMCA chapter is no longer the most comprehensive digital trade chapter. A United States-Japan agreement (separate from the trade agreement) goes further, including coverage of information and communications technology that uses cryptography.[121] Parties to the agreement may not require the suppliers to "transfer or provide access

---

[116]   USMCA, Annex 19-A.

[117]   USMCA, Annex 19-A(3).

[118]   USMCA, Annex 19-A(4).

[119]   USMCA, Art. 19.15.

[120]   USMCA, Art. 19.18.

[121]   Agreement Between the United States of America and Japan Concerning Digital Trade, October 7, 2019, https://ustr.gov/sites/default/files/files/agreements/japan/Agreement_between_the_United_States_and_Japan_concerning_Digital_Trade.pdf; see "U.S.-Japan Digital Trade Agreement Includes New ICT, Tax, Security Language" (2019), World Trade Online, October 7, https://insidetrade.com/daily-news/usmca-incorporates-new-digital-trade-chapter-cybersecurity-provisions.

to any proprietary information relating to cryptography."[122] Among the exceptions, no party under the agreement can be required to allow data access if it would jeopardize a party's "essential security interests."[123]

V INVESTMENT RELATING TO INTELLECTUAL PROPERTY AND SERVICES

Investment issues, particularly the reduction of the protection of foreign investment in most sectors involving Mexico and its elimination after a three-year transition period as between the US and Canada, were discussed in Chapter 3. However, it is notable that investment disputes often arise within the IP and services sectors. NAFTA's Chapter 11 specifically covered intangible property.[124] The Industry Advisory Committee expressed "serious concerns" about the exclusion of investment protection:

> Many foreign investments have a significant intellectual property component and many IP-intensive industries must make foreign investments in order to compete effectively in those markets. ITAC-13 believes it is not beneficial to the U.S. economic interest to curtail rights for U.S. companies to protect their IP investments in overseas markets.[125]

---

[122] Ibid., Art. 21.

[123] Ibid., Art. 4(a).

[124] See NAFTA, Art. 1139 (including in the definition of "investment" "(g) real estate or other property, tangible or intangible, in the expectation or used for the purpose of economic benefit or other business purposes").

[125] Report of the Industry Trade Advisory Committee on Intellectual Property, September 27, 2018, https://ustr.gov/trade -agreements/free-trade-agreements/united-states-mexico-canada -agreement/advisory-committee, 33.

Several Chapter 11 cases have focused on alleged violations of intellectual property rights.[126]

Similar issues arise from the relationship between services and investment, since many cross-border and financial services activities cannot be undertaken without investments, sometimes substantial ones, in the host country. In the most obvious example, the dispute between the US and Mexico over cross-border trucking addressed the US's failure to permit Mexican trucks to enter the US *and* a prohibition on Mexican investment in US trucking enterprises, both of which were overturned by the Chapter 20 panel.[127]

At the conclusion of the USMCA negotiations, the Services Advisory Committee on USMCA objected strongly to the reduction of investor–state dispute settlement (ISDS) protections with Mexico and their elimination with Canada:

> [T]he new Trade Agreement eliminates the ability of most businesses to enforce many of the Agreement's core protections through ISD [against Mexico], limits recourse to ISDS to only existing investments, and adds new procedural hurdles to any company seeking to use neutral enforcement mechanisms …
>
> Additionally, the Committee is alarmed that no ISDS protections would be available for business concerns in Canada, based on the assertion that such protections are not needed due to Canada's well-regarded legal protections. The Committee rejects this view for three reasons: (1) other countries with less robust legal systems will demand the same treatment (i.e., no ISDS mechanism); (2) US investors will have to rely on the US government to enforce the Trade Agreement's investment protections

---

[126] See, for example, *Eli Lily and Co. v. Government of Canada*, ICSID Case no. UNCT/14/2 (March 16, 2017), https://icsid .worldbank.org/en/Pages/cases/casedetail.aspx?CaseNo=UNCT/14/ 2. For a review of the case, see Thomas Musmann (2017), "Eli Lilly v. Canada—The First Final Award Ever on Patents and International Investment Law," Kluwer Patent Blog, April 4, http:// patentblog.kluweriplaw.com/2017/04/04/eli-lilly-v-canada-the-first -final-award-ever-on-patents-and-international-invest-ment-law/.

[127] *In the Matter of Cross-Border Trucking Services.*

not subject to ISDS, which will politicize the process, as well as prevent investors from "being made whole"; and (3) it is out of step with the approach taken by other major jurisdictions—such as the EU—in the investment chapters of their FTAs—which will leave our competitors' investments more secure than ours.[128]

Presumably, the impact of eliminating ISDS for IP and services will not become fully apparent until several years after USMCA has entered into force, when the three-year grace period for NAFTA Chapter 11 will no longer be available to US companies providing IP and services to Mexico and Canada. Given the enormous importance of IP and services exports for the US, as noted in the introduction to this chapter, it is not unreasonable to predict that this omission will be among the costliest for the US and US enterprises of any of the USMCA changes.

---

[128] "Report of the Industry Trade Advisory Committee on Services," September 27, 2018, https://ustr.gov/trade-agreements/ free-trade-agreements/united-states-mexico-canada-agreement/ advisory-committee, 7.

8.   Updating NAFTA drawing on the TPP

I   INTRODUCTION

As Chapter 1 indicated, significant portions of USMCA have been taken either verbatim or with some modifications from the CPTPP, a very logical approach given that NAFTA was negotiated more than 27 years ago (in 1991–92) and what was at the time the world's most modern and deepest FTA was the TPP as negotiated by the Obama Administration on behalf of the United States along with 11 other countries.[1] Many of the most important CPTPP/TPP innovations have been discussed in other chapters of this book (in addition to mention in Chapter 1). These include protection of the environment (Chapter 4); investor protections in Mexico's petroleum sector (Chapter 5); intellectual property, telecommunications services and perhaps most important, digital trade (Chapter 7).

However, this is not to suggest that other changes adopted from TPP, many of which have been based on post-NAFTA

---

[1]   The Trans-Pacific Partnership became the Comprehensive and Progressive TPP (CPTPP) after US withdrawal, with the other 11 parties agreeing on a list of modifications. See texts, www .international.gc.ca/trade-commerce/trade-agreements-accords -commerciaux/agr-acc/cptpp-ptpgp/text-texte/index.aspx?lang =eng&_ga=2.137201392.1186738.1570397124-1128694463 .1562952965. In most respects the original TPP text remains as negotiated and signed on February 4, 2016.

trade agreements concluded by the United States,[2] are unimportant either to the NAFTA parties or to their stakeholders. While it is difficult at this early date to accurately predict which ones will have a significant impact on future North American trade, several of them have the potential to have a major impact. USMCA also confirms that it may be easier to reach agreement on some innovations where there are only three parties at the table, compared to 12 with the original TPP (even if all the NAFTA parties were among the 12).

II   SMALL AND MEDIUM-SIZED ENTERPRISES

The USMCA's Chapter 25 expands somewhat on TPP's Chapter 24 although the USMCA chapter, like that of CPTPP, is largely aspirational. (SMEs were not addressed in NAFTA.) The TPP chapter was limited to information sharing and the creation of an SME Committee. Information-sharing is to consist on the creating of a website that would make available the entire agreement and its annexes (already available at multiple sources), a vague obligation to provide website links to the equivalent websites of other parties and their agencies and other "appropriate entities" that would be useful to traders or investors, preferably in English.[3] The SME Committee was designed to assist SMEs in "taking advantage of the commercial opportunities under this agreement."[4] The committee is required to meet within one year of the entry into force of

---

[2]   See, e.g., United States-Dominican Republic-Central American Free Trade Agreement [Costa Rica, Dominican Republic, El Salvador, Guatemala, Honduras, Nicaragua and the United States], August 5, 2004, www.sice.oas.org/Trade/CAFTA/CAFTADR_e/ CAFTADRin_e.asp (addressing corruption in Chapter 18, Section B).

[3]   CPTPP, Arts 24.1, 24.2.

[4]   CPTPP, Art. 24.2.

CPTPP; further meetings are "as necessary,"[5] which means that any future meetings are subject to the views of the parties and the committee members, an approach that does not give one a great deal of confidence that the committee will have much of an impact. Matters arising under the SME chapter are exempt from state-to-state dispute settlement.[6]

USMCA expands this somewhat by requiring that the parties, "recognizing the fundamental role of SMEs in maintaining dynamism and enhancing competitiveness of their respective economies, shall foster close cooperation between SMEs of the Parties and cooperate in promoting jobs and growth in SMEs." The parties also emphasize the "integral role of the private sector" in SME coordination.[7] (This could have been more difficult in CPTPP given the fondness of Brunei, Malaysia and Vietnam for the state-controlled sectors of the economy.) USMCA also goes beyond CPTPP by committing the parties more specifically to increasing SME trade and investment opportunities through cooperative measures to strengthen small business support infrastructure; promoting SMEs owned and operated by under-represented groups; enhancing cooperation among the parties for information exchange and best practices; and encouraging the use of web-based platforms to share information.[8]

The USMCA provisions to some extent reflect an understanding of how difficult it is to encourage and support SMEs so that they can operate internationally. I discussed this problem with colleagues at a conference in Nova Scotia in September 2019, and with several small business stakeholders, primarily in the hospitality industry. Most queried in this unscientific evaluation were aware of NAFTA and the fact that it may soon be replaced. However, most of them had not taken

---

[5] CPTPP, Art. 24.2.4.
[6] CPTPP, Art. 24.3.
[7] USMCA, Art. 25.1.
[8] USMCA, Art. 25.2.

any direct advantage of NAFTA and had no idea whether anything in USMCA would lead to more business with Americans and (much less likely) Mexican nationals. None of them had even heard of the Comprehensive Economic and Trade Agreement (CETA) between the European Union and Canada, which entered into provisional force in September 2017, despite efforts by the Canadian government and business groups to publicize it.[9]

There are of course many other provisions in USMCA that would assist SMEs as well as larger enterprises in taking advantage of North American trade. These include, among others, enhanced customs and trade facilitation provisions (to a limited degree); the increased de minimis thresholds for packages; better access for dairy; greater labor obligations for Mexico; better IP enforcement; better regulatory cooperation; and coverage of digital trade.[10] Still, the situation under USMCA once it enters into force is mixed:

> The USMCA does provide for some new trade promoting opportunities for SMEs, but there are equally as many challenges and uncertainties. Not every sector will be impacted in the same way or to the same extent ... SMEs and businesses around the country still have work to do in order to analyze the changes and assess the impacts on their finances, supply chains, and investment decisions if and before the agreement enters into force, most likely sometime in 2020.[11]

---

[9]   Comprehensive Economic and Trade Agreement Between Canada, of the One Part, and the European Union and Its Member States [EU-Canada], October 30, 2016, www.international.gc.ca/trade-commerce/trade-agreements-accords-commerciaux/agr-acc/ceta-aecg/text-texte/toc-tdm.aspx?lang=eng.

[10]   "USMCA (NAFTA 2.0): What It Means for SMEs" (2018), Trade Moves LLC, October 22, www.trademoves.net/trademoves -blog/usmca-nafta-20-what-it-means-for-smes.

[11]   Ibid.

III   REGULATION OF STATE-OWNED ENTERPRISES AND DESIGNATED MONOPOLIES

NAFTA addressed competition, monopolies and state enterprises together in one short chapter,[12] mostly in a hortatory fashion and without dealing effectively with any of the three. Most significantly, while neither monopolies nor state enterprises were barred, each NAFTA party was obligated through regulatory control and administrative supervisions to assure that any monopoly "acts in a manner that is not inconsistent with the Party's obligations under this Agreement wherever such a monopoly exercises any regulatory, administrative or other governmental authority that the Party has delegated to it in connection with the monopoly good or service, such as the power to grant import or export licenses, approve commercial transactions or impose quotas, fees or other charges," and acts in a non-discriminatory manner toward investors, goods and service providers.[13] Similar language applies to state enterprises.[14]

USMCA expands on party obligations in these areas although it remains to be seen after USMCA has been in force for several or more years whether the requirements can be effectively enforced. The chapter includes a definition of state-owned enterprises (SOEs), similar to that found in CPTPP[15] but considerably more detailed, perhaps reflecting the United States' serious concerns with the WTO's approach to SOEs, where the Appellate Body has imposed unreasonable standards for demonstrating that Chinese SOEs are "public

---

[12]   NAFTA, Chapter 15.
[13]   NAFTA, Art. 1502.3.
[14]   NAFTA, Art. 1503.2.
[15]   CPTPP, Art. 17.1.

bodies" and thus subject to the WTO's subsidies disciplines.[16] In USMCA an enterprise is an SOE if a party owns more than 50 percent of the share capital directly or indirectly; controls directly or indirectly more than 50 percent of the voting rights; has the power to control the enterprise through any ownership interest, including a minority interest; or holds the power to appoint a majority of the board of directors.[17] For many observers such bright-line rules make much more sense that the vagueness of the WTO Agreement on Subsidies and Countervailing Duties, which has given the Appellate Body an opportunity to exclude from the term "public body," and thus from WTO subsidies disciplines, many SOEs effectively controlled and heavily subsidized by the government.

Interestingly, the USMCA chapter applies to SOEs, state enterprises and monopolies that could affect trade or invest-ment within North America or activities "that cause adverse effects in the market of a non-Party."[18] Essential elements, inter alia, are intended to assure that a party's SOE "acts in accordance with commercial considerations in its purchase or sale of a good or service," and that the enterprise "accords to a good or service supplied by an enterprise of another Party treatment no less favorable than it accords to a like good or

---

[16] These concerns have been most recently stated by the US Trade Representative's Office July 16, 2019 referring to *China— Countervailing Duties*, https://ustr.gov/about-us/policy-offices/press-office/press-releases/2019/july/statement-wto-appellate-report-china, "Today's appellate report recognizes that the United States has proved that China uses State-Owned Enterprises (SOEs) to sub-sidize and distort its economy. Nonetheless, the majority in the report says that the United States must use distorted Chinese prices to measure subsidies, unless the U.S. provides even more analysis than the hundreds of pages in these investigations. This conclusion ignores the findings of the World Bank, OECD working papers, eco-nomic surveys, and other objective evidence, all cited by the United States."

[17] USMCA, Art. 22.1.

[18] USMCA, Art. 22.2.1.

a like service supplied by enterprises of the Party, of any other Party or of a non-Party" and treats covered investments in a non-discriminatory manner as well.[19] As in NAFTA, similar rules apply to designated monopolies.[20] Small entities, with revenues of less than about $250 million, are excepted.[21]

Other provisions of the lengthy chapter include requirements that courts be provided with jurisdiction over civil claims against enterprises based on commercial activity carried on in a party's territory and restrictions on subsidies.[22] Among other transparency requirements, within six months after the entry into force of USMCA, each party must publish a list of such enterprises on an official website, and update the list annually.[23] USMCA creates an SOE and designated monopolies committee, similar to the Working Group on Trade and Competition under NAFTA.[24]

Energy issues have been discussed in Chapter 5. However, USMCA was signed on November 30, 2018, one day before Andrés Manuel López Obrador (AMLO) became president. This is significant, because one of AMLO's key policies to date has been to significantly increase the powers and authority of Mexico's petroleum monopoly, PEMEX. As observers have noted,

> Pemex is the centerpiece of Mr. López Obrador's aspiration to overturn what he sees as more than three decades of "neoliberal" economic policy. One of his first moves after taking office was

---

[19]   USMCA, Art. 22.4.1(a), (b).
[20]   USMCA, Art. 22.4.2. (Applicable to private enterprises enjoying monopoly status through government approval.)
[21]   USMCA, Art. 22.13.5; Annex 22-A.
[22]   USMCA, Arts 22.5, 22.6.
[23]   USMCA, Art. 22.10.
[24]   See USMCA, Art. 22.2; NAFTA, Art. 1504.

to order the oil company to add the motto "For the recovery of sovereignty" to its Mexican-eagle logo.[25]

These policies have been followed even though many are skeptical as to whether Pemex can effectively construct its new \$8 billion gasoline refinery and halt Mexico's decline in oil production of the past 15 years when no major new oilfields are scheduled to come on line. Most of this is to be accomplished without significant participation of the private sector, some of whom have been alienated by a three-year moratorium on new lease auctions, inter alia.[26]

There is no evidence to date that the expansion of Pemex and the reduction of private enterprise participation in oil exploration and development is a violation of USMCA's Chapter 22 on SOEs. However, the situation bears watching.

IV   COMPETITION LAW

As noted earlier in this chapter, NAFTA itself did not deal effectively with competition law. In USMCA, competition law is addressed in a chapter separately from monopolies and state enterprises. It is worth noting that dealing in substantive detail with competition issues is difficult in international agreements because of conceptual and enforcement differences among major nations, both developed and developing.[27] USMCA, however, reflects what is probably the most modern attempt to deal with competition issues in a regional trade

---

[25]   Jude Webber and Michael Stott (2019), "Mexico: Lopez Obrador Makes a Big Bet on Oil," *Financial Times*, October 3, www .ft.com/content/d5c3c1c0-e432-11e9-b112-9624ec9edc59.

[26]   Ibid.

[27]   See, for example, D. Daniel Sokol, "Troubled Waters Between U.S. and European Antitrust" (2017) *Michigan Law Review*, **115**, 955; Francisco Gonzalez de Cossio (2003), "International Aspects of Competition Law," www.unis.edu.gt › fetch › international-competition.

agreement to which the United States is a party. The basic principle requires that "Each Party shall maintain national competition laws that proscribe anticompetitive business conduct to promote competition in order to increase economic efficiency and consumer welfare and shall take appropriate action with respect to that conduct." It must also "endeavor to apply its national competition laws to all commercial activities in its territory" with a party having the right of "applying its national competition laws to commercial activities outside its borders that have an appropriate nexus to its jurisdiction."[28]

Other aspects of the chapter are designed to encourage procedural fairness in enforcement, cooperation and coordination between national authorities, making competition "enforcement and advocacy policies as transparent as possible," and obligatory consultations on the request of any party.[29] Another provision requires parties to "adopt or maintain national consumer protection law or other laws or regulations that proscribe fraudulent and deceptive commercial activities."[30] Matters arising under this competition chapter are excluded from dispute settlement under the investment chapter, Chapter 14 (which applies only to US-Mexico disputes) or general state-to-state dispute settlement.[31]

CPTPP's competition chapter was similar in most respects. The most significant difference compared to USMCA was the inclusion of a provision designed to require "each Party should adopt or maintain laws or other measures that provide an independent private right of action."[32] Remedies are not specified, presumably because most other nations do not accept US laws that provide for treble damages in private

---

[28] USMCA, Arts 21.1.1, 21.1.2.
[29] USMCA, Arts 21.2, 21.3, 21.5, 21.6.
[30] USMCA, Art. 21.4.2.
[31] USMCA, Art. 21.7.
[32] CPTPP, Art. 16.3.2.

anti-trust actions.[33] CPTPP also provided a lukewarm technical cooperation requirement, indicating that "the Parties shall consider undertaking mutually agreed technical cooperation activities, subject to available resources."[34]

V   COMPETITIVENESS AND BUSINESS FACILITATION

The United States explained the purpose of the Competitiveness and Business Facilitation chapter in TPP as follows:

> The Competitiveness and Business Facilitation chapter creates mechanisms by which governments can make the assessments and get the information they need to assess the agreement's overall contribution to its participants' competitiveness. To do so, it establishes means to regularly review whether implementation of the agreement is leading to the anticipated gains in regional competitiveness ... [35]

(NAFTA had no equivalent committee.)

In TPP, it was evident from the language that effective encouragement of good supply management practices was the major focus of the chapter, with the Competitiveness Committee obligated to "explore ways to promote the development and strengthening of supply chains within the free trade area."[36] A distinct provision was included requiring the

---

[33]   See Leon B. Greenfield and David F. Olsky (2007), "Treble Damages: To What Purpose and to What Effect?" British Institute of International and Comparative Law, February 2, www.wilmerhale.com/en/insights/publications/treble-damages-to-what-purpose-and-to-what-effect-february-2-2007.

[34]   CPTPP, Art. 16.5.

[35]   USTR, Transpacific Partnership, Chapter 22 Summary, Competitiveness and Business Facilitation, 2016, https://ustr.gov/trade-agreements/free-trade-agreements/trans-pacific-partnership/tpp-full-text.

[36]   TPP, Art. 22.2.3(d).

committee to "explore ways in which this Agreement may be implemented so as to promote the development and strengthening of supply chains in order to integrate production, facilitate trade and reduce the costs of doing business within the free trade area."[37] The committee, which was mandated to meet within one year of the date of entry into force of the agreement (but thereafter only "as necessary"), was composed only of government representatives, although it was directed to "establish mechanisms appropriate to provide continuing opportunities for interested persons of the Parties to provide input on matters relevant to enhancing competitiveness and business facilitation."[38]

The competitiveness chapter of USMCA, while in some respects resembling the TPP, is less ambitious. It makes no mention of supply chains or the facilitation of their development, for reasons unknown. Here, as in TPP, the committee is composed entirely of government officials and is not required to convene again after the first meeting.[39] The committee may seek advice from appropriate experts but stakeholders have no direct input.[40] Parties individually are directed to establish opportunities for interested persons to provide input on matters relating to enhancing competitiveness.[41] One might have wished that the mechanisms for stakeholder input had been developed in more detail in the chapter. It is of course possible that the three USMCA governments will make effective use of the Competitiveness Committee, but there is certainly no guarantee that it will have any impact, particularly if private stakeholder input is not actively solicited.

---

[37] TPP, Art. 22.3.1.
[38] TPP, Arts 22.2, 22.4.
[39] USMCA, Art. 26.1.2.
[40] USMCA, Art. 26.1.8.
[41] USMCA, Art. 26.2.

VI   ADDRESSING CORRUPTION

Although missing in NAFTA, anti-corruption provisions have been a part of most US FTAs since CAFTA-DR, including USMCA. Including coverage in USMCA makes obvious sense. While none of the three parties is free from corrupt activities, Mexico has long battled endemic corruption from the presidential level to that of the local policeman. As one observer summarizes the situation:

> Corruption is a significant risk for companies operating in Mexico. Bribery is widespread in the country's judiciary and police. Business registration processes, including getting construction permits and licenses, are negatively influenced by corruption. Organized crime continues to be a very problematic factor for business, imposing large costs on companies … Mexico's anti-corruption laws are almost never enforced, and public officials are rarely held liable for illegal acts. New anti-corruption laws were passed in 2017, but their effectiveness has not been proven yet.[42]

This status is confirmed by Transparency International, which in 2018 ranked Mexico 138th out of 180 reviewed countries.[43] (Canada ranks no. 9, the United States, no. 22.[44])

Moreover, during the presidential campaign, President López Obrador made rooting out of corruption one of the key objectives of his presidency, although it is unclear whether he has made any progress. During the early months of his presidency there were no major prosecutions of public officials and more than 70 percent of the government contracts

---

[42]   "Mexican Corruption Report" (2018), Gan Integrity, July, www.ganintegrity.com/portal/country-profiles/mexico/.

[43]   "Mexico"   (2018),   Transparency   International,   www.transparency.org/cpi2018.

[44]   Ibid.

were awarded directly, without competitive bids.[45] Thus, at this writing one may reasonably question whether AMLO's Administration will be able to reduce endemic corruption in Mexico, or even whether he is serious about doing so.

In CPTPP, transparency and corruption were combined in a single chapter, as has often been the case in earlier US FTAs.[46] It is a separate chapter in USMCA. Innovations are limited, with the parties reaffirming their adherence to the Organisation for Economic Co-operation and Development (OECD), United Nations and similar conventions against foreign bribery, along with principles developed by the Asia-Pacific Economic Cooperation Forum (APEC) and the Group of Seven.[47]

VII   GOOD REGULATORY PRACTICES AND REGULATORY COHERENCE

As tariffs have gradually been reduced, better regulatory practices and increased conformity of such regulations among nations have become increasingly important to international traders, even though such efforts in trade agreements have had only limited success. In analyzing the effects of a "hard" Brexit, for example, in sectors where tariffs are low the non-tariff barriers reflected by compliance paperwork and other administrative requirements could cost more than new

---

[45]   See Azam Ahmed and Kirk Sample (2019), "A New Revolution? Mexico Still Waiting as Lopez Obrador Nears Half-Year Mark," *New York Times*, May 10, www.nytimes.com/2019/05/10/world/americas/amlo-mexico-lopez-obrador.html.

[46]   CPTPP, Ch. 26; CAFTA-DR, Ch. 18.

[47]   USMCA, Arts 27.2.2, 27.2.3.

MFN tariffs.[48] In commenting on the regulatory coherence chapter of the TPP, USTR noted the objectives:

> Through the Regulatory Coherence chapter, the United States is seeking to foster an open, fair, and predictable regulatory environment for U.S. businesses operating in Asia-Pacific markets, including through principles that are central features of the U.S. regulatory process, such as transparency, impartiality, and due process as well as coordination across the government to ensure a coherent regulatory approach … [49]

The terms, whether "good regulatory practices" or "regulatory coherence," encompass several related areas as the quotation indicates. Arguably, a first attempt in this area was in NAFTA, where the parties addressed what at the time was an important aspect of transparency, "Publication, Notification and Administration of Laws."[50] Under TPP, the parties focused on "promoting mechanisms for effective interagency consultation and coordination" as well as implementation of "core good regulatory practices." In the TPP, the United States and other parties recognized that regulatory coherence was an ongoing process setting up a committee that was designed to give the parties and their stakeholders opportunities "to report on implementation, share experiences on best practices and consider potential areas for cooperation."[51]

USMCA expands considerably on TPP, addressing in much greater scope and detail an area of great importance to the USMCA stakeholders who rely on effective supply chain management to take full advantage of the benefits of

[48] See Alex Chadwick (2017), "The Realities of Trade After Brexit," Baker and McKenzie, www.bakermckenzie.com/-/media/files/insight/publications/brexit_tradeflows.pdf, 2.

[49] USTR, Trans-Pacific Partnership Chapter 25 Summary, 2016, https://ustr.gov/trade-agreements/free-trade-agreements/trans-pacific-partnership/tpp-full-text.

[50] NAFTA, Ch. 18.

[51] USTR, Commentary on Chapter 25.

duty-free, quota-free North American trade. The commitment is well summarized at the outset of the chapter:

> The Parties recognize that implementation of government-wide practices to promote regulatory quality through greater transparency, objective analysis, accountability, and predictability can facilitate international trade, investment, and economic growth, while contributing to each Party's ability to achieve its public policy objectives ... The application of good regulatory practices can support the development of compatible regulatory approaches among the Parties, and reduce or eliminate unnecessarily burdensome, duplicative, or divergent regulatory requirements. Good regulatory practices also are fundamental to effective regulatory cooperation.[52]

These objectives are supported by requirements, inter alia, to create a central regulatory coordination body in each country; processes for international consultation, coordination and review; disseminate reliable and high-quality information; as well as early planning for new regulations.[53] As elsewhere (for example, the SME chapter) a dedicated website is an obligation to include all information required to publish a regulation.[54] Transparent development of regulations, a concept that can be traced to NAFTA as noted above, is also obligatory.[55] The regulatory process is to be enhanced through export advisory groups and the encouraging of regulatory impact assessments,[56] long a feature of US practice.[57] While the

---

[52]   USMCA, Art. 28.2.

[53]   USMCA, Arts 28.3–28.6.

[54]   USMCA, Art. 28.7.

[55]   USMCA, Art. 28.9.

[56]   USMCA, Arts 28.10–28.11.

[57]   See John Morrall and James Broughel (2014), "The Role of Regulatory Impact Analysis in Federal Rulemaking," Mercatus Center, April 10, www.mercatus.org/publications/regulation/role-regulatory-impact-analysis-federal-rulemaking (observing that "Regulatory impact analysis (RIA) is a tool regulators use to help guide them through the decision-making process when promulgating regu-

term "regulatory coherence" appears to have been generally avoided in USMCA, regulatory "compatibility and coherence" are encouraged.[58] USMCA establishes a "Committee on Good Regulatory Practices" essentially similar to the TPP's "Committee on Regulatory Coherence."[59]

Whether the chapter is unique or is a model for coverage of good regulatory practices in future trade agreements remains to be seen. Efforts to achieve a greater degree of regulatory coherence were a major area of disagreement in the now-dormant Transatlantic Trade and Investment Partnership (TTIP) negotiations between the EU and the Obama Administration.[60] It has been suggested that the USMCA chapter was drafted with the understanding that it could be a model for a similar chapter in planned trade agreement discussions between the United States and the EU, if those discussions ever move forward.[61]

VIII   SANITARY AND PHYTOSANITARY MEASURES AND TECHNICAL BARRIERS TO TRADE

A   Introduction to SPS and TBT

Logically, SPS could have been dealt with in Chapter 6 of this book, with other provisions affecting agriculture, but given the close structural relationship between the SPS chapter and the chapter on technical barriers to trade, both are addressed here.

---

lations" that has been used in the United States by executive branch agencies since 1981).

[58]   USMCA, Art. 28.17.

[59]   USMCA, Art. 28.18; TPP, Art. 25.6.

[60]   See "Analysts: USMCA Good Regulatory Practices Chapter a Baseline for EU Deal" (2018), World Trade Online, November 15, https://insidetrade.com/daily-news/analysts-usmca-good-regulatory -practices-chapter-baseline-eu-deal.

[61]   Ibid.

Given that NAFTA negotiations were completed in the fall of 1992, several years before the Uruguay Round of Multilateral trade negotiations was complete,[62] it was not surprising that SPS measures were included in NAFTA's chapter on agriculture, and TBT provisions in a separate chapter, both in somewhat different structure than found in the WTO agreements.[63] As the Agricultural Advisory Committee noted, "The existing NAFTA was groundbreaking as it was one of the first free trade agreements that establish the framework of rules and disciplines leading to the development, adoption, and enforcement of sanitary and phytosanitary measures (SPS measures)."[64]

The SPS and TBT chapters of CPTPP and USMCA were designed not only to update NAFTA but to update the WTO SPS and TPT Agreements, which were also somewhat out of date after nearly 25 years[65] but could not be modernized because of the failure of the Doha Round of multilateral trade negotiations. Despite the similar approaches in the agreement, SPS provisions deal exclusively with human, animal and plant safety issues, while the TBT provisions deal with technical regulations, standards and conformity assessments of all other products.

---

[62] Marrakesh Agreement Creating the World Trade Organization, Including the TBT Agreement and SPS Agreement in Annex 1A, April 15, 1995, www.wto.org/english/docs_e/legal_e/04-wto_e.htm.

[63] See NAFTA, Ch. 7, Section B; Ch. 9 (standards related measures).

[64] Agricultural Policy Advisory Committee Report, September 27, 2018, https://ustr.gov/trade-agreements/free-trade-agreements/united-states-mexico-canada-agreement/advisory-committee.

[65] See WTO Legal Texts, www.wto.org/english/docs_e/legal_e/legal_e.htm (Agreement on Sanitary and Phytosanitary Measures, Agreement on Technical Barriers to Trade).

B **Sanitary and Phytosanitary Measures**

The WTO's SPS Agreement and the SPS chapter of USMCA are essentially a set of procedures to deal with a dichotomy. Governments must protect humans, animals and plants from health risks and at the same time should avoid using spurious suggestions of risks in order to protect domestic agriculture. As USTR has succinctly stated the problem:

> The United States supports SPS measures taken by governments to protect their people, animals and plants from health risks. Unfortunately, governments often seek to disguise measures that are discriminatory, unduly burdensome, or not based on scientific evidence as legitimate SPS measures. These measures create significant barriers to U.S. agricultural exports, and USTR is committed to identifying and removing these barriers.[66]

In the TPP, where the SPS provisions were the model for and closely resemble those in USMCA, USTR further explained the approach:

> This [ensuring the safety of food supplies] involves ensuring that our partners use science and risk analysis as a foundation for SPS measures, which mirrors U.S. food and agricultural safety policy. As examples, they must use appropriate import check and restriction policies focused on direct threats to health and safety, avoid duplicative or unnecessary testing requirements where food already meets accepted international standards, and use transparent procedures for developing regulations—including opportunities for public comment.[67]

---

[66] USTR, "Sanitary and Phytosanitary Measures and Technical Barriers to Trade," https://ustr.gov/issue-areas/agriculture/sanitary -and-phytosanitary-measures-and-technical-barriers-to-trade.

[67] USTR, Trans-Pacific Partnership, Chapter 7 Summary, Sanitary and Phytosanitary Measures, 2016, https://ustr.gov/trade -agreements/free-trade-agreements/trans-pacific-partnership/tpp-full -text.

The approach followed in essentially all SPS mechanisms, given the difficulty at the outset in determining whether a country's measure restricting agricultural imports is truly designed to protect human, animals or plants, or rather to protect domestic producers, is to require the country to show that there is a strong scientific basis for the measure. They must also give weight to internationally accepted standards over those that have been developed by individual countries.

In the past, the United States and Canada were parties to a long-running dispute between the North American beef producers and the EU over the EU's ban on the importation of beef fattened with growth hormones. Despite efforts over many years the EU was never able to demonstrate that there was any health risk to humans by ingesting beef grown with hormones, and the Appellate Body of the WTO so decided, but for political and environmental reasons the EU refused to permit imports of such beef. In 2013, the United States and the EU reached an agreement or "mutually acceptable solution" which permits the exportation by the United States of quantities of beef that have not been fattened with hormones.[68]

TPP was said to have incorporated

> new rules that will ensure that science-based SPS measures are developed and implemented in a transparent, predictable, and non-discriminatory manner, while at the same time preserving the ability of U.S. and other … regulatory agencies to take necessary steps to ensure food safety and protect plant and animal health.[69]

---

[68]   *European Communities—Measures Concerning Meat and Meat Products (Hormones)*, WT/DS26/AB/R, 2013, www.wto.org/english/tratop_e/dispu_e/cases_e/ds26_e.htm. (DS48 was a similar complaint brought by Canada.) See also, Renee Johnson (2015), "The U.S.-EU Beef Hormone Dispute," Congressional Research Service, January 14, https://fas.org/sgp/crs/row/R40449.pdf.

[69]   Ibid.

The USMCA chapter also incorporates the definitions from the WTO's SPS Agreement,[70] with some innovations of its own, presumably reflecting the willingness of all three USMCA parties to go beyond what had been agreed only a few years earlier in TPP. According to the Report of the Agricultural Policy Advisory Committee, the major changes in USMCA are

> those provisions which increase transparency on the development and implementation of SPS measures; advance science-based decision making; improve processes for certification, regionalization and equivalency determinations; conduct systems-based audits; improve transparency for import checks and additional measures to ensure more expeditious border crossing; and enhance compatibility of measures.[71]

In USMCA, as with earlier SPS versions, the focus is on procedures designed to assure that restrictions are based on science and risk analysis, with a preference for the use of international standards as noted above, rather than more arbitrary efforts to protect local producers.[72] Efforts are made to encourage adaptation to regional conditions, with recognition of pest- or disease-free areas, so as to encourage trade in those areas.[73] Transparency concerns are evident throughout.[74] Import checks must be based on actual potential risk, with the parties required to inform importers and exporters within five days (down from a week under TPP) if a shipment is being restricted or prohibited for reasons related to food safety or animal or plant health.[75]

---

[70] USMCA, Art. 9.1.

[71] Agricultural Policy Advisory Committee Report, September 27, 2018.

[72] USMCA, Art. 9.6.

[73] USMCA, Art. 9.8.

[74] See, e.g., USMCA, Art. 9.13.

[75] USMCA, Art. 9.11.

Emergency measures are permitted but only if parties disclose the scientific basis for such measures.[76] Since most countries maintain certification requirements the chapter requires that the information required relates only to SPS issues, is based on recognized international standards and is otherwise appropriate.[77] Other provisions address equivalency (where different testing procedures achieve the importing party's level of protection) and "enhanced compatibility,"[78] along with information exchange, food safety audits and consultations. A Committee on Sanitary and Phytosanitary Measures is created, to meet annually unless otherwise decided.[79] Such committee work is apparently to be supplemented by technical working groups that can function on either an ongoing or an ad hoc basis.[80] Disputes over SPS measures are subject to state-to-state dispute settlement under USMCA, Chapter 31, with the panel encouraged to seek advice from experts chosen by the panel in consultation with the disputing parties.[81]

C   Technical Barriers to Trade

Like the SPS Agreement, the USMCA TBT chapter builds on NAFTA, the WTO and TPP. Thus, the USMCA chapter incorporates the WTO's TBT Agreement and its explanatory notes by reference.[82] It also reflects one of the earliest treatment of standards issues in any trade agreement, in NAFTA Chapter 9.[83] Chapter 9 was raised by Mexico in a Chapter 20 state-to-state dispute, *Cross-Border Trucking Services*

---

[76]   USMCA, Art. 9.14.
[77]   USMCA, Art. 9.12.
[78]   USMCA, Arts 9.7, 9.9.
[79]   USMCA, Art. 9.18.
[80]   Ibid.
[81]   USMCA, Art. 9.20.
[82]   USMCA, Art. 11.1.1.
[83]   NAFTA, Ch. 9.

and Investment.[84] Mexico had argued, inter alia, that the US failure to implement its cross-border trucking services and investment obligations was not justified by the standards chapter.[85] That argument, however, was not discussed in detail in the report because the United States chose not to rely on Chapter 9 as a defense.[86] Rather, the panel, believing it necessary to address Chapter 9 because both Mexico and Canada (in the latter's submission to the panel) noted that "under Article 904, the United States has the right to set a level of protection relating to safety concerns, through the adoption of standards-related measures, notwithstanding any other provision of this Chapter ..." and must be "in accordance with this Agreement" in Article 904.[87]

As with the WTO SPS Agreement, many WTO members believed that the TBT Agreement could be improved beyond its original version, and specifically provided in the agreement itself that the TBT Committee would review the agreement in three years, and every three years thereafter, "with a view to recommending an adjustment of the rights and obligations of this Agreement where necessary to ensure mutual economic advantage and balance of rights and obligations."[88] Such reviews never progressed beyond very preliminary stages, with the result that the United States and many other countries have sought (successfully) to include improved TBT provisions in regional trade agreements, such as CPTPP and USMCA.

---

[84] Final Report of the Panel, *Cross-Border Trucking Services*, Secretariat File no. USA-MEX-98-2008-01, February 6, 2001, www.nafta-sec-alena.org/Home/Dispute-Settlement/Decisions-and-Reports.

[85] Ibid., paras 5, 126.

[86] Ibid., para. 183.

[87] Ibid., paras 271–2.

[88] Agreement on Technical Barriers to Trade, Annex 1A of the Agreement Establishing the World Trade Organization, April 15, 1994, Art. 15.4, www.wto.org/english/docs_e/legal_e/17-tbt_e.htm.

The TBT chapter should be read in conjunction with the section of this chapter discussing good regulatory practices. While the TBT chapter of USMCA is considerably more detailed and far-reaching that the CPTPP chapter, the importance of technical barriers to United States trade interests is well set out in USTR's commentary on the CPTPP chapter:

> TPP's Technical Barriers to Trade (TBT) chapter helps create an open, transparent, stakeholder-based system of standards-setting … It ensures that technical standards-setting, conformity assessment procedures, and technical regulations are fair and transparently developed, with opportunities for meaningful input and "bottom-up" participation in standards-setting.[89]

The Industry Trade Advisory Committee on Standards and Technical Trade Barriers (Standards Committee) provides a useful summary of the achievements of the USMCA negotiations in its report: "Chapter 11 Technical Barriers to Trade (TBT) and Chapter 28 Good Regulatory Practices [discussed in section G of this chapter] are exceptional examples of trade agreement modernization—reinforcing the core of the WTO TBT Agreement and expanding beyond the achievements of the former Trans-Pacific Partnership text."[90] The Standards Committee faulted USTR only for failing to tie industry-specific annexes in Chapter 12 explicitly to the TBT chapter, and noted that other chapters such as Chapter 8 (energy) and 19 (digital trade) are directly affected by standards issues.[91]

---

[89] USTR, Trans-Pacific Partnership, Chapter 8 Summary, 2016, https://ustr.gov/trade-agreements/free-trade-agreements/trans-pacific-partnership/tpp-full-text.

[90] Report of the Industry Trade Advisory Committee on Standards and Technical Barriers, September 27, 2018, https://ustr.gov/trade-agreements/free-trade-agreements/united-states-mexico-canada-agreement/advisory-committee.

[91] Ibid.

The USMCA chapter reflects several structural differences from CPTPP. For example, for business, as reflected in the report of the Standards Committee, it is important to have U.S. standards treated as international standards under USMCA. Thus, standards which satisfy the "Code of Good Practice principles of standards development (e.g., balance, openness, due process, etc.) are in fact 'international.'"[92] This objective is reinforced in USMCA Chapter 11, since it requires the USMCA parties to "apply the TBT Committee Decisions on International Standards" and prohibits the parties from applying "additional principles or criteria other than those in the TBT Committee Decision on International Standards in order to recognize a standard as an international standard."[93] It may well be that achieving greater regulatory "alignment" was simpler for USTR in USMCA than CPTPP because Mexico and Canada, over the NAFTA years in particular, have already embraced many US origin technical standards because of the duty-free, quota-free regional trade.

Still, the basic approach of USMCA does not in principle differ from earlier agreements. Thus, in addition to incorporation of the WTO TBT Agreement, USMCA supports international standards, guides and regulations in regulatory alignment.[94] A party that has not used international standards in the preparation and implementation of technical regulations can be challenged for failing to do so.[95] The chapter also encourages USMCA parties to permit subcontractors and non-governmental bodies to prepare conformity assessments

---

[92]   Ibid. See Decision of the WTO TBT Committee (G/TBT/1/ Rev. 10), June 22, 1995, https://docs.wto.org/dol2fe/Pages/FE _Search/FE_S_S009-DP.aspx?language=E&CatalogueIdList= 234947,129845,121467,101299,15476&CurrentCatalogueIdIndex= 3&FullTextHash=1&HasEnglishRecord=True&HasFrenchRecord= True&HasSpanishRecord=True.

[93]   USMCA, Arts 11.4.2, 11.4.3.

[94]   USMCA, Art. 11.4.1.

[95]   USMCA, 11.5.6.

and favors mutual recognition of such assessments.[96] It also forms a Committee on Technical Barriers to Trade (TBT Committee), again composed of government representatives, to "strengthen their joint work in the fields of technical regulations, standards, and conformity assessment procedures."[97]

Some have expressed concerns that in drafting these provisions the United States has given Canada and Mexico an disproportionate role in US drafting of US regulations (and vice versa).[98] However, this appears to be a minor risk, given the economic domination of USMCA by the United States and the fact that for Mexico and for Canada, some 75 percent of total exports go to the United States. This does not assure complete conformity in standards and technical regulations, but it gives all parties an incentive not to diverge significantly from a common approach.

D   Standards Set Out in Sectoral Annexes

A separate USMCA chapter addresses technical standards for chemicals, cosmetics, information and communications technology, energy performance standards, medical devices and pharmaceuticals, as defined therein.[99] It thus impacts to some extent products treated in other USMCA chapters, such as those affecting technical barriers to trade, communications, intellectual property and good regulatory practices among

---

[96]   USMCA, Arts 11.7.7, 11.9.1, 11.9.2.

[97]   USMCA, Art. 11.11.1.

[98]   Tori K. Whiting and Gabriella Beaumont-Smith (2019), "Backgrounder: An Analysis of the United States-Mexico-Canada Agreement," Heritage Foundation, January 28, www.heritage.org/trade/report/analysis-the-united-states-mexico-canada-agreement, 24.

[99]   USMCA, Ch. 12.

others.[100] The sections of the chapter generally apply along the following lines (with chemical substances as the example):

> This Annex applies to the preparation, adoption, and application of technical regulations; standards; conformity assessment procedures; measures relating to hazard communication, labeling, and communication of information on the use and storage of chemical substances and chemical mixtures, and on response in the workplace to hazards and exposures; and import and export permits for chemical substances and chemical mixtures by a Party's central level of government ...[101]

The various subchapters also require the parties to publish online information regarding central government competent authorities charged with implementing and enforcing measures related to the sector and state the objectives of enhancing regulatory compatibility. Exchange of information on methodologies for assessing chemical substances (in this instance) is also mandated.[102]

---

[100] See USMCA, Chs 11, 18, 20 and 28.

[101] USMCA, Art. 12.A.2.

[102] See, e.g., USMCA, Arts 12.A.3, 12.A.4, 12.A.5.

9. Carryover provisions from NAFTA

This chapter discusses several provisions of NAFTA that in large part have been carried over to USMCA. Here, as in other areas where the NAFTA provisions have found their way into USMCA, changes have been made, in some cases significant ones, as with the addition of pharmaceutical industry-related provisions to the more generally applicable provisions for publication and administration. In my experience, it is safer to assume that there have been changes when NAFTA provisions have been incorporated into USMCA rather than the reverse.

I   GOVERNMENT PROCUREMENT

The NAFTA provisions on government procurement were drafted at a time (1991–92) when the WTO's Government Procurement Agreement was still in draft form, but when the GATT Tokyo Round Government Procurement Code was in force among a limited group of GATT parties.[1] NAFTA's Chapter 10 contains the usual elements of government procurement, which are designed to ensure a high degree of transparency in the bidding process and national treatment for goods and services procurements that exceed certain minimum thresholds.[2] NAFTA also includes detailed tender-

---

[1]   Agreement on Government Procurement, 1979, www .worldtradelaw.net/tokyoround/procurementcode.pdf.download.

[2]   NAFTA, Art. 1002.

ing and bid-challenging procedures[3] along with mechanisms for technical cooperation and programs for small businesses.[4] As with most such agreements, governments agree to apply the agreement only to a positive list of government entities. Perhaps the greatest shortcoming of NAFTA's procurement provisions was its failure to include Canada's provinces and the US states.[5] Among the benefits for the United States under the NAFTA procurement chapter was the success of US insurance providers in providing coverage for about two-thirds of Mexican government employees.[6]

However, the results of the USMCA negotiations were unfortunate. The USMCA chapter on procurement applies only to the United States and Mexico.[7] Procurements between the United States and Canada are thus governed by the WTO's Government Procurement Agreement (GPA),[8] the United States and Canada being among the current 48 members to which the agreement is applicable. (Mexico is not among them.[9]) Under the GPA, 37 American states and the Canadian provinces and territories are (voluntarily) covered.[10] For Mexican and Canadian procurement in each other's terri-

---

[3]   NAFTA, Arts 1008–17.

[4]   NAFTA, Arts 1020, 1021.

[5]   NAFTA, Annex 1001.a-1.

[6]   Report of the Industry Trade Advisory Committee on Services, September 27, 2018, https://ustr.gov/trade-agreements/free-trade-agreements/united-states-mexico-canada-agreement/advisory-committee.

[7]   USMCA, Art. 13.2.3.

[8]   Agreement on Government Procurement, Annex 4(b) to the WTO Agreement, April 15, 1994, as revised through April 6, 2014, www.wto.org/english/tratop_e/gproc_e/gpa_1994_e.htm.

[9]   WTO, Parties, Observers and Accessions, www.wto.org/english/tratop_e/gproc_e/memobs_e.htm.

[10]   GPA Coverage Schedules, United States, Annex 2; Canada, Annex 2, www.wto.org/english/tratop_e/gproc_e/gp_app_agree_e.htm.

tories, the CPTPP procurement rules are applicable.[11] They include lower thresholds carried over from NAFTA that are not entirely replicated in the WTO's GPA. For example,

> Canada applies a GPA threshold of $180,000 for its procurement of goods and services by federal agencies, in contrast to its NAFTA thresholds of $25,000 for goods ... and $80,000 for services. For the procurement of goods and services by its government enterprises, Canada applies a threshold of $492,000 under the GPA and $400,000 under NAFTA.[12]

It is also noted that NAFTA used a negative list approach where no agencies are excluded unless listed, while the GPA used the positive list approach, where only the entities listed in a party's annex are included.

Thus, as observers have rather caustically noted, "Government procurement contracts in North America will be dictated by a 'hodge-podge' of international agreements that could make things complicated for businesses and potentially raise costs for taxpayers."[13] As usual, these complications pose a greater challenge for SMEs than for larger MNEs. Given that SMEs seeking to take advantage of government procurements internationally are most likely to begin with procurements in neighboring Canada and Mexico, the potential complications are unfortunate. It is difficult to know at this time whether Mexican bidders will have competitive advantages in bidding on Canadian procurements. More generally, since government procurements are financed by national or local taxpayers, steps which may decrease competition from

---

[11]   See CPTPP, Ch. 15. In CPTPP, Canada's provinces and territories were covered; US states were not included in the US annex.

[12]   "USMCA—Modernized NAFTA: Procurement" (2019), Perspectives on Trade, October 5, https://trade.djaghe.com/?p=5174.

[13]   Megan Cassella (2018), "'Buy American' Makes Its Way into USMCA," Politico, www.politico.com/newsletters/morning-trade/2018/10/29/buy-american-makes-its-way-into-usmca-392939.

Canada for US procurements are unfortunate if minimizing costs is an objective.[14] Of course, for those who favor "Buy American" under all circumstances, if USMCA provides even a slight disincentive for foreign competitors, that could be considered a benefit.

The results do not bode well either for an increasingly global procurement market. As the Advisory Committee for Automotive and Capital Goods observed, "U.S. exporters to Canada would enjoy less access to Canadian government tenders than potential bidders in the European Union or Trans-Pacific Partnership (TPP) member countries (including major competitors like Japan, Singapore and Australia) enjoy."[15] Should the United States ultimately decide on the basis of "Buy American" views to withdraw from the WTO/GPA, "which is not inconceivable," the United States would lose access to the Canadian government market.[16] Such access would have been preserved if the USMCA procurement provisions had applied to Canada.

Insofar as Mexico and the United States are concerned, the USMCA chapter incorporates many of the updates in CPTPP, changes which could apparently not be achieved in the broader WTO GPA negotiations that took place a few years ago. One addition of possible significance, particularly to SMEs, is the requirement that notices of procurement opportunities be

---

[14] See, e.g., Tori K. Whiting and Gabriella Beaumont-Smith (2019), "Backgrounder: An Analysis of the United States-Mexico-Canada Agreement," Heritage Foundation, January 26, www.heritage.org/trade/report/analysis-the-united-states-mexico-canada-agreement, 24 (commenting on the potential USMCA impact on Canadian bidding for US contracts).

[15] "Addendum to the Earlier (September 28, 2019) Report of the Industry Trade Advisory Committee on Automotive Equipment and Capital Goods," October 24, 2018, https://ustr.gov/trade-agreements/free-trade-agreements/united-states-mexico-canada-agreement/advisory-committee, 6.

[16] Ibid.

offered in many instances through a single electronic portal.[17] However, the general agency coverage does not appear to vary much from TPP or NAFTA.

At minimum, some American providers of goods and services to government entities will face additional administrative costs because different systems will be used for submitting bids to Mexico (USMCA) and to Canada (GPA). While the similarities in procedures are substantial, details and bidding thresholds differ as noted above. Also, to the extent that a prime contractor in one USMCA party (e.g., Canada) desires to use a subcontractor from another USMCA party (e.g., Mexico) for a project in the United States, the bidding process could be considerably more complex than it was under NAFTA. To some extent the problem would be mitigated if Mexico were to become a party to the GPA, but this seems highly unlikely given that Mexico is not even one of the 34 WTO members that have sought observer status under the GPA.[18] If anything, the López Obrador Administration appears to be moving in the opposite direction, reducing the opportunities for private enterprise, foreign or domestic, in government contracts.[19]

II   TRADE REMEDIES

NAFTA's Chapter 19 mechanism providing for review of national anti-dumping and countervailing duty decisions by binational panels has been discussed in detail in Chapter 3 of

---

[17]   USMCA, Arts 13.6.2(b), 13.20.3(b).

[18]   WTO, GPA Parties, Observers and Accessions, www.wto.org/english/tratop_e/gproc_e/memobs_e.htm.

[19]   For example, the administration's new gasoline refinery is to be "state-directed, centrally-driven, reliant on national production and free of foreign influence," Jude Webber and Michael Stott (2019), "Mexico: Lopez Obrador Makes a Big Bet on Oil," *Financial Times*, October 3, www.ft.com/content/d5c3c1c0-e432-11e9-b112-9624ec9edc59.

this book. However, other mechanisms and principles relating to regional trade contained in USMCA also merit brief mention.

NAFTA, like virtually all prior US trade agreements and the General Agreement on Tariffs and Trade, contains so-called "safeguard" measures or "emergency" actions, to protect domestic producers against unexpected increasing imports.[20] As far as I am aware, no trade agreement concluded by the United States between 1947 and 2019, including TPP,[21] omitted safeguard provisions applicable to trade in industrial products.[22] NAFTA contemplated both bilateral and global safeguard actions. For global actions, NAFTA generally preserved the rights of the parties to bring safeguard actions under GATT and the WTO Safeguards Agreement.[23] However, when applying global safeguards a NAFTA party could not include other NAFTA parties unless that party "account[s] for a substantial share of total imports" and "contribute[s] importantly to the serious injury or threat thereof" as a result of the imports. If a NAFTA party was not among the top five suppliers of the product, its exports to the other NAFTA party were also excluded.[24]

---

[20] NAFTA, Ch. 8; GATT, Art. XIX.

[21] See TPP, Ch.6, Sec. A.

[22] A recent exception is the United States-Japan Trade Agreement, October 7, 2019, https://ustr.gov/countries-regions/ japan-korea-apec/japan/us-japan-trade-agreement-negotiations/us -japan-trade-agreement-text. That agreement, of very limited scope, includes only safeguards for agricultural trade, in a side letter. No safeguards provision exists for industrial goods trade, although either party may terminate the agreement on four months' notice under Article 10.

[23] GATT, Art. XIX; Agreement on Safeguards, Annex 1A of the Agreement Establishing the World Trade Organization, April 15, 1994, www.wto.org/english/docs_e/legal_e/25-safeg_e.htm.

[24] NAFTA, Art. 802.2. Exclusion of restrictions on imports of steel from Canada, Mexico, Israel and Jordan (the latter two under FTAs with similar safeguard provisions) was challenged success-

NAFTA incorporated separate safeguard provisions for use within NAFTA,[25] although they have been used on only one occasion, prompting a dispute over restriction of broom corn brooms by the United States, litigated under NAFTA's Chapter 20 provisions, and won by Mexico.[26] These bilateral safeguards were limited to use during the transition period to duty-free trade, where it could be shown that the imports were a "substantial cause of serious injury."[27] Since the transition period to duty-free treatment expired for essentially all products no later than January 1, 2008,[28] the bilateral action safeguards in NAFTA have long since become irrelevant.

In USMCA, the parties retain their rights under GATT and the WTO Safeguards Agreement.[29] USMCA also retains the NAFTA party exclusions noted above.[30] This contrasts with the CPTPP safeguard provisions, where similar exclusions for other CPTPP parties were not included, although the non-global safeguards under CPTPP were only applicable during the transitional period.[31]

USMCA also preserves the rights of the parties to bring dumping and countervailing duty cases under GATT/WTO

---

fully by multiple WTO parties as being inconsistent with WTO safeguard rules because those imports had been used by US authorities in determining whether serious injury had resulted. See *United States—Definitive Safeguard Measures on Imports of Certain Steel Products*, WT/DS252/AB/R, adopted December 10, 2003, www.wto .org/english/tratop_e/dispu_e/cases_e/ds248_e.htm.

[25]   NAFTA, Art. 801.

[26]   See *U.S. Safeguard Action Taken on Broom Corn Brooms from Mexico, USA-MEX-1997-2008-01*, January 30, 1998, www.nafta-sec -alena.org/Home/Dispute-Settlement/Decisions-and-Reports.

[27]   NAFTA, Art. 801.1.

[28]   NAFTA, Annex 302.2.1(d).

[29]   USMCA, Art. 10.2.

[30]   USMCA, Arts 10.2.1, 10.2.2.

[31]   CPTPP, Art. 6.3. Under CPTPP, the length of the transitional period varies considerably among parties. See CPTPP, Art. 2 and various annexes.

rules and their own unfair trade laws, as was the case under NAFTA and CPTPP, as with most other regional trade agreements.[32] One innovation in USMCA that does not exist in either NAFTA or CPTPP is a requirement for cooperation in preventing evasion of trade remedy laws, several provisions focused primarily on duty evasion cooperation.[33]

III TEMPORARY ENTRY FOR BUSINESS VISITORS

NAFTA provided no broad rights for workers who are citizens of one of the NAFTA parties to work in either of the others. USMCA follows the same approach, although in some areas the language is different; it provides for temporary entry for business persons, with many limitations. As with the General Agreement on Trade in Services (GATS), the movement of natural persons (so-called "Mode 4") is effectively limited to persons of one member entering the territory of another member to supply professional services (e.g. accountants, lawyers, doctors or teachers) even if members could, if they wished, permit more open immigration. In this respect WTO members are free to impose measures regarding citizenship, residence or access to the employment market on a permanent basis.[34]

---

[32] USMCA, Art. 10.5; NAFTA, Art. 1902; CPTPP, Art. 6.8. The United States-Japan Agreement, October 7, 2019, https://ustr.gov/ countries-regions/japan-korea-apec/japan/us-japan-trade-agreement -negotiations/us-japan-trade-agreement-text, explicitly preserves the parties' rights to impose global safeguards but incorporates no specific language on dumping or countervailing duty actions. See Art. 5.2.

[33] USMCA, Arts 10.6, 10.7.

[34] See General Agreement on Trade in Services (GATS), Annex 1b of the WTO Agreement, April 15, 1994, www.wto.org/english/ docs_e/legal_e/26-gats_01_e.htm; WTO, "The General Agreement

The USMCA temporary entry chapter thus must be read in conjunction with the USMCA's cross-border services chapter, Chapter 16, discussed in Chapter 7 of this book. Overall, the USMCA services chapter makes few substantive changes to its NAFTA counterpart. Not surprisingly given the enormous sensitivity of immigration issues in North America (and elsewhere), the scope of the USMCA chapter consists of limitations rather than authorizations:

1. This Chapter applies to measures affecting the temporary entry of business persons of a Party into the territory of another Party.
2. This Chapter does not apply to measures affecting natural persons seeking access to the employment market of another Party, nor does it apply to measures regarding citizenship, nationality, residence or employment on a permanent basis.
3. Nothing in this Agreement prevents a Party from applying measures to regulate the entry of natural persons of another Party into, or their temporary stay in, its territory, including those measures necessary to protect the integrity of, and to ensure the orderly movement of natural persons across, its borders, provided that those measures are not applied in a manner as to nullify or impair the benefits accruing to any Party under this Chapter.[35]

In addition, the range of business visas available under USMCA, as under NAFTA, closely resembles the structure of US immigration law.[36] Thus the covered categories include business visitors; traders and investors; intra-company transferees; and professionals.[37] While all of these are non-resident visas, some visa holders, such as treaty traders and investors, may remain in the host country, for example, the United

---

on Trade in Services (GATS): Objectives, Coverage and Disciplines," www.wto.org/english/tratop_e/serv_e/gatsqa_e.htm.

[35]   USMCA, Art. 16.2.
[36]   USMCA, Annex 16-A.
[37]   Ibid.

States, as long as their trader or investor status remains valid, which could be years or decades.

Similarly, visas for professionals such as lawyers and accountants, among others ("1B visas"), are usually valid for three years, renewable for another three years, and are often a route to permanent residence. Thus, the "temporary" aspect must be taken with a grain of salt. Detailed requirements are set out for professionals; the list in USMCA was not expanded from NAFTA. For example, to qualify for a USMCA visa as a lawyer (including a notary in Quebec) an individual must hold an "LL.B., J.D., LL.L., B.C.L. or Licentura Degree (five years); or membership in a state/provincial bar."[38] In most cases a baccalaureate or similar degree, licentura degree or state/provincial license is required, in some cases with three years' experience.[39]

USMCA, like NAFTA, provides for a "Trade National" (TN) visa for professionals who have a job offer in the United States. It is estimated that in 2017 some 30,000–40,000 Canadian citizens were working in the United States on a TN visa.[40] For Canadian citizens the visa may be obtained with the necessary job offer and proof of citizenship at the US/ Canada border of the airport port of entry; for Mexican citizens, application at a US consulate is required. The TN visa is not available for permanent residents, only citizens, and remains available for three years.[41] Nor does it apply to those

---

[38] USMCA, Ch. 16, App. 2.

[39] Ibid.

[40] "USMCA Immigration to US: USMCA TN Visa for Canadians" (2018), VisaPlace News, www.visaplace.com/blog -immigration-law/uncategorized/usmca-immigration-us-usmca-tn -visa-canadians/.

[41] See USMCA, Annex 16-A, Section D; para. 1. "Skilled Workers and Professionals Keep Visa Rights Under NEW USMCA Trade Deal," Foreign Worker Canada, www.canadianimmigration .net/news-articles/skilled-workers-and-professionals-keep-visa -rights-under-new-usmca-trade-deal/.

who are self-employed. It is suggested that continuation of the TN visa program was a significant victory in the negotiations for Mexico and Canada, given the US Administration's "Buy American, Hire American" policies, but the provisions are of course a boon to Americans who wish to pursue professional employment in Canada or Mexico.[42] As the United States government advises, eligible persons for TN visas are (a) citizens of Canada and Mexico; with (b) a profession that qualifies under the regulations (and Annex 16-A Section D professionals list); for (c) a US position that requires a professional; for whom (d) a full or part-time job has been prearranged with a US employer; and who (e) possess the necessary professional qualifications.[43] One of the major advantages of the TN visa is fewer administrative burdens, for both visa applicants and their prospective employers in all three USMCA parties.

IV   PUBLICATION AND ADMINISTRATION

The NAFTA negotiators appear to have been desirous of achieving greater transparency generally in the publication, notification and administration of laws at a time before the Internet, when Mexico in particular had not established a solid record of publication of laws and regulations.[44] Lack of transparency has been an endemic problem for many years for the US government and stakeholders involved in overseas trade and investment. It is, for example, a major problem for US economic relations with China. As one study (concerning China) noted, "In general, the absence of clear and transparent rules and policies—in financial markets, as well

---

[42]   Ibid.

[43]   "TN NAFTA Professionals," US Citizenship and Immigration Services, www.uscis.gov/working-united-states/temporary-workers/tn-nafta-professionals; USMCA, Annex 16-A, Section D.

[44]   NAFTA, Ch. 18.

as for activities such as commerce, capital investment, and trade—is a major problem because it dissuades participation, adds uncertainty, and can even foster corruption."[45] Arguably, the same could have been said about Mexico at the time of the NAFTA negotiations in 1991–92.

NAFTA's short (3-page) chapter focused on establishing contact points among the parties, prior notification of actual or proposed measures that "the Party considers might materially affect the operation of this Agreement or otherwise substantially affect that other Party's interests under this Agreement."[46] Equally significantly, NAFTA required a form of administrative due process, whereby persons of another party receive reasonable notice when an administrative proceeding affecting their interests is initiated, and are afforded, with some limitations, "a reasonable opportunity to present facts and arguments in support of their positions prior to any final administrative action."[47] Also significant is an obligation for each party, but aimed primarily at Mexico (since both Canada and the United States had the necessary courts and administrative procedures in place), to

> establish or maintain judicial, quasi-judicial or administrative tribunals or procedures for the purpose of the prompt review and, where warranted, correction of final administrative actions regarding matters covered by this Agreement. Such tribunals shall be impartial and independent of the office or authority entrusted with administrative enforcement and shall not have any substantial interest in the outcome of the matter.[48]

---

[45] Ben S. Bernanke and Peter Olson (2016), "China's Transparency Challenges," Brookings, March 8, www.brookings.edu/blog/ben-bernanke/2016/03/08/chinas-transparency-challenges/.

[46] NAFTA, Art. 1803.1.

[47] NAFTA, Art. 1804.

[48] NAFTA, Art. 1805.1.

Chapter 29 of USMCA builds upon this foundation in some-what greater detail, with a new focus on the pharmaceuti-cal products and medical device industry. Requirements for notice, the availability of administrative proceedings con-ducted in accordance with generally recognized principles of procedural due process and review, and appeal requirements closely resemble those in NAFTA.[49]

The most significant addition compared to NAFTA, and to other US FTAs with provisions like those in NAFTA, is a sep-arate section devoted to transparency and procedural fairness (TPF) for pharmaceutical products and medical devices. The reasons the US pharmaceutical industry sought (and received) such additional protections are summarized as follows:

> The purpose of a TPF chapter for medical technology is to give the manufacturer the opportunity to understand the basis for a reimbursement decision and to provide evidence to the govern-ment body making the reimbursement decision ... [W]e should seek provisions that are designed to provide transparency to the process by which national (but not state or provincial) health care authorities in the NAFTA countries set reimbursement rates for medical devices at the national level. In the case of Mexico, these provisions should also apply to the Government's decisions about which products to list on its national formulary ..."[50]

The chapter has the stated objectives of protecting public health, promoting research and development, providing timely and affordable access to pharmaceuticals and the need to recognize the value of pharmaceuticals and medical devices through "the operation of competitive markets."[51] Procedural fairness requirements emphasize timely action by the national

---

[49]   USMCA, Arts 29.2, 29.3, 29.4.

[50]   Industry Trade Advisory Committee on Chemicals, Pharmaceuticals, Health/Science Products and Services, September 27, 2019, https://ustr.gov/trade-agreements/free-trade-agreements/united-states-mexico-canada-agreement/advisory-committee, 9.

[51]   USMCA, Art. 29.6.

health care authorities, full disclosure of procedural rules, opportunities for applicant comments, and provision of sufficient written information to understand the authorities' listing of new products for reimbursement. Independent review processes are also required, as is the provision of written information to the public, subject to protection of confidential information.[52]

Other provisions address dissemination of information and consultations.[53] A key exclusion, presumably sought by Mexico, Canada, or both, makes the procedural fairness section inapplicable to government procurement of pharmaceutical products and medical devices.[54] The parties also confirm that the purpose of this section is transparency and procedural fairness, "not to modify a Party's system of health care in any other respects or a Party's rights to determine health expenditure priorities."[55]

Despite the limitations and exceptions in the section, its obligations once again reflect the importance of the pharmaceutical sector to the US export economy as well as its political power. It will be interesting to see how faithfully these provisions are implemented by Mexico and Canada, particularly now that biologic drug protection in USMCA has been eliminated.[56]

---

[52] USMCA, Art. 29.7.

[53] USMCA, Arts 29.8, 29.9.

[54] USMCA, Ch. 29, fn. 5.

[55] USMCA, Ch. 29, fn. 1.

[56] Protocol of Amendment to the Agreement Between the United States of America, the United Mexican States, and Canada, December 10, 2019, para. 7E (deleting USMCA, Art. 20.49), https://ustr.gov/sites/default/files/files/agreements/FTA/USMCA/Protocol-of-Amendments-to-the-United-States-Mexico-Canada-Agreement.pdf.

V   GENERAL EXCEPTIONS

This section addresses many but not all exceptions placed by the drafters in Chapter 32. Exceptions for cultural industries for Mexico, which did not exist in NAFTA, are included in that chapter. The prohibition on FTAs with Communist countries (e.g., China) is discussed in the "significant USMCA innovations" report, as is the section on indigenous peoples' rights.

NAFTA incorporated various general exceptions, most of which were based on GATT exceptions. These included the general exceptions in GATT Article XX and the national security exception in GATT Article XXI.[57] Both of these were incorporated in somewhat modified form in USMCA.[58] I note that GATT Article XXI has taken on greater significance in recent years as the Trump Administration imposed tariffs or quotas on grounds that they were necessary in order to maintain US national (economic) security on imports of steel and aluminum from most countries[59] (although Mexico and Canada were later excluded because both countries were refusing to move forward on ratifying USMCA as long as the tariffs remained in place).[60] It is perhaps for this reason that the "essential security" language in USMCA does not incorporate the limitations of the exceptions in either GATT Article XXI or NAFTA, presumably to give the United States—the only USMCA party that has invoked the GATT clause—somewhat

---

[57]   USMCA, Arts 2101, 2102.

[58]   USMCA, Arts 32.1, 32.2.

[59]   Presidential Proclamation on Adjusting Imports of Steel into the United States, March 8, 2018, www.whitehouse.gov/presidential -actions/presidential-proclamation-adjusting-imports-steel-united -states/.

[60]   Bill Chappell (2019), "U.S. Will Lift Tariffs on Steel and Aluminum from Canada and Mexico," NPR, May 17, www.npr.org/ 2019/05/17/724357441/u-s-to-lift-tariffs-on-canadas-and-mexico-s -steel-and-aluminum.

more flexibility in using the essential security as a basis for unilateral actions.

Both NAFTA and USMCA also include limitations on the application of the trade agreement to national taxation measures, largely to preserve the integrity of tax treaties and the parties' ability to maintain domestic revenue policies and cooperate internationally on tax matters through existing treaty mechanisms.[61] While NAFTA maintains an exception based loosely on GATT Article XII to safeguard the balance of payments,[62] USMCA includes a broader "temporary safe-guards measures" provision. There, the agreement explicitly "does not prevent a Party from adopting or maintaining a restrictive measure with regard to payments or transfers for current account transactions in the event of serious balance of payments and external financial difficulties or threats thereto" or for restrictions on capital movements in similar circumstances.[63] This concept of an exception for external financial difficulties appears to be derived at least in part from a trade agreement the United States concluded with Chile in 2003.[64]

Both NAFTA and USMCA incorporate limitations on the parties' obligations to furnish information that would conflict with national law, impede law enforcement, be contrary to the public interest, or prejudice legitimate public or private commercial interests.[65] The NAFTA language focuses more on personal privacy or personal financial information.[66] Reflecting the enormous changes that have taken place through the growth in digital trade, along with personal

---

[61] NAFTA, Art. 2103; USMCA, Art. 32.3.

[62] NAFTA, Art. 2104.

[63] USMCA, Art. 32.4.2.

[64] United States-Chile Free Trade Agreement, Annex 10-C, June 6, 2003, https://ustr.gov/trade-agreements/free-trade-agreements/chile-fta/final-text.

[65] USMCA, Art. 32.7.

[66] NAFTA, Art. 2105.

privacy concerns since NAFTA was concluded, USMCA makes provisions for the protection of personal information, requiring each party to maintain legal frameworks for the purpose, taking into "account principles and guidelines of relevant international bodies."[67] Other procedural requirements are also discussed, along with soft obligations on promoting compatibility, information exchanges and cooperation among government agencies.[68] Parties are obligated to give non-discriminatory treatment to requests by natural persons of any party to records held by the central governments.[69]

---

[67]   USMCA, Art. 32.8.
[68]   USMCA, Arts 32.8.6, 32.8.7.
[69]   USMCA, Art. 32.9.

10. Other significant USMCA innovations

As in the case of Chapter 9 discussing carryover provisions, it should not be assumed that the provisions discussed in this Chapter 10 are the *only* significant USMCA innovations. Among others are the new automotive rules of origin (Chapter 2) and the elimination of investor–state dispute settlement for United States-Canada relations and the restriction of ISDS in many matters affecting US persons with claims against Mexico (Chapter 3). Several of the provisions discussed in this chapter could have very significant impact on the interpretation, application and longevity of USMCA in the future.

I   LIMITATIONS ON CURRENCY MANIPULATION

There is more than a little irony in the fact that the first US FTA chapter on currency manipulation is found in an agreement where none of the parties (except perhaps the United States) have a history of manipulating their currencies. As one observer has noted, "The United States, Mexico, and Canada already have floating exchange rate regimes and currently meet the transparency and reporting requirements under Chapter 33, so the practical impact of Chapter 33 on current policies and practices of the three countries is limited."[1] Under the circumstances, the chapter is probably more significant

---

[1]   Stephanie Segal (2018), "USMCA Currency Provisions Set a New Precedent," Center for Strategic and International Studies,

as a model for future trade agreements with countries where currency manipulation has been a major US concern.

Given this history, it was no surprise that in the "Phase One" agreement between the United States and China concluded in January 2020, currency manipulation was extensively addressed.[2] The fact that, as of August 2019, China has been formally branded as a currency manipulator (rescinded in February 2020) even though it did not meet the criteria in US law,[3] further reinforces the utility of the US negotiators having recently dealt with the issue in USMCA. While one might have expected that the US trade agreement with Japan would have addressed currency manipulation, since Japan has been so accused in the past, that agreement is silent on the subject.[4]

USMCA was not the United States' first effort to address exchange rate policies in a trade agreement. While the CPTPP contains no chapter on currency manipulation, a joint declaration of the original TPP parties (including the United States)

October 5, www.csis.org/analysis/usmca-currency-provisions-set -new-precedent.

[2]   Economic and Trade Agreement Between the United States of America and the People's Republic of China, January 15, 2020, https://ustr.gov/sites/default/files/files/agreements/phase%20one %20agreement/Economic_And_Trade_Agreement_Between_The _United_States_And_China_Text.pdf, Ch. 5.

[3]   "Treasury Designates China as a Currency Manipulator" (2019), US Dept of the Treasury, August 5, https://home.treasury .gov/news/press-releases/sm751.

[4]   US-Japan Trade Agreement, October 7, 2019, https://ustr.gov/ countries-regions/japan-korea-apec/japan/us-japan-trade-agreement -negotiations/us-japan-trade-agreement-text; see Leika Kihara, "Japan May Face Trump's Heat as Currency Manipulator: Ex-FX Diplomat," Reuters, www.reuters.com/article/us-japan-usa-trade -currency/japan-may-face-trumps-heat-as-currency-manipulator-ex -fx-diplomat-idUSKBN1H51BB.

was released in November 2015 at the same time as the text.[5] That declaration incorporated some of the same principles now found in USMCA, including adherence to International Monetary Fund (IMF) requirements; transparency and reporting; and macroeconomic policy consultations.[6] The declaration was to become effective for each party's relevant authority "immediately after entry into force for the country of that Authority."[7] However, the joint declaration appears to have disappeared when the TPP was replaced by the CPTPP.[8]

The USMCA chapter on "Macroeconomic Policies and Exchange Rate Matters" is summarized by USTR as follows:

> The chapter will address unfair currency practices by requiring high-standard commitments to refrain from competitive devaluations and targeting exchange rates, while significantly increasing transparency and providing mechanisms for accountability. This approach is unprecedented in the context of a trade agreement, and will help reinforce macroeconomic and exchange rate stability.[9]

The chapter confirms the commitment of the USMCA parties to market-determined exchange rates and adherence to IMF requirements.[10] It contains various transparency and reporting requirements including public disclosure of data on international reserve balances and intervention in foreign exchange

---

[5]   "Joint Declaration of the Macroeconomic Policy Authorities of Trans-Pacific Partnership Countries," November 5, 2015, www.treasury.gov/initiatives/Documents/TPP_Currency_November%202015.pdf.

[6]   Ibid., Secs I, II and III.

[7]   Ibid., Sec. V.

[8]   See Stephanie Segal, "USMCA Currency Provisions."

[9]   USTR (2018), "United States-Mexico-Canada Trade Fact Sheet: Modernizing NAFTA into a 21st Century Trade Agreement," https://ustr.gov/trade-agreements/free-trade-agreements/united-states-mexico-canada-agreement/fact-sheets/modernizing.

[10]   USMCA, Arts 33.4.1, 33.4.2.

markets, both on a monthly basis.[11] A Macroeconomic Committee consisting of government officials of the three parties will meet at least annually to "monitor the implementation of this Chapter and its further elaboration."[12] "Expedited bilateral consultations" are available if a party believes that another party is failing to comply with policy and reporting requirements.[13] Disputes over a party's alleged failure to comply with the chapter are subject to state-to-state dispute settlement under Chapter 31.[14]

II   RESTRICTIONS ON TRADE AGREEMENTS WITH CHINA

Among the most unusual and unexpected provisions in USMCA is effectively a ban against Mexico or Canada concluding a trade agreement with a "non-market country," for example, China. Under the USMCA language a non-market economy country is one which "a Party [e.g., the United States] has determined to be a non-market economy [NME] for purposes of its trade remedy laws"; and "with which no Party has signed a free trade agreement."[15] Both of these limitations are significant. Although the language does not mention China, it is one of several countries (including Vietnam) that have been designated NMEs for purposes of trade remedies.[16] The second proviso is important because at

---

[11]   USMCA, Art. 33.5.

[12]   USMCA, Art. 33.6.

[13]   USMCA, Art. 33.7.

[14]   USMCA, Art. 33.8.

[15]   USMCA, Art. 32.10.1.

[16]   See 19 U.S.C. Sec. 1677(18)(B) (2000). Applicable factors include

> (i) the extent to which the currency of the foreign country is convertible into the currency of other countries; (ii) the extent to which wage rates in the foreign country are determined by free bargaining between labor and management; (iii) the extent

the time USMCA was signed both Mexico and Canada had signed the CPTPP (March 8, 2018), which included among its parties another NME, Vietnam.

The restrictions require that if Mexico or Canada considers such negotiations with China it must provide three months' notice to the other parties with "as much information as possible regarding the objectives for those negotiations" and an opportunity for the other parties to review the proposed text 30 days before signature so the reviewing parties may "assess its potential impact on this agreement."[17] Most significantly, if a party enters into such a trade agreement with an NME, the other parties have the option to terminate USMCA with regard to that party on six months' notice and replace it with a bilateral agreement between the remaining two parties.[18]

The NME trade agreement ban has met with criticism in both the United States and elsewhere. The Heritage Foundation argues that "A trade agreement should not prevent the Party countries from advancing efforts to liberalize with trade, especially with countries [i.e., China] which have so much to do in terms of lower trade barriers."[19] The Asia Pacific Foundation of Canada complained (with perhaps some exaggeration), "There are no two ways about it. Washington wants to limit

---

to which joint ventures or other investments by firms of other foreign countries are permitted in the foreign country; (iv) the extent of government ownership or control of the means of production; (v) the extent of government control over the allocation of resources and over the price and output decisions of enterprises; and (vi) such other factors as the administering authority considers appropriate.

[17] USMCA, Arts 32.10.2, 32.10.3, 32.10.4.

[18] USMCA, Art. 32.10.5.

[19] Tori K Whiting and Gabriella Beaumont-Smith (2019), "Backgrounder: An Analysis of the United States-Mexico-Canada Agreement," Heritage Foundation, January 28, www.heritage.org/trade/report/analysis-the-united-states-mexico-canada-agreement, 55.

the trade options of its allies and to isolate China. And it is just getting started."[20]

US insistence on the restriction may have been triggered not only by the US-China trade war that was already well under way when USMCA was concluded on September 30, 2018, but as a result of the fact that Canada and China had begun exploratory talks toward a bilateral trade agreement in September 2016. Former Mexican President Peña Nieto in September 2018 attended a meeting in China for the ninth summit of the BRICS (Brazil, Russia, India, China and South Africa), at a time when Mexico and China were enjoying "a close and rosy relationship."[21] One necessarily wonders whether the Trump Administration will seek similar restrictions in future trade agreements where the US also has a significant negotiating advantage, although none is found in the United States-Japan Agreement and would be virtually inconceivable in any agreement that might emerge with the EU or with the United Kingdom after Brexit. One of the challenges for both Mexico and Canada will be making efforts to develop mutually beneficial economic relations with China to the extent possible without seriously alienating the United States. Given that many believe that United States-Chinese economic competition and rivalries are likely to affect the world economy for decades, this provision may be only the first in which US efforts to isolate China conflict with Mexican and Canadian economic objectives.

---

[20]   Alex Lo (2018), "USMCA Trade Pact: For Canada and Mexico, Throwing China Under Bus Was a No-Brainer," This Week in Asia, October 6, www.scmp.com/week-asia/opinion/article/2167145/usmca-trade-pact-canada-and-mexico-throwing-china-under-bus-was-no.

[21]   Ibid.

III   SUNSET PROVISIONS

USMCA provides that "A Party may withdraw from this Agreement by providing written notice of withdrawal to the other Parties. A withdrawal shall take effect six months after a Party provides written notice to the other Parties. If a Party withdraws, this Agreement shall remain in force for the remaining Parties."[22] This is substantively identical to the parallel language in NAFTA.[23] In both cases the issue whether a US President can withdraw from NAFTA (or from USMCA) under the US Constitution without congressional approval, as President Trump repeatedly threatened to do, has not been resolved.[24] There appears to be little question that under international law the president may withdraw after the relevant notice has been given and the six-month period has elapsed.[25] In any event, no party to NAFTA or USMCA could be forced to remain a party for more than six months after its decision to withdraw. Short of withdrawal, the parties to most US trade agreements have specifically contemplated amendments, and all have a Free Trade Commission or something similar that could be tasked with considering modifications.[26]

Under such circumstances, most trade agreements, including, as far as I can determine, all those that have been negoti-

---

[22]   USMCA, Art. 34.6

[23]   NAFTA, Art. 2205.

[24]   See Brandon J. Murrill (2019), "The President's Authority to Withdraw the United States from the North American Free Trade Agreement (NAFTA) Without Further Congressional Action," Congressional Research Service, March 5, www.everycrsreport.com/reports/R45557.html.

[25]   See Vienna Convention on the Law of Treaties, May 23, 1969, Arts 54–56, www.oas.org/legal/english/docs/Vienna%20Convention%20Treaties.htm.

[26]   See, e.g., NAFTA, Art. 2001 (Free Trade Commission), Art. 2202 (amendments).

ated by the United States since the beginning (Israel, in 1986), have included no fixed date of termination or sunset clause.

Why then did the United States insist on a separate sunset provision, a "ticking time bomb" in the words of several observers,[27] one that would terminate USMCA 16 years after its entry into force unless the parties confirm that they wish to extend it for another 16 years? USTR, in its principal fact sheet, did not mention the sunset clause for which it has so steadfastly fought despite Canadian and Mexican opposition.[28] Perhaps the best that can be said for the provision is that it is far less potentially damaging than the five-year sunset clause originally sought by the United States,[29] likely reflecting the Trump Administration's skepticism about any international agreement that actually or potentially restricts the government's unilateral actions. The original five-year plan was, as explained by Commerce Secretary Wilbur Ross, designed to force regular, "systematic re-examination" of the revised agreement.[30]

The essential elements of the sunset clause can be summarized as follows: (a) USMCA terminates 16 years after entry into force unless each party confirms that it wants the agreement to continue for a further 16 years; and (b) on the sixth anniversary of its entry into force, a "joint review" of the agreement must be conducted by the Commission created under USMCA, with any party able to provide "recommen-

---

[27]   Simon Lester and Inu Manak (2018), "New NAFTA's Sunset Clause Is a Ticking Time Bomb," Cato Institute, November 7, www .cato.org/publications/commentary/new-naftas-sunset-clause-ticking -time-bomb.

[28]   USTR, "United States-Mexico-Canada Trade Fact Sheet."

[29]   Lester and Manak, "New NAFTA's Sunset Clause Is a Ticking Time Bomb."

[30]   David Lawder (2017), "U.S. Pushes for 'Sunset Clause' to Re-Examine NAFTA Every Five Years," Bloomberg News, October 12, www.bnnbloomberg.ca/u-s-pushes-for-sunset-clause-to -re-examine-nafta-every-five-years-1.883334.

dations for action."[31] If (c), each party confirms in writing it wishes to extend the agreement, no further action is required until the end of the next six-year period.[32] However, (d), if any party dissents, a further joint review is required each subsequent year, again unless and until all parties have agreed on a 16-year extension.[33] Even if there is an extension, (e) joint reviews are required every six years thereafter.[34]

According to the implementing legislation, the president is required to consult with appropriate congressional committees and stakeholders before each joint review takes place, and to keep the committee apprised of any progress and intended actions.[35] However, the Congress has no veto over any actions that are taken by the president to withdraw (or remain).

Support for a sunset clause in an agreement as politically sensitive as NAFTA or USMCA reflects in my view a stunning level of naivety and lack of basic understanding of how businesses operate. Naivety because such agreements, including any amending protocols, must be ratified by the United States Congress. One needs only to look at USMCA, which was signed on November 30, 2018 but could not even be submitted to Congress until almost year later, on December 13, 2019, because of the time required to reach a political agreement with Congress on changes to the agreement and to the content of the implementing legislation.[36] Does it really make sense, even if the three USMCA parties could agree on changes, to force Congress and the president to go through a ratification process every five years or so?

---

[31] USMCA, Arts 34.7.1, 34.7.2.

[32] USMCA, Art. 34.7.3.

[33] USMCA, Art. 34.7.4.

[34] USMCA, Art. 34.7.5.

[35] USMCA Implementation Act, December 13, 2019, H.R. 5430, 116th Congress, 1st Session, www.congress .gov/bill/116th-congress/house-bill/5430/text#toc-H7B2A 937BE4154D6CAD827CE4149F1E70, Sec. 611.

[36] Ibid.

The concept also flies in the face of the basic fact that businesses by and large do not invest in new or expanded facilities when economic uncertainty abounds. North American business investment has been sluggish because of the uncertainty as to whether NAFTA would be terminated or replaced by the Trump Administration.[37] Such uncertainty was resolved only when it became apparent that USMCA would be approved by all three USMCA parties and enter into force by July 1, 2020.[38]

It is difficult to understand how even a 16-year sunset clause would eliminate the threat of another period of business uncertainty, even if it does not occur for some years. Under the best of circumstances, all three parties might confirm after the six-year joint review that they wish to extend USMCA for another 16 years. If not, joint reviews would have to be conducted by the Commission each year for the remainder of the six-year period, or until all parties agree, or until USMCA terminates under the provision. It is difficult to imagine how any policy that could result in business uncertainty on a potentially continuing basis beginning in 2026 would benefit the United States or its USMCA partners. One can make a rea-

---

[37]   See Leah Schnurr and Andrea Hopkins (2018), "Bank of Canada Says NAFTA Uncertainty Weighing on Investment," Reuters, May 16, www.reuters.com/article/us-canada-cenbank/bank-of-canada-says-nafta-uncertainty-weighing-on-investment-idUSKCN1IH2AV.

[38]   The Protocol Replacing the North American Free Trade Agreement with the Agreement Between the United States of America, the United Mexican States, and Canada, November 30, 2018 (to which USMCA is annexed), Art. 2, https://ustr.gov/sites/default/files/files/agreements/FTA/USMCA/Text/USMCA_Protocol.pdf, provides that USMCA will enter into force on the first day of the third month following the last notification by a party of its approval of the agreement. As of January 31, 2020, Mexico and the United States had ratified the agreement, and it was expected that Canada would complete its parliamentary approval process by the end of April.

sonable argument that North American business investment and employment, already suffering from what promises to be a long-term trade conflict with China, will not benefit from yet another layer of economic uncertainty!

IV   INDIGENOUS PEOPLES' RIGHTS

The Preamble to USMCA, for the first time in a trade agreement concluded by the United States,[39] recognizes, inter alia, "the importance of increased engagement by indigenous peoples in trade and investment ..."[40] More significantly, USMCA, at Canada's insistence, includes a general exception applicable to the entire USMCA, for obligations to indigenous peoples, protecting legal obligations of Canada or other parties to indigenous groups:

> Provided that such measures are not used as a means of arbitrary or unjustified discrimination against persons of the other Parties or as a disguised restriction on trade in goods, services, and investment, this Agreement does not preclude a Party from adopting or maintaining a measure it deems necessary to fulfill its legal obligations to indigenous peoples.[41]

---

[39]   Similar provisions have existed since 2001 in all New Zealand's trade agreements beginning with Singapore, including the CPTPP, for the obligations of the New Zealand government to the Maori in the Treaty of Waitangi. See Waitangi Tribunal Report on the Trans-Pacific Partnership Agreement (Wai 2522, 2016), https://forms.justice.govt.nz/search/Documents/WT/wt_DOC_104833137/Report%20on%20the%20Trans-Pacific%20Partnership%20Agreement%20W.pdf.

[40]   USMCA, Preamble, clause 17.

[41]   USMCA, Art. 32.5. A footnote clarifies that for Canada "the legal obligations include those recognized and affirmed by section 35 of the *Constitution Act 1982* or those set out in self-government agreements between a central or regional level of government and indigenous peoples."

Other chapters of USMCA are also relevant to the interests of indigenous peoples. Specifically, indigenous handicraft goods are eligible for duty-free treatment.[42] Other USMCA chapters that protect the environment and encourage corporate social responsibility and responsible business conduct as it relates to the environment address matters of particular importance to indigenous groups.[43] While some have criticized USMCA for not explicitly referring to the United Nations Declaration on the Rights of Indigenous Peoples (UNDRIP) despite its endorsement by the USMCA parties, it is arguable that the general reference to obligations to indigenous peoples encompasses those legally binding principles.[44]

---

[42]   USMCA, Art. 6.2. An excellent summary of the benefits of USMCA for indigenous groups is Kevin O'Callaghan, Emilie Bundock and Madison Grist (2018), "USMCA Aims to Protect the Interests of Indigenous Peoples in International Trade," Fasken Indigenous Bulletin, October 23, www.fasken.com/en/knowledge/2018/10/van-usmca-aims-to-protect-the-interests-of-indigenous-peoples-in-international-trade/.

[43]   USMCA, Ch. 24, esp. Art. 24.13.

[44]   See O'Callaghan, Bundock and Grist, "Indigenous Peoples."

11. USMCA's future in context

As this book went to press (January 2020) several other trade disputes existed that if resolved could increase the effectiveness of USMCA as a platform for North American production of autos and other goods, and if not resolved could have the opposite effect. This chapter briefly considers what, in the author's view, are the most significant of these factors.

I   SECTION 232 (STEEL, ALUMINUM AND AUTOS)

Although in May 2019 the Trump Administration lifted steel and aluminum tariffs imposed in 2018 on imports from Canada and Mexico, tariffs or quotas remain or have been reimposed not only on imports from China but also on those from producers in Argentina, Brazil, the EU, Japan, South Korea and others. These tariffs increase the cost of manufacturing in the United States of products that use these metals, particularly autos but many others ranging from nails to home appliances, making those produced in the United States more expensive that those produced in other countries (including Mexico and Canada). Proposed Section 232 tariffs on auto and auto parts imports have been continuously postponed by the Trump Administration and may no longer be under serious consideration given the repeated delays in taking tariff action.[1]

---

[1]   See David Lewder (2019), "Trump Can No Longer Impose 'Section 232' Auto Tariffs After Missing Deadline, Experts," Reuters, November 19, www.reuters.com/article/us-usa-trade-autos/trump-can-no-longer-impose-section-232-auto-tariffs-after-missing

It may be that the trade agreement concluded with Japan[2] and the prospect of swift retaliation from the European Union encouraged the administration to reconsider; whatever the reason, a serious additional threat to the North American auto industry has to date been avoided if in fact the Section 232 tariffs are no longer being considered.

As noted in Chapter 2 and elsewhere in this volume, stricter auto and auto parts rules of origin under USMCA,[3] including those designed to encourage a shift of protection from Mexico to the United States, will inevitably increase production costs in the United States and elsewhere in North America, raising vehicle prices for both local sales and exports. Thus, in the final analysis, auto production in North America may have greater difficulty competing with producers in Asia and Europe who export their vehicles to North America.

-deadline-experts-idUSKBN1XT0TK (suggesting that under the 1962 Trade Expansion Act provision the period for acting on the study that began in May 2018 expired as of November 14, 2019).

[2]　　US-Japan Trade Agreement, October 7, 2019 (not yet in force), https://ustr.gov/countries-regions/japan-korea-apec/japan/us-japan-trade-agreement-negotiations/us-japan-trade-agreement-text. The agreement does not mention autos and auto parts, but it may be that an understanding exists between the parties that such tariffs will not be applied.

[3]　　These include regional content requirements increasing from 62.5 percent to 75 percent; $16 minimum hourly wages for 40 percent of auto and 45 percent of light truck production; and a requirement that 70 percent of the steel parts used in auto and auto parts production be derived from steel "melted and poured" in North America. While many would consider wage increases stimulated by the USMCA's labor provisions highly beneficial, if those provisions result in higher wage costs for auto and auto parts production, the finished product costs will also increase.

II   US-CHINA TRADE WAR AND ONGOING ECONOMIC RIVALRIES

The ongoing trade "war" with China, even though as of January 15, 2020 a truce had been reached through a "first-phase" agreement,[4] has also increased the cost of many intermediate goods imported into the United States for domestic production as well as for finished products that have become more expensive for US consumers. It is notable that the January 2020 agreement does not eliminate tariffs imposed by the United States on Chinese imports under Section 301 of the 1974 Trade Act since mid 2018, although it postpones additional tariffs and reduces some of those imposed earlier.[5] Tariffs will remain indefinitely at 25 percent for about $250 billion of imports and 7.5 percent (down from 15 percent earlier) for another $120 billion worth.[6]

The heavily managed trade agreement commits China to purchase an additional $200 million worth of US products each year for the next two years, including billions in natural gas and other energy products, and some $40 billion of agri-

---

[4]   Economic and Trade Agreement Between the Government of the United States of America and the Government of the People's Republic of China, January 15, 2020, https://ustr.gov/sites/default/files/files/agreements/phase%20one%20agreement/Economic_And _Trade_Agreement_Between_The_United_States_And_China_Text .pdf.

[5]   See USTR (2019), "United States and China Reach Phase One Trade Agreement," December 12, https://ustr.gov/about-us/policy -offices/press-office/press-releases/2019/december/united-states -and-china-reach (stating that some $250 billion worth of Chinese imports will remain subject to 25 percent tariffs, while tariffs on another $120 billion of Chinese imports will fall to 7.5 percent).

[6]   See Chad P. Bown (2019), "Phase One China Deal: Steep Tariffs Are the New Normal," Peterson Institute, December 19, www .piie.com/blogs/trade-and-investment-policy-watch/phase-one-china -deal-steep-tariffs-are-new-normal.

cultural products.[7] China has also agreed to provide additional protection against forced technology transfer, to improve protection of intellectual property,[8] and to improve US financial institution access to the Chinese markets.[9] Still, even with the agreement, the average tariffs on Chinese imports have increased to 19.3 percent from 3.0 percent two years ago and still affect two-thirds of all US imports from China.[10] The accords seek to increase Chinese purchases of American farm products as noted above, but some observers doubt that it will in practice do much more than restore the status quo before the trade war began.[11]

Despite what most believe to be a serious need to protect high-tech US products and technology from Chinese national security threats, and to restrain China's rampant illegal subsidies, such problems are left for a future Phase Two agreement to be negotiated in the unspecified future. Nor does the agreement resolve the standoff between the United States and China over Huawei's attempts to market 5G telecommunications equipment throughout the world, sales of which are resolutely opposed by the United States.[12] Under the Phase One agreement US penalty tariffs will continue to disrupt supply chains for an extended period of time even for goods that

---

[7]   US-China Agreement, Chs 3, 6.

[8]   US-China Agreement, Chs 1, 2.

[9]   US-China Agreement, Ch. 4.

[10]   See Chad P. Bown, "Phase One China Deal."

[11]   See Josh Zumbrun and Kirsk Maltais (2019), "China's Farm-Purchase Targets Under Trade Deal Face Skeptics," *Wall Street Journal*, December 18, www.wsj.com/articles/chinas-farm -purchase-targets-under-trade-deal-face-skeptics-11576665004 (suggesting that the $200 million export target could be achieved only if US exporters sent 100 percent of their soy, oil exports and liquefied natural gas to China).

[12]   See Steven Musil, Sean Keane and Corinne Reichert (2020), "US Presses British Officials to Block Huawei from 5G Network," CNET, January 15, www.cnet.com/news/us-presses-british-officials -to-block-huawei-from-5g-network/.

have no national security implications, and make some goods manufactured in the United States less competitive with their counterparts abroad, discouraging domestic consumption and, because of increased production costs, reducing US exports of many products, particularly automobiles.

Although a more comprehensive settlement of China-United States trade frictions seems highly unlikely in the foreseeable future, even the Phase One agreement should help to free North American investors and workers to take fuller advantage of the potential benefits of USMCA. Those enterprises currently producing goods in China for export to the United States should realize that high tariffs on many Chinese goods are the new normal, to exist for at least another year and perhaps much longer. This presumably means that they will seek alternative manufacturing sites in Vietnam, Mexico or elsewhere. Mexico could benefit from these shifts if López Obrador's anti-foreign investment policies do not scare them off, but in many instances sourcing changes will be costly and the higher production costs in alternative markets may increase the costs of both intermediate and final goods to consumers in North America.

More generally in my view, the economic and trade rivalries between the United States and China, particularly in the "Made in China 2025" areas where China seeks parity or even dominance, such as robots, artificial intelligence, semiconductors and electric vehicles, can be expected to continue for at least the next three or four decades. This unpleasant fact makes the smooth functioning of USMCA even more important for the parties and for the economic well-being of their stakeholders.

III   EMASCULATION OF THE WTO'S DISPUTE SETTLEMENT SYSTEM

As of December 10, 2019, the WTO's Appellate Body ceased to function; while three judges are required to hear each case, only one remained, due to US blocking of appointments and reappointments.[13] In my view one would have to be an incurable optimist to believe that the ongoing dispute between most members and the United States regarding the alleged overstepping of the appellate body, particularly its alleged "diminishing rights and obligations" of WTO members,[14] can be resolved in the foreseeable future. Various factors, including but not limited to the fact that the 164-member WTO makes decisions by consensus (meaning that not only the US but also such powerful members as China, India and Russia must agree), suggest that serious reform of the WTO, such as that which would be required in such areas as appellate body procedures, rules affecting anti-dumping and subsidies actions, and more generally its ability to deal with non-market economies, are years away.

Another implicit vote of the US lack of confidence in the WTO and endorsement of unilateral action is found in the US-China Agreement, which contains none of the traditional provisions for third-party dispute settlement. Rather, the agreement's "bilateral evaluation and dispute resolution" mechanism[15] is no more than a bilateral consultation mechanism which would leave the United States, should it decide that China was not acting in good faith to implement the provisions of the agreement, to retaliate with yet more tariffs.

It also seems clear that the Trump Administration will continue to flout WTO rules in other ways, with its unilateral

---

[13] See Keith Johnson (2019), "How Trump May Finally Kill the WTO," Foreign Policy, December 9, https://foreignpolicy.com/2019/12/09/trump-may-kill-wto-finally-appellate-body-world-trade-organization/.

[14] See Bryce Baschuk (2019), "What's Next for the WTO After Sabotage by the U.S.," *Washington Post*, December 11, www.washingtonpost.com/business/whats-next-for-the-wto-after-sabotage-by-the-us/2019/12/11/db45de8e-1bd3-11ea-977a-15a6710ed6da_story.html.

[15] US-China Agreement, Ch. 4.

Section 232 actions based on dubious "national security" concerns with steel and aluminum, and pursuing a Section 301 action against China without resort to the dispute settlement process. While the Airbus penalty tariffs were authorized by the WTO, the planned tariffs against French products relating to taxation of digital goods were not. Others may feel that they too can flout WTO rules without consequence, as China has been doing for years in the areas of illegal subsidies and intellectual property.

Under the original USMCA the demise of WTO dispute settlement posed a serious risk for Canada and Mexico, since the USMCA dispute settlement mechanism was no better than NAFTA's Chapter 20 (which permitted the United States to block panels essentially at will). However, under the December 10 amendments this becomes somewhat more difficult.[16] Assuming that all three parties promptly appoint their rosters of panelists, and assuming that the United States plays by the rules, Canada and Mexico as well as the United States have a reasonable chance of establishing a functioning system for resolving trade disputes even though the WTO's mechanism is no longer operative.

IV   UNPREDICTABILITY OF THE CURRENT US AND MEXICAN ADMINISTRATIONS

As is evident from other parts of this book, particularly with regard to President López Obrador's "Mexico First" energy policies (Chapter 5) and the Trump Administration's originally proposed drastic revisions to NAFTA (Chapter 1 and

---

[16] Protocol of Amendment to the USMCA, December 10, 2019, https://ustr.gov/sites/default/files/files/agreements/FTA/USMCA/ Protocol-of-Amendments-to-the-United-States-Mexico-Canada -Agreement.pdf, amendments to Chapter 31. See also Chapter 3 of this book for discussion of the changes.

elsewhere), neither government's actions in areas relating to intra-regional trade have achieved a high level of predictability. There is thus always the risk that one or both will take unexpected actions affecting regional trade and investment. Prior such occurrences include the Trump Administration's threat in June 2019 to impose tariffs of up to 25 percent on all Mexican source imports if Mexico failed to take effective steps to counter illegal immigration from El Salvador, Guatemala and Honduras to the United States via Mexico.[17] It seems likely that Mexico as well as other countries, whether allies or foes, will periodically be the targets of the Trump Administration's unilateralist foreign policy, with economic sanctions or high tariffs being the result.

On the Mexican side, López Obrador's decision immediately after taking office in December 2018 to cancel the Mexico City airport project and to postpone new oil leases for three years has raised concerns for actual and potential investors.[18] As of the end of January 2020, these concerns remain, as reflected in the López Obrador Administration's threat to cancel existing contracts of many clean power generators or remove long-standing subsidies for use of the government's electricity transmission monopoly lines. Either could force the owners, primarily European and US energy companies, to cease operations[19] and to seek international arbitration

---

[17]   David Nakamura, John Wagner and Nick Miroff (2019), "Trump Announces Migration Deal with Mexico, Averting Threatened Tariffs," *Washington Post*, June 7, www.washingtonpost.com/politics/trump-could-decide-over-the-weekend-to-hold-off-on-tariffs-white-house-official-says/2019/06/07/6adb7d86-892d-11e9-98c1-e945ae5db8fb_story.html.

[18]   See Chapter 3 of this book.

[19]   See Amy Stillman (2019), "Mexico's Renewable Power Suppliers Face Risks Under Grid Proposal," Bloomberg News, December 22, https://business.financialpost.com/pmn/business-pmn/mexicos-renewable-power-suppliers-face-risks-under-grid-proposal. See also the discussion in Chapter 5 of this book.

under NAFTA or Mexico's bilateral investment treaties with Italy and Spain. The anti-business investment climate could discourage new investment in Mexico at a time when it is desperately needed to strengthen the economy and create new jobs and exports.

Given the ongoing challenges of governing both nations, the personalities of the two presidents, and the devotion of both to "America First" or "Mexico First" populism, it is almost certain that similar disruptive events will occur on one or both sides of the border in the future. If both governments can effectively deal with them when they arise, serious consequences may be avoided. However, it seems naive to assume that President López Obrador will always defer to President Trump whenever such events occur, as with the migration issue noted above and in the willingness of the Mexican government to back down when it was faced with proposals under US implementing legislation for labor attachés that raised sovereignty concerns in December 2019.[20] Such risks therefore seem inevitable in the future, particularly if the Mexican economy, flat in 2019, does not begin to recover in 2020. Also, as indicated in Chapter 4 of this book, the complex and intrusive rapid-response labor dispute resolution mechanism could generate conflicts between the United States and Mexico, should the United States use the mechanism as an excuse for restricting imports, or Mexican authorities object to alleged intrusions on Mexico's sovereignty.

Under such circumstances, the uncertainties that should be largely resolved for North American investment and employment by the entry into force of USMCA will not be entirely dissipated, particularly if AMLO's opposition to private foreign investment and Mr Trump's threats to Mexico persist.

---

[20] See Chapter 4 of this book.

V   THE CORONAVIRUS PANDEMIC

This book is not an appropriate place for a lengthy discussion of the ramifications of the COVID-19 pandemic for the USMCA or North American trade, in part because as of May 2020 (when this section was added) it was impossible to predict the full impact. However, several salient points bear noting. First, the WTO has predicted that world merchandise trade in 2020 will fall by between 12 percent and 32 percent compared to 2019, with nearly all regions suffering double-digit declines. The impact is expected to be more pronounced in sectors with complex value chains, such as automotive products.[21] Thus, the highly integrated North American auto industry, already challenged by the USMCA's new and stricter rules of origin[22] and the temporary closure of many auto factories in North America due both to COVID-19 concerns and declining consumer demand, will face new and unexpected hurdles as a result of the pandemic.[23] Second, with at least 20 million people out of work in the United States alone,[24] and with a recession expected in all three NAFTA/USMCA parties,

---

[21]   World Trade Organization, "Trade Set to Plunge as COVID-19 Pandemic Upends Global Economy," Press Release, April 8, 2020, https://www.wto.org/english/news_e/pres20_e/pr855_e.htm.

[22]   See ch. 2.

[23]   See "Rep. Kind: USTR Considering Flexibility for USMCA's Auto Terms," *World Trade Online*, April 14, 2020, https://insidetrade .com/daily-news/rep-kind-ustr-considering-flexibility-usmca%E2 %80%99s-auto-terms. ("Several industry groups and senators have warned that automakers and parts makers need more time to adjust to uniform regulations needed to guide the application of the complex automotive rules of origin. Those negotiations have faced delays due to technical issues as well as efforts to fight the COVID-19 pandemic, as some companies have shifted their focus to the manufac-turing of medical goods. Many auto companies have also temporarily closed production facilities.")

[24]   Eric Morath and Sarah Chaney, "U.S. Jobless Claims top 20 Million Since Start of Shutdowns," *The Wall Street Journal*, April

demand for many consumer products including but not limited to automobiles may be depressed for several years or more.[25] Unfortunately, it seems highly unlikely that the extreme economic and social destruction caused by COVID-19 will be fully rectified unless and until a vaccine for the virus or other preventative measures are widely available throughout North America,[26] developments that could require a year or more.

Most significantly for the future of today's long supply chains, the pandemic, for which China has been widely blamed, has added substantial pressure for the "reshoring" of supply lines that rely today on China (or in some instances other Asian countries). This is particularly critical for personal protective equipment, and pharmaceuticals and materials used in their manufacture. At the present time, estimates suggest that some 80 percent of active ingredients and 40 percent of finished drugs sold in the United States are sourced outside the United States, and China is the second-largest source of drugs imported into the United States (after India).[27]

This adds to the U.S.-China trade war and to other political, environmental and economic pressures to bring supplies of these products, along with those that raise national security

---

16, 2020, https://www.wsj.com/articles/u-s-unemployment-claims -likely-continued-at-record-levels-11587029401.

[25] See John Muellbauer, "The Coronavirus Pandemic and US Consumption," *Vox CEPR Policy Portal*, April 11, 2020, https:// voxeu.org/article/coronavirus-pandemic-and-us-consumption (suggesting that the impact of the COVID-19 pandemic will impose shocks on both supply and consumer demand that "are far grimmer than at any time in the 2008 global financial crisis").

[26] See Lauren Krouse, "When Will the Novel Coronavirus Pandemic Be Over?", *Women's Health*, April 28, 2020, https://www .womenshealthmag.com/health/a31406983/when-will-coronavirus -end/.

[27] Yanz Huang, "The Coronavirus Outbreak Could Disrupt the U.S. Drug Supply," *Council on Foreign Relations*, March 5, 2020, https://www.cfr.org/in-brief/coronavirus-disrupt-us-drug-supply -shortages-fda.

concerns, and closer to home, with shorter supply chains confined to the United States or more sensibly to North America (where three countries provide significant opportunities to diversify sources as well). COVID-19 thus may increase the percentage of U.S., Canadian and Mexican total trade and investment that takes place within North America in the future and reduce the region's imports from elsewhere (as well as exports from the United States in particular to China). Without USMCA, this evolving process would have been even more costly and difficult to implement; with USMCA it will still be challenging and economically disruptive but seems more likely to occur without causing serious, long-term injury to the North American economies, their enterprises, workers and consumers.

Selected bibliography

USMCA PRIMARY AND GOVERNMENT MATERIALS

Protocol of Amendment to the USMCA (December 10, 2019), https://ustr.gov/sites/default/files/files/agreements/FTA/USMCA/Protocol-of-Amendments-to-the-United-States-Mexico-Canada-Agreement.pdf.

Protocol Replacing the North American Free Trade Agreement with the Agreement Between the United States of America, the United Mexican States and Canada (November 30, 2018), https://ustr.gov/sites/default/files/files/agreements/FTA/USMCA/Text/USMCA_Protocol.pdf.

United States-Mexico-Canada Agreement (November 30, 2018, amended December 10, 2019), https://ustr.gov/trade-agreements/free-trade-agreements/united-states-mexico-canada-agreement/agreement-between.

"United States-Mexico-Canada Agreement," US Dept of Commerce, International Trade Administration, www.trade.gov/usmca/.

USMCA, "Creating More Balanced and Reciprocal North American Trade," https://ustr.gov/usmca.

USMCA Advisory Committee Reports, https://ustr.gov/trade-agreements/free-trade-agreements/united-states-mexico-canada-agreement/advisory-committee.

USTR, "USMCA Fact Sheets," https://ustr.gov/trade-agreements/free-trade-agreements/united-states-mexico-canada-agreement/fact-sheets.

CPTPP/TPP PRIMARY AND GOVERNMENT MATERIALS

Comprehensive and Progressive Agreement for Trans-Pacific Partnership, August 3, 2018, www.international.gc.ca/trade

-commerce/trade-agreements-accords-commerciaux/agr-acc/
cptpp-ptpgp/text-texte/index.aspx?lang=eng&_ga=2.171950688
.1186738.1570397124-1128694463.1562952965.

Presidential Memorandum Regarding Withdrawal of the United
States from the Trans-Pacific Partnership Negotiations and
Agreement, January 23, 2017, www.whitehouse.gov/presidential
-actions/presidential-memorandum-regarding-withdrawal-united
-states-trans-pacific-partnership-negotiations-agreement/.

NAFTA PRIMARY AND GOVERNMENT MATERIALS

Global Affairs Canada, "NAFTA Chapter 11 Cases," www
.international.gc.ca/trade-agreements-accords-commerciaux/
topics-domaines/disp-diff/nafta.aspx?lang=eng.

NAFTA Secretariat, "NAFTA, Status Report of Panel Proceedings,"
www.nafta-sec-alena.org/Home/Dispute-Settlement/Status
-Report-of-Panel-Proceedings.

NAFTA Secretariat, North American Free Trade Agreement,
December 15, 1992, www.nafta-sec-alena.org/Home/Texts-of-the
-Agreement/North-American-Free-Trade-Agreement.

OTHER INTERNATIONAL AGREEMENTS

Agreement Establishing the World Trade Organization, April 15,
1995 (with annexed agreements), www.wto.org/english/docs_e/
legal_e/legal_e.htm.

Central America-United States-Dominican Free Trade Agreement
(Dominican Republic, El Salvador, Guatemala, Honduras,
Nicaragua, United States), August 5, 2015, http://bit.ly/2FPw4l3.

United States-Japan Trade Agreement, October 7, 2019, https://
ustr.gov/countries-regions/japan-korea-apec/japan/us-japan-trade
-agreement-negotiations/us-japan-trade-agreement-text.

OTHER GOVERNMENT MATERIALS

Government of Canada (2018), "Trade Remedies and Related
Dispute Settlement (Chapter 19) Summary," October, http://bit
.ly/2Vp7WfU.

US Customs and Border Protection (2018), "Section 232 Tariffs on
Aluminum and Steel," http://bit.ly/2K7ufFE.

US Dept of State (undated), "United States Bilateral Investment Treaties," www.state.gov/e/eb/ifd/bit/117402.htm.

USMCA Trade Advisory Committee Reports (2018), USTR, September–October, https://ustr.gov/trade-agreements/free-trade-agreements/united-states-mexico-canada-agreement/advisory-committee.

USTR (2018), "Trump Administration Announces Intent to Negotiate Trade Agreements with Japan, the European Union and the United Kingdom," October, https://ustr.gov/about-us/policy-offices/press-office/press-releases/2018/october/trump-administration-announces.

USTR (2018), United States-Japan Trade Agreement (USJTA) Negotiations," December, http://bit.ly/2FPP9Us.

USTR (2018), "United-States-Mexico-Canada Trade Fact Sheet: Rebalancing Trade to Support Manufacturing," October, https://ustr.gov/about-us/policy-offices/press-office/fact-sheets/2018/october/united-states%E2%80%93mexico%E2%80%93canada-trade-fa-0.

USTR (2019), "Changes in Existing Law Required to Bring the United States into Compliance with Obligations Under the Agreement Between the United States of America, the United Mexican States and Canada (USMCA), January 29, www.finance.senate.gov/imo/media/doc/USMCA%20Changes%20To%20Existing%20US%20Law%20Document.pdf.

USTR (2019), "Notice of Modification of Section 301 Action: China's Acts, Policies, and Practices Related to Technology Transfer, Intellectual Property, and Innovation," March 5, www.federalregister.gov/documents/2018/12/19/2018-27458/notice-of-modification-of-section-301-action-chinas-acts-policies-and-practices-related-to.

USTR (2019), "United States-European Union Negotiations," January, http://bit.ly/2VrjcbG.

OTHER SOURCES

Angulo, Sharay (2018), "Most Mexican Auto Exports Can Meet New NAFTA Rules, Says Minister," *Reuters*, August 27, www.reuters.com/article/us-trade-nafta-mexico-autos/most-mexican-auto-exports-can-meet-new-nafta-rules-says-minister-idUSKCN1LC2HC.

"Chamber [of Commerce]: Elements of USMCA should not be viewed as model for new FTAs" (2019), World Trade Online, January 9, http://bit.ly/2YQV2sX.

de Mestral, Armand and Robin Morgan (2016), "Does Canadian Law Provide Remedies Equivalent to NAFTA Chapter 11 Arbitration?" CIGI Investor–State Arbitration Series Paper no. 4, May, 11, http://bit.ly/2YMgz6a.

Dziczek, Kristin, Bernard Swiecki, Yen Chen, Valerie Brugeman, Michael Schultz and David Andrea (2017), "NAFTA Briefing: Trade Benefits to the Automotive Industry and Potential Consequences of Withdrawal from the Agreement," Center for Automotive Research, January, www.cargroup.org/publication/nafta-briefing-trade-benefits-to-the-automotive-industry-and-potential-consequences-of-withdrawal-from-the-agreement/.

Elliott, Kimberly Ann (2018), "Can the World Trade Organization Be Saved?" *World Politics Review*, October 16, http://bit.ly/2YMiffY.

Gantz, David A. (1995), "Implementing the NAFTA Rules of Origin: Are the Parties Helping or Hurting Free Trade?" *Arizona Journal of International and Comparative Law*, **12**, 367.

Gantz, David A. (2009), "The United States and Dispute Settlement Under the North American Free Trade Agreement: Ambivalence, Frustration and Occasional Defiance," in Cesare P.R. Romano (ed.), *The Sword and the Scales: The United States and International Courts and Tribunal*, New York: Cambridge University Press, pp. 356, 381.

Gantz, David A. (2018), "The Risks and Rewards of Renegotiating the North American Trade Relationship," *Maryland Journal of International Law*, **33**, 127.

Hufbauer, Gary Clyde, and Euijin Jung (2018), "Higher de Minimis Thresholds: A Win in the USMCA," Peterson Institute for International Economics, *Trade and Investment Policy Watch* blog, October 15, https://piie.com/blogs/trade-investment-policy-watch/higher-de-minimis-thresholds-win-usmca.

Johnson, Renee (2015), "The U.S.-EU Beef Hormone Dispute," Congressional Research Service, January 14, https://webcache.googleusercontent.com/search?q=cache:B7zp-YjK7tIJ:https://fas.org/sgp/crs/row/R40449.pdf+&cd=1&hl=en&ct=clnk&gl=us&client=firefox-b-1-d.

Martin, Eric, Josh Wingrove and Andrew Mayeda (2017), "U.S. Demands on NAFTA Said to Risk Scuttling Trade Talks," International Trade Report (BBNA), **34**, 1316.

"Mexico's Ambassador Suggests USMCA Parties Get a Head Start on Dispute-Settlement Rosters" (2019) World Trade Online, September 5, https://insidetrade.com/daily-news/mexicos-ambass ador-suggests-usmca-parties-get-head-start-dispute-settlemen t-rosters.

Negroponte, Diana Villiers (2018), "Mexico's Energy Reforms Become Law", Brookings, August 14, www.brookings.edu/ articles/mexicos-energy-reforms-become-law/.

Schott, Jeffrey J. (2018), "For Mexico, Canada, and the United States, a Step Backward on Trade and Investment," Peterson Institute for Int'l Economics, October 2, https://piie.com/blogs/ trade-investment-policy-watch/mexico-canada-and-united-states -step-backwards-trade-and.

Shaiken, Harley (2017), "Improved Workers' Rights for Mexicans Will Benefit Americans," *New York Times*, January 30, www .nytimes.com/roomfordebate/2017/01/30/new-terms-for-nafta-7/ improved-workers-rights-for-mexicans-will-benefit-americans.

Whiting, Tori K., and Gabriella Beaumont Smith (2019), "Backgrounder: An Analysis of the United States-Mexico-Canada Agreement," Heritage Foundation, January 28, www.heritage.org/ trade/report/analysis-the-united-states-mexico-canada-agreement.

Wingrove, Josh, and Eric Martin (2017), "U.S. Proposes Gutting NAFTA Legal Dispute Tribunals," Bloomberg Markets, October 14 (subscription), https://bloom.bg/2Uo23Cr.

JUDICIAL DECISIONS AND LEGISLATION

Certain Softwood Lumber Products from Canada, Case nos. USA-CDA-1992-1904-01, USA-CDA-1992-1904-02, http://bit .ly/2IctBE3.

Certain Softwood Lumber Products from Canada, Case nos. USA-CDA-2002-1904-02, USA-CDA-2002-1904-03, USA-CDA-2002-1904-07, USA-CDA-2005-1904-01, USA-CDA-2006-1904-04, USA-CDA-2006-1904-05, http://bit.ly/2IctBE3.

Cross-Border Trucking Services, USA-Mex-1998-2008-1, February 6, 2001, 6–7 (paras 21, 22), NAFTA Decisions and Reports, www.nafta-sec-alena.org/Home/Dispute-Settlement/Decisions -and-Reports.

Loewen Group, Inc. and Raymond L. Loewen v. United States of America, ICSID Case no. ARB(AFT)/98/3, http://bit.ly/2UiIewU.

Section 301 of the Trade Act of 1974, as amended, Pub. L. 93-618, 19 U.S.C. Sec. 2411.

United States—Sections 301–310 of the Trade Act 1974, WT/
DS152/AB/R, adopted January 27, 2010.

Index